CURRENCIES, CAPITAL, AND CENTRAL BANK BALANCES

The Hoover Institution gratefully acknowledges the following individuals and foundations for their significant support of the **Working Group on Economic Policy** *and this publication:*

Lynde and Harry Bradley Foundation

Preston and Carolyn Butcher

Stephen and Sarah Page Herrick

Michael and Rosalind Keiser

Koret Foundation

William E. Simon Foundation

John A. Gunn and Cynthia Fry Gunn

CURRENCIES, CAPITAL, AND CENTRAL BANK BALANCES

EDITED BY

JOHN H. COCHRANE
KYLE PALERMO
JOHN B. TAYLOR

CONTRIBUTING AUTHORS

Adrien Auclert	Raphael Bostic	Sebastian Edwards
Peter R. Fisher	Esther L. George	Gita Gopinath
Oleg Itskhoki	Robert S. Kaplan	Mickey D. Levy
Lorie K. Logan	Prachi Mishra	William Nelson
Jonathan D. Ostry	Monika Piazzesi	Charles I. Plosser
Randal K. Quarles	Raghuram Rajan	Thomas J. Sargent
Martin Schneider	George P. Shultz	John B. Taylor
Paul Tucker	Kevin Warsh	John C. Williams

WITH ADDITIONAL DISCUSSANTS

HOOVER INSTITUTION PRESS

STANFORD UNIVERSITY   STANFORD, CALIFORNIA

Hoover Institution Press Publication No. 697

Hoover Institution at Leland Stanford Junior University, Stanford, California 94305-6003

First printing 2019

26 25 24 23 22 21 20 19   9 8 7 6 5 4 3 2 1

Manufactured in the United States of America

The paper used in this publication meets the minimum requirements of the American National Standard for Information Sciences—Permanence of Paper for Printed Library Materials, ANSI/NISO Z39.48-1992. ⊚

Cataloging-in-Publication Data is available from the Library of Congress.
ISBN-13: 978-0-8179-2234-4 (cloth)
ISBN-13: 978-0-8179-2236-8 (EPUB)
ISBN-13: 978-0-8179-2237-5 (Mobipocket)
ISBN-13: 978-0-8179-2238-5 (PDF)

Contents

Preface

John H. Cochrane, Kyle Palermo, and John B. Taylor

This book focuses on two related monetary policy issues that are crucial to the future of central banks and the entire international monetary system, which includes over 150 central banks. We are pleased and grateful that top central bank officials from the United States—including five current and three former members of the Federal Open Market Committee—and from other countries joined the discussion and contributed to this book, along with monetary economists from academia and private financial institutions. There is much to be learned from the formal papers, the lead discussants, the policy panels, and the many questions and comments which are included in this book

The first policy issue concerns the international flow of money and capital and the resulting behavior of exchange rates—the price of one money, or currency, in terms of another. The key policy questions are whether capital flow management—government restrictions on cross-border loans and investments—can reduce harmful capital and exchange rate volatility; whether any such potential stabilization is worth its cost in market distortions, financial repression, and increased instability as people try to guess the actions of capital flow managers; and whether alternatives such as better and more rules-based international coordination of monetary policies can alleviate some of the conditions that lead countries to wish to control capital.

The second policy issue concerns the size of central bank balance sheets and their potential role as a separate monetary policy instrument beyond the policy interest rate set by central banks. A central bank balance sheet increases when the central bank purchases assets (such as government bonds or foreign currency bonds), borrows from commercial banks, and gives out central bank reserves in return. The first key policy question is whether central bank balance sheets should stay large or whether they should be reduced, either to the minimum—in which the economy remains satiated in interest-paying reserves—or to a smaller level, through which interest rates are then market-determined given the central bank's supply of non-interest-bearing reserves. The second key policy question is whether a radical expansion of the balance sheet should become a standard part of monetary policy any time short-term rates are constrained by the lower bound, whether such expansion should be reserved to an emergency action in case of financial panic, or whether it should be eschewed altogether.

The two issues interact because central bank balance sheet operations can affect exchange rates and capital flows. Moreover, the issues are currently on the policy agenda. The G20 Eminent Persons Group will make recommendations about policy toward capital flow later this year. The G20 central banks and finance ministries are then to follow up with decisions and implementation. The Fed is in the process of making key decisions about the ultimate size of its balance sheet, which will help set the stage for decisions at other central banks in the future. This book, like the policy conference at the Hoover Institution upon which it is based, aims to examine relevant research, debate the policy options, and present theory-based and fact-based analyses with which policy makers can make informed decisions on these and related issues.

CAPITAL FLOWS AND CURRENCIES IN THE INTERNATIONAL MONETARY SYSTEM

The book begins with two chapters on the international monetary system, which lead into an in-depth discussion of current IMF policy and policy advice relating to international capital flows. In *International Rules of the Monetary Game*, Raghuram Rajan, former governor of the Reserve Bank of India, in joint research with Prachi Mishra, develops a framework for international policy evaluation that shows the benefits of a rules-based system. He argues that monetary rules can prevent central banks' unconventional monetary policies from adversely affecting other countries and thereby interfering with the international system. In commenting on the paper, Tom Sargent stresses the broader reasons for a rules-based monetary system based on his own extensive research.

In *Dollar Dominance in Trade and Finance*, Gita Gopinath shows how private international financial intermediaries tend to focus on certain currencies, with the US dollar currently the dominant currency of choice. The dollar is often used for invoicing even when trade is between two non-US entities. Foreign as well as American banks often take dollar deposits and make dollar loans. The theoretical explanation is built on the idea that the dollar can serve as both a unit of account and a store of value and that attempts by countries to intervene to obtain such an advantage for their own currency often fail. In his comments, Adrien Auclert shows that there are many other predictions and ways to test the model.

With these two papers as general background, Jonathan Ostry, Sebastian Edwards, and John Taylor present their views on *Capital Flows, the IMF's Institutional View, and Alternatives*, chaired by George Shultz, who began the discussion by offering the view that, "The problem isn't capital flows; the problem is the central banks creating more money than is useful in their own countries, and it's slopping around." Ostry argues in favor of the IMF's Institutional View in which capital flow management measures artfully restrict the flow of capital across international borders. Taylor raises concerns about such restrictions and argues in favor of a rules-based international system along the lines advocated by Rajan. Edwards, based in part on the experience in Chile, notes that the transition to a world with open capital markets may take time. His bottom line is that the IMF should urge countries to "aim toward having no controls." Of course, there may be dangers getting there," he continues, "but we will help you deal with those problems."

CENTRAL BANK BALANCE SHEETS AND FINANCIAL STABILITY

In *Monetary Policy with a Layered Payment System*, Monika Piazzesi and Martin Schneider reconcile the standard idea that, faced with negative nominal rates on reserves or deposits, banks or individuals will swap them for currency with the fact that rates on both have, in practice, been negative. They offer a model that treats reserves and deposits as mechanisms for overcoming financial frictions, with banks and end users valuing low-return assets because they raise collateral ratios and offer a convenient medium of exchange, respectively. Discussant Oleg Itskhoki takes a deep dive into Piazzesi and Schneider's model, explaining the many underlying details of what he calls a "rich and insightful paper" and exploring some questions about its underlying details and opportunities to empirically test its assumptions.

In his chapter on *Liquidity Regulation and the Size of the Fed's Balance Sheet*, Randal Quarles, vice chairman for supervision of the Federal Reserve Board of Governors, looks at how bank demand for reserves will affect the size of the Fed's post-normalization balance sheet, which includes assets that banks use to meet liquidity coverage ratio (LCR) requirements. Discussant Paul Tucker follows with a call for policy makers to approach central and private banks through the lens of a Money-Credit Constitution which binds them to the goal of ensuring a secure monetary system. He also proposes a potential solution to the core problem raised by Quarles about the quantity of reserves demanded by banks: let banks decide for themselves under a voluntary reserves averaging program similar to that used by the Bank of England before the financial crisis.

Lorie Logan, Peter Fisher, Mickey Levy, and William Nelson then weigh in on *The Future of Central Bank Balance Sheets* chaired by Kevin Warsh who urged panelists to "question the prudence of unconventional policies' standing in the central bank's conventional toolkit," and to be "candid about our choices and humble about what we know of the Fed's incomplete experiment, even a decade later." There are two basic possibilities. First, the Fed could aim for a balance sheet in which reserves do not pay interest and the supply of reserve balances is low enough that the interest rate is determined by the demand and supply of reserves. Sometimes called the corridor approach, it's what the Fed used for decades before the global financial crisis. Second, the Fed could aim for a supply of reserves well above the quantity demanded at a zero rate and then set the interest rate through interest on excess reserves. This method is sometimes called a floor system.

Logan, with current experience at the New York Fed trading desk, argues for the second view, emphasizing that markets would be less volatile if the Fed sticks to a floor system. Fisher, who used to run the New York Fed trading desk, disagrees, saying that operational considerations for staying "big" are not convincing and that the rationale is orthogonal to the case made for going big in the first place. Nelson, who is familiar with operational considerations from his time at the Federal Reserve Board, argues in favor of the first approach. Levy notes the "economic and political risks of maintaining an outsized balance sheet" and concludes, "Of particular concern is the Fed's exposure to Congress's dysfunctional budget and fiscal policy making in the face of mounting government debt and debt service costs."

MONETARY REFORM AS SEEN FROM THE FOMC

In the symposium on *Monetary Policy and Reform in Practice*, one former and three current Federal Reserve Bank presidents take this volume into practical territory. Moderator Charles Plosser kicks off the discussion by reminding us that this was a chance for "real-life policy makers" to weigh in on challenges facing the Fed today, and for audience members to "prod them with some questions and see what their reactions will be." Kansas City Fed President Esther George discusses our very different and often-paradoxical post-crisis world in which low rates, a big Fed balance sheet, deepening fiscal deficits, and structural drags on long-run growth prospects are matched by an economy growing above trend at full employment. "Whatever the 'new normal' is, monetary policy is not yet there," she explains, warning that the Fed must use today's good economic times to resolve uncertainties about responses to future crises while shoring up our financial system.

Robert Kaplan of the Dallas Fed zeroes in on a number of the structural issues raised in George's paper. The Dallas Fed, he explains, forecasts a growth climate that is much less rosy when we zoom out to the medium term. He surveys some of the trends it is watching most closely, including declining labor force participation, declining education and skills, high government debt and unfunded liabilities, and how these trends will affect Fed tools such as the balance sheet and macroprudential policy.

Atlanta Fed President Raphael Bostic focuses on challenges to implementing policy without complete data. It's crucial that the Fed not repeat mistakes it made prior to the 2008 financial crisis when it missed financial red flags because it wasn't closely monitoring the housing market, he explains. The Atlanta Fed is working to reduce the risks of missing warning signs in the future by collecting "on-the-ground" intelligence from business leaders, public officials, and community groups.

LONG-RUN POLICY FRAMEWORKS

Federal Reserve Bank of New York President John Williams leans into the theme of this volume with a discussion of how policy makers can best maintain price stability and anchored inflation expectations—not this year or next year, but under a long-run policy framework. Focusing on the challenges policy makers face in pursuing these goals in a persistently low-rate environment, Williams explores some of the global downward pressures on r-star and where he thinks the rate will go in the future. He caps his paper off with an even bigger-picture discussion of how central banks should approach policy, not as a reaction to short-run problems, but under a big-picture framework that focuses on long-run goals and incorporates a healthy dose of analysis, dialogue, and weighing of different options.

PART I

CHAPTER ONE

INTERNATIONAL RULES OF THE MONETARY GAME

Prachi Mishra and Raghuram Rajan

In order to avoid the destructive beggar-thy-neighbor strategies that emerged during the Great Depression, the postwar Bretton Woods regime attempted to prevent countries from depreciating their currencies to gain an unfair and sustained competitive advantage. The system required fixed, but occasionally adjustable, exchange rates and restricted cross-border capital flows. Elaborate rules on when a country could move its exchange rate peg gave way, in the post-Bretton Woods world of largely flexible exchange rates, to a free-for-all where the only proscribed activity was sustained unidirectional intervention by a country in its exchange rate, especially if it was running a current account surplus. For more normal policies, a widely held view at that time was that each country, doing what was best for itself in a regime of mobile capital, would end up doing what was best for the global equilibrium. For instance, a country trying to unduly depreciate its exchange rate through aggressive monetary policy would see inflation rise to offset any temporary competitive gains. However, even if such automatic adjustment did ever work, and our paper does not take a position on this, the global environment has changed. Today, we have:

The views represent those of the authors and not of the Reserve Bank of India, IMF, or any of the institutions to which the authors belong.

- Weak aggregate demand, in part because of poorly understood consequences of population aging and productivity slowdown
- A more integrated and open world with large capital flows
- Significant government and private debt burdens
- Sustained low inflation.

The pressure to avoid a consistent breach of the lower inflation bound and the need to restore growth to reduce domestic unemployment could cause a country's authorities to place more of a burden on unconventional monetary policies (UMP) as well as on exchange rate or financial market interventions/repression. These may have large adverse spillover effects on other countries. The domestic mandates of most central banks do not legally allow them to take the full extent of spillovers into account and may force them to undertake aggressive policies so long as they have some small, positive domestic effect. Consequently, the world may embark on a suboptimal collective path. We need to reexamine rules of the game for responsible policy in such a context. This paper suggests some of the issues that need to be considered.

THE PROBLEM WITH THE CURRENT SYSTEM

All monetary policies have external spillover effects. If a country reduces domestic interest rates, its exchange rate also typically depreciates, helping exports. Under normal circumstances, the "demand creating" effects of lower interest rates on domestic consumption and investment are not small relative to the "demand switching" effects of the lower exchange rate in enhancing external demand for the country's goods. Indeed, one could argue that the spillovers to the rest of the world could be positive on net, as the enhanced domestic demand draws in substantial imports, offsetting the higher exports at the expense of other countries.

Matters have been less clear in the post-financial crisis world and with the unconventional monetary policies countries have adopted. For instance, if the interest rate-sensitive segments of the economy are constrained by existing debt, lower rates may have little effect on enhancing domestic demand but continue to have demand-switching effects through the exchange rate. Similarly, the unconventional "quantitative easing" policy of buying assets such as long-term bonds from domestic players may certainly lower long rates but may not have an effect on domestic investment if aggregate capacity utilization is low. Indeed, savers may respond to the increased distortion in asset prices by saving more. And if certain domestic institutional investors such as pension funds and insurance companies need long-term bonds to meet their future claims, they may respond by buying such bonds in less distorted markets abroad. Such a search for yield will depreciate the exchange rate. The primary effect of this policy on domestic demand may be through the demand-switching effects of a lower exchange rate rather than through a demand-creating channel. (See, for example, Taylor 2017 for evidence on the exchange rate consequences of unconventional monetary policy in recent years and the phenomenon of balance sheet contagion among central banks.)

Other countries can react to the consequences of unconventional monetary policies, and some economists argue that it is their unwillingness to react appropriately that is the fundamental problem (see, for example, Bernanke 2015). Yet concerns about monetary and financial stability may prevent those countries, especially less institutionally developed ones, from reacting to offset the disturbance emanating from the initiating country. It seems reasonable that a globally responsible assessment of policies should take the world as it is, rather than as a hypothetical ideal.

Ultimately, if all countries engage in demand-switching policies, we could have a race to the bottom. Countries may find it hard

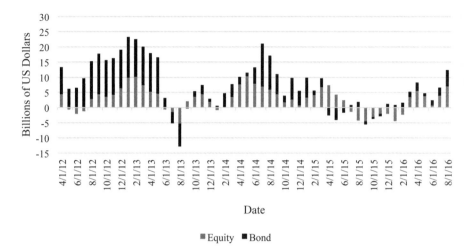

FIGURE 1.1.1. Nonresident Portfolio Inflows to Emerging Market Economies.
Source: IMF, "Global Financial Stability Report," October 2016

to get out of such policies because the immediate effect for the country that exits might be a serious appreciation of the exchange rate and a fall in domestic activity. Moreover, the consequences of unconventional policies over the medium term need not be benign if aggressive monetary easing results in distortions to asset markets and debt buildup, with an eventual disastrous denouement.

Thus far, we have focused on exchange and interest rate effects of a country's monetary policy on the rest of the world. A second, obviously related, channel of transmission of a country's monetary policy to the rest of the world in the post-Bretton Woods system has been through capital flows. These have been prompted not just by interest differentials but also by changes in institutional attitudes toward risk and leverage, influenced by sending country monetary policies. Figure 1.1.1, for example, shows that post-global crisis capital flows to EMs have been large. This is despite great reluctance on the part of several EMs to avoid absorbing the inflows.

As a consequence, local leverage in emerging economies has increased (figure 1.1.2). The increase could reflect the direct effect

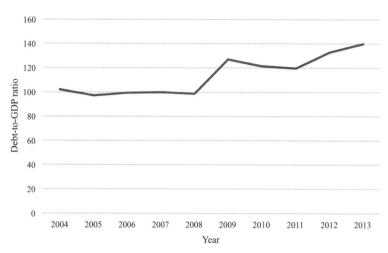

FIGURE 1.1.2. Corporate Debt-to-GDP Ratio for Emerging Economies
Source: IMF, "Global Financial Stability Report," October 2016

of cross-border banking flows, changes in global risk aversion stemming from source country monetary policy (Rey 2013; Baskaya et al. 2017; Morais, Peydro, and Ruiz 2015), the promise of abundant future liquidity on borrowing capacity (see Diamond, Hu, and Rajan 2017, for example), or the indirect effects of an appreciating exchange rate and rising asset prices, which may make it seem that emerging market (EM) borrowers have more equity than they really have (see Shin 2016, for example).

The unintended consequence of such flows is that they are significantly influenced by the monetary policies of the sending countries and may reverse quickly—as they did during the Taper Tantrum in 2013. This means that they are not a reliable source of financing, which then requires emerging market central banks to build ample stocks of liquidity (that is, foreign exchange reserves) for when the capital flows reverse. Moreover, the liquidity insurance provided by emerging market central banks to their borrowers is never perfect, so when capital flows reverse, they tend to leave financial and economic distress in their wake. Capital flows, driven or pulled back by the monetary policy stance in industrial countries, create risk on the way in and distress on the way out. They constitute both a costly spillover and a significant constraint on emerging market monetary flexibility.

The bottom line is that simply because a policy is called monetary, unconventional or otherwise, it may not be beneficial on net for the world. That all monetary policies have external spillovers does not mean that they are all justified. What matters is the relative magnitude of demand-creating versus demand-switching effects and the magnitude of other net financial sector spillovers, that is, the net spillovers (see Borio 2014; Borio and Disyatat 2009, 292; Rajan 2013 and 2014, for example).

Of course, a central contributor today to policy makers putting lower weight on international spillovers is that almost all central banks have purely domestic mandates. If they are in danger of violating the lower bound of their inflation mandate, for example, they are required to adopt all possible policies to get inflation back on target, no matter what their external effect. Indeed, they can even intervene directly in the exchange rate in a sustained and unidirectional way, although internationally this could be seen as an abdication of international responsibility according to the old standards. The current state of affairs means that central banks find all sorts of ways to justify their policies in international fora without acknowledging the unmentionable—that the exchange rate may be the primary channel of transmission and external spillovers may be significantly adverse. Unfortunately, even if they do not want to abdicate international responsibility, their domestic mandates may give them no other options. In what follows, we will examine sensible rules of monetary behavior assuming the domestic mandate does not trump international responsibility.

PRINCIPLES FOR SETTING NEW RULES

Monetary policy actions by one country can lead to measurable and significant cross-border spillovers. Such spillovers can influence countries to undertake policies that shift some of the cost of the policy to foreign countries. This temptation to shift costs can create inefficiencies when countries set their policies unilaterally. If countries agree on a set of new rules or principles that describe the limits of acceptable behavior, it can reduce inefficiencies and lead to higher welfare in all the countries. This does not mean countries have to coordinate policies, only that they have to become better global citizens in foregoing policies that have large negative external effects. We had such a rule in the past—no sustained unidirectional intervention in the exchange rate—but with the plethora of new unconventional policies, we have to find new, clear, and mutually acceptable rules.

What would be the basis for the new rules? As a start, policies could be broadly rated based on analytical inputs and discussion. To use a driving analogy, polices that have few adverse spillovers and are even to be encouraged by the global community could be rated green; policies that should be used temporarily and with care could be rated orange; and policies that should be avoided at all times could be rated red. To establish such ratings, the effects of any policy have to be seen over time, rather than at a point in time. We will discuss the broad principles for such ratings in this section. We will then discuss whether the tools economists have today allow empirical analysis to provide a clear-cut rating of policies. (To preview the answer, it is "No!") We will then argue that it may still be possible to make progress, once broad principles of the sort discussed in this section are agreed on.

A number of issues would need to be considered in developing a framework to rate policies.

- Should a policy that has any adverse spillovers outside the country of origin be totally avoided? Or should the benefits in the country of origin be added to measure the net global effects of the policy? In other words, should we consider the enhancement to global welfare or the net spillovers to others only in judging policy?
- Should the measurement of spillovers take into account any policy reactions by other countries? In other words, should the policy be judged based on its partial equilibrium or general equilibrium effects?
- Should domestic benefits weigh more and adverse spillovers weigh less for countries that have run out of policy options and have been stuck in slow growth for a long time? Should countries be allowed "jump starts" facilitated by others?
- Should spillovers be measured over the medium term or evaluated at a point in time?
- Should spillovers (both positive and negative) be weighted more heavily for poorer countries that have weaker institutions and less effective policy instruments?
- Should spillovers be weighted by the affected population or by the dollar value of the effect?

Some tentative answers follow.

In general, policies that have net adverse outside spillovers over time could be rated red and should be avoided. Such policies obviously include those that have small positive effects in the home country (where the policy action originates) combined with large negative effects in the foreign country (where the spillovers occur). For example, if unconventional monetary policy actions lead to a feeble recovery in some of the advanced countries leading to small positive effects on exports to emerging markets, but large capital flows to, and asset price bubbles in, the EMs, these policies could be rated red. Global welfare would decrease with this policy.

If a policy has positive effects on both home and foreign countries, and therefore on global welfare, it would definitely be rated green. Conventional monetary policy would fall in this category, as it would raise output in the home economy and create demand for exports from the foreign economy. A green rating for such policies would, however, assume that the stage of the financial and credit cycle in the home and foreign economies is such that financial stability risks from low interest rates are likely to be limited.[1]

It is possible to visualize other policies that have large positive effects for the originating country (because of the value of the policy or because of the country's relative size) and sustained small negative effects for the rest of the world. Global welfare, crudely speaking, may go up with the policy, even though welfare outside the originating country goes down. While it is hard to rate such policies without going into specifics, these may correctly belong in the orange category: permissible for some time but not on a sustained basis. Even conventional monetary policies to raise growth in the home economy could fall in the orange category if countries are at a financial stage where low interest rates lead to significant financial stability risks in the home and foreign economies.

Clearly, foreign countries may have policy room to respond, and that should be taken into account. Perhaps the right way to measure spillovers to the foreign country is to measure their welfare without the policy under question and their welfare after the policy is implemented and response initiated. So, for instance, a home country A at the zero lower bound may initiate quantitative easing (QE) and a foreign country B may respond by cutting interest rates to avoid capital inflows and exchange rate appreciation. The spill-

---

1. One example of what could be rated green is the framework suggested by Taylor (2017) wherein countries would announce their rules-based monetary policies—with opt-outs in cases of emergency. Such a framework would have the added benefit of allowing countries to set reasonable reaction functions to source country policies.

over effects of QE would be based on B's welfare if QE were not undertaken versus B's welfare after QE is initiated and it responds. A policy could also be rated green if it acts as a booster shot for an economy stuck in a rut and if it can jump-start that economy (for example, Lars Svensson's proposal for Japan to engage in exchange rate targeting in order to alter inflationary expectations), but creates temporary negative spillovers for the foreign economy. Even if there are temporary adverse spillovers on foreign countries, the policy—through its effect on home economy growth and demand for foreign goods—can eventually provide offsetting large positive spillovers to the rest of the world. Of course, it is important that the home economy, after receiving the booster shot and picking up growth, not follow policies (such as holding down its exchange rate longer term) that minimize positive spillovers to other countries. A policy rated red on a static basis could thus be deemed green based on commitments over time. This also means that policies should be rated over the medium term rather than on the basis of one-shot static effects.

What we have just argued is that countries stuck in a rut for a long time and with few other options should temporarily be allowed policies that may have adverse spillovers. But what if the policy is sought to be employed over the medium term? Here, "rut" is a relative term both over time and across countries. If a stagnant, rich country is allowed a free pass, should historically stagnant, and therefore poor, countries have a permanent pass to do whatever is in their best interests? It would be difficult to carve out exceptions to developed countries based on relative stagnation, or deviations from trend growth, without admitting a whole lot of other exceptions.

In this vein, poorer countries typically have weaker institutions—for example, central banks with limited credibility and budgetary frameworks that are not constrained by rules and watchdogs. As a result, their ability to offset spillovers with policies is typically more limited. Furthermore, poorer citizens live closer to the minimum margin of sustainability and poorer countries typically have weaker safety nets. So there is a case for weighting spillovers to poor countries more. However, it will be difficult to determine precisely what weight to place. Nevertheless, this facet could be kept in mind in deciding how to rate a policy when it is on the borderline.

A related problem is whether spillovers should be measured in aggregate monetary terms or in "utils" weighted by population. Once again, determining utilities may be hard, so perhaps at first pass it may be better to evaluate the dollar value of spillovers without attempting a further translation in utilities. This will certainly facilitate adding up across countries and over time to see the net effect of policies.

Overall, whether policies are rated red, green, or orange would depend on a number of factors such as the stage of the financial and business cycle in the home and foreign countries; whether the policy action constitutes a booster shot to jump-start the economy or gives only a mild boost and has to be employed for a sustained period; whether standard transmission channels are clogged to warrant the use of unconventional policies; whether the foreign country has room to adopt buffering policies; whether the spillovers affect poor countries which have weak institutions and less room to respond, etc.

Finally, some examples of policies that could be rated could include the following.

- Direct or "evident" exchange rate manipulation, e.g., through massive intervention in the foreign exchange market which aims to depreciate a country's exchange rate or not let it appreciate, or keep it "undervalued" relative to some benchmark.
- Other indirect policies that have similar beggar-thy-neighbor effects. Unconventional monetary policies could potentially belong to this category.

- Policies that can have financial sector spillovers such as capital flows, high credit growth, and asset price bubbles. These could also be considered as generating large adverse spillovers through the financial system. Low interest rate policies for long periods in advanced economies could fall in this category.

In sum then, at first pass it may be reasonable to consider the following for such policies.

a) Focus on spillovers over time.

b) Measure spillovers as the welfare of a receiving country if a policy is implemented, after it undertakes policies in response, less its welfare if the policy were not implemented.

c) Allow policies that do not impose net adverse external spillover effects over time and discourage policies that do have net adverse external spillover effects over time, with some tolerance for a subset of policies that have large domestic benefits and are intended to be carried on for a short while.

d) Do not carve out exceptions for any country, regardless of its stage in the business cycle.

e) Give more weight to spillovers to poor countries at the margin.

f) Measure spillovers in dollar terms.

Before concluding this section, let us address five common reactions to any suggestion of rules of the game.

Central banks already take into account spillback effects of their policies, even if they have a domestic mandate. This is true, but the spillback effects (the partial consequences of their policies as they flow back to the source country, for example, through lower growth and thus lower imports of trading partners) may be only a fraction of the spillover effects. What matters for the world as a whole is that countries internalize spillover effects.

Central banks already discuss their policies at various forums and strive to communicate and be transparent. Yes, but open communication and transparency still are tantamount to saying, "It's our policy, and your problem."

Taking spillover effects into account would make policy making, which is already hard, overly complicated and impossible to communicate. Yes, but presumably countries already take spillback effects into account, which involves estimating policy reaction functions of other countries. How much more complicated will it be to take spillover effects into account?

Rules will constrain only the systemically important central banks. Probably, though smaller countries will also have obligations. It is a reality that the consequences of monetary policy are asymmetric and depend on a country's importance. Often, this is a source of privilege and power. We are suggesting some commensurate obligations.

Any rules will affect a central bank's ability to deliver on its domestic mandate. True, which is why we will eventually have to explore how domestic mandates sit with international obligations in this integrated world. In many other areas of international interaction (e.g., carbon emissions), we rarely argue that a country is free to do what is best domestically even if it imposes costs on the rest of the world. It cannot be that monetary policy gets a free pass simply because monetary mandates were put in place when spillovers were less of a concern.

Before we discuss how we could move forward, let us discuss what we can glean from the literature. A more technical description of the principles that could guide us in setting new rules of the game is provided in the appendix.

THE STATE OF THE LITERATURE

Of course, even if we have agreement on broad principles of rating, we need to measure the effects of policies. Unfortunately, the state of the art here is more art than science. Models may reflect the policy biases (unconscious or otherwise) of those devising them and are at a sufficiently early stage that it would be difficult to draw strong conclusions from them. Perhaps, therefore, more empirical analysis (rather than theoretical models) on the lines of Kamin (2016) should be emphasized and seen as an input to a dialogue, with the analysis being refined as we understand actual outcomes better.

Simulation of Spillover Scenarios: Global Models

The International Monetary Fund (IMF) has used several global models, such as GIMF, FSGM, and GPM, to simulate different spillover scenarios.[2] These are dynamic general equilibrium models with many regions and many sectors. These models are used to measure spillovers from monetary policies in advanced countries. The US Federal Reserve has also developed a multicountry dynamic general equilibrium model called SIGMA, which has also been used for analysis of spillovers.

Easy monetary conditions in advanced economies can lead to capital inflows, exchange rate appreciation, rapid credit growth, and asset price bubbles in emerging markets. On the other hand, monetary normalization or a rise in interest rates in advanced economies can cause capital outflows and exchange rate depreciation in the EMs. Several spillover scenarios can be simulated using these global models. These scenarios include, for example, a growth-driven exit with complications where long-term interest rates

---

2. Global Integrated Monetary and Fiscal Model, Flexible System of Global Models, and Global Protection Model.

jump up as monetary policy is tightened and capital outflows from emerging markets are intense; and an exit without growth where monetary policy is tightened despite a lack of growth momentum in the United States. In these scenarios, emerging economies could see growth fall below the baseline.

While these global models provide a useful framework to understand spillovers, they are already complicated, with multiple sectors, regions, and parameters, even without realistic depictions of institutional or financial sector vulnerabilities. Moreover, the predictions from these models are not sufficiently clear-cut and often depend on the underlying assumptions. The choice of scenarios that are played up prominently in policy documents could be influenced by the desired answers. We need to understand far more about the reliability of these models and their sensitivity to alternative assumptions before countries will trust them to be applied for policy judgments.

Two-country Models of International Policy Spillovers

There is also a strand of literature that considers policy spillovers in two-country frameworks. For example, Haberis and Lipinska (2012) consider how monetary policy in a large, foreign economy affects optimal monetary policy in a small, open economy ("home") when both economies are close to a zero lower bound. They show that more stimulatory foreign monetary policy *worsens* the home policy maker's trade-offs between stabilizing inflation and the output gap when home and foreign goods are close substitutes. An exchange rate channel of monetary transmission is key to the argument. A looser foreign policy leads to a relatively more appreciated home real exchange rate, which induces large expenditure-switching away from home goods when goods are highly substitutable—just at a time (e.g., at the zero lower bound, or ZLB) when home policy is trying to boost demand for home goods. Fujiwara, Sudo, and Teranishi (2010), Eichengreen et al. (2011), Bodenstein, Erceg, and Guerrieri (2009), and Erceg and Linde (2011), among others, also study spillovers in two-country models. Fujiwara, Sudo, and Teranishi (2010) and Eichengreen et al. (2011) study explicit policy coordination. Eichengreen et al., for example, argue that monetary spillovers at the ZLB should be internalized in a coordinated global monetary policy. Ostry and Ghosh (2013), however, note that real-world examples of international policy coordination are rare. They argue that the most compelling reasons why we do not see more coordination in practice are asymmetry in country size, disagreement about the economic situation and cross-border effects of policies, and often policy makers' failure to recognize that they face trade-offs across different objectives.

More recently, Bernanke (2015) lays out a simple two-country model of spillovers to show that a flexible exchange rate can largely insulate emerging markets from both internal and external shocks in the medium run. He argues that even the existence of financial stability spillovers does not invalidate the basic implication of the "trilemma," that exchange rate flexibility can help insulate domestic output from foreign monetary policies; and any remaining spillovers should be tackled by regulatory and macroprudential measures. We agree that a flexible exchange rate and targeted macroprudential policies are usually the best tools available for containing any building vulnerabilities that may threaten a developed country's growth or the stability of its financial system. There may, however, be limits to their use, especially in emerging markets where monetary and fiscal institutions have modest credibility or, relatedly, where there is a high extent of dollarization (see, for example, Akinci and Queralto 2018). For instance, the well-documented "fear of floating" in emerging markets (see Calvo and Reinhart 2000) is not because policy makers are not sufficiently conversant with modern macroeconomic theory but because the different political and institutional environments in an emerging market make it costlier to follow policy advice that works well in a developed country.

Spillovers and policy coordination have also been considered extensively in the international trade literature. Bagwell and Staiger (2002), in their pioneering work, develop a two-good, two-country general equilibrium model to analyze terms of trade spillovers from tariff policies and to provide a rationale for policy coordination among countries. A large number of papers build on the approach in Bagwell and Staiger to understand spillovers and externalities in international trade.

The simple two-country models provide a useful framework to understand the mechanisms through which policies in one country can affect others, but they may be less suited for "measuring" spillovers. Therefore, in what follows, we discuss several econometric models that have been used in the literature on spillovers.

Structural VARs

There is a significant body of evidence that uses structural VARs (vector autoregression) to analyze spillovers. The identification in such models is based on sign restrictions or through the heteroskedasticity method introduced by Rigobon and Sack (2003). IMF (2014) and IMF (2015), for example, estimate a structural VAR using long-term bond yields and stock prices for the United States, the United Kingdom, the euro area, and Japan (G4) using daily data and sign restrictions for identification of the shocks. The dynamic interactions between the dependent variables and external shocks are then modeled using a panel VAR, estimated with monthly data. The dependent variables include local long-term sovereign yields, the nominal effective exchange rate, and industrial production. The external shocks are the G4 money or real shock. The results show that money and real shocks have different spillover implications.

Money shocks cause a significant co-movement in long-term bond yields, whereas the real shock implies a much smaller co-movement of yields. While the real shock has an overall benign spillover on EMs, the money shock has adverse spillovers on EMs. Yue and Shen (2011) instead exploit heteroskedasticity in the bond market data and estimate an SVAR to study international transmission of shocks across advanced economies. Employing daily data on ten-year government bond yields for the United States, Germany, Japan, and the United Kingdom over the period 1989–2010, they find that shocks to US long-term markets exert a significant influence on foreign bond yields. On average, nearly 30 percent of the shock to US bond yields is directly transmitted to foreign bond yields.

Global Vector Autoregression Model

The global vector autoregression (GVAR) model was developed by Pesaran, Schuermann, and Weiner (2004) and by Dees et al. (2007). For each country, the conventional VAR model is extended with the addition of a set of foreign variables. These variables are constructed as weighted averages of the same variables of all the country's trading partners. All individual countries' VAR models are collected and estimated as a single VAR model. The dynamic properties of the model are then used to analyze how shocks are propagated across countries. IMF (2014), for example, uses GVARs to analyze the spillover implications of a potential slowdown in EMs. Cashin, Mohaddes, and Raissi (2012) also use GVARs to analyze spillovers from macroeconomic shocks in systemic economies to the Middle East and North Africa region, as well as outward spillovers from a GDP shock in the Gulf Cooperation Council countries and MENA (Middle East and North Africa) oil exporters to the rest of the world. Chen et al. (2015) instead use a global vector error correction model (GVECM) to study the impact of US quantitative easing on both emerging and advanced economies.

The GVECM framework is similar to GVAR, the only difference being that it accounts for co-integration between the variables in the model using an error correction term. Chen et al. (2015) find that the estimated effects of US QE are diverse. While the US monetary policy contributed to overheating in Brazil, China, and some other emerging economies in 2010 and 2011, it supported the respective recoveries in 2009 and 2012, pointing to unevenly distributed benefits and costs of monetary policy spillovers.

Factor Augmented Vector Autoregression Model (FAVAR)

FAVAR is another econometric methodology similar to VAR which has been used in the literature to measure spillovers. The methodology was developed by Aasveit, Bjørnland, and Thorsrud (2013). It is a standard VAR augmented with two unobserved factors. The unobserved factors are identified and estimated by employing the principal component method. To identify the vector of structural shocks, a combination of zero and sign restrictions is used. IMF (2014), for example, uses a FAVAR framework to analyze the spillovers of a slowdown in EM growth to commodity prices. The framework is applied to identify specific oil-demand as opposed to oil-supply shocks where production data are available at a monthly frequency.

Event Studies

A rising body of literature uses event study methodology to analyze the international transmission of shocks. The methodology pools events such as monetary policy announcements made by the FOMC and evaluates market reactions in emerging markets around these events. Several studies also assess the importance of macroeconomic fundamentals and other country characteristics in the transmission of shocks to financial markets in EMs. Although there is some debate about whether these studies accurately capture long-run effects (after all, they are predicated on the market reacting "efficiently" to the long-run consequences of policy), these studies generally find that countries with stronger macroeconomic fundamentals are affected less during the episodes of volatility, relative to countries with weaker fundamentals.

Other Empirical Studies

A growing literature on transmission of unconventional monetary policies to emerging markets examines correlations in market outcome variables across countries. Hofmann and Takáts (2015), for example, referring to a range of country-specific studies, conclude that interest rates and asset prices have become increasingly correlated globally during the period of unprecedented monetary easing by the major advanced economies. Both the short- and long-term interest rates of EMs have been heavily influenced by those in the advanced economies, particularly the United States. Rey (2013, 2014), more generally, provides evidence for strong common movements in gross capital flows and credit growth around the world.

Recently, Kamin (2016) in an ongoing study uses some back-of-the-envelope estimates to provide evidence for an exchange rate channel of monetary transmission in the United States. He shows that a US monetary easing that lowers US Treasury yields by 25 basis points causes the dollar to depreciate by 1 percent. However, he finds that while a 25 basis point decline in yields lowers foreign output by 0.05 percent through the "demand switching" channel, it increases foreign output through the "demand creating" channel by exactly the same magnitude. More studies along these lines, perhaps by academics (see more on this below), should be encouraged and should be seen as inputs into a policy dialogue.

Spillovers from Exchange Rate "Movements"

Studying the effects of exchange rates is a hardy perennial of international macroeconomics. But nearly all the empirical research is focused on the impact on the country whose exchange rate changes. There is less evidence, however, on the effect of exchange rate movements on the exports of competitor countries, which in its adverse manifestation is dubbed the "beggar-thy-neighbor" effect. In a world besieged by accusations of "currency wars" and "negative spillovers," owing to the extensive recourse to unconventional monetary policies and exchange rate depreciations, measuring this effect is important.

Competitor country effects from exchange rate changes have been discussed in the literature, albeit without much systematic empirical examination of the phenomenon. For example, de Blas and Russ (2010) theoretically examine third-country effects of relative price shocks. Feenstra, Hamilton, and Lim (2002) conjecture that China's significant devaluation in 1994 curtailed export growth for South Korean chaebols. Similarly, Forbes and Rigobon (2002) survey the evidence for contagion through a trade channel, where sudden devaluation by one country may spread crisis to other countries that compete with it in a common export market.[3]

Summary of the Empirical Literature

To summarize, there is a fast-growing empirical literature on estimating spillovers. A large body of the literature, however, seems to have focused on analyzing the international transmission of outcome variables like government bond yields or exchange

---

3. See also Avdjiev, Koch, and Shin (2017) for international spillovers of exchange rate movements through the financial sector.

rates rather than measuring cross-border spillovers from specific policies. Where studies have tried to measure spillovers from specific policies, *identifying* the spillover effects remains a challenge. Identifications through sign restrictions or through heteroskedasticity methods are essentially statistical techniques and may not have much economic interpretation. Event studies help in identification, but data on market variables at very high frequency (e.g., intraday data used typically in advanced economies around particular events) may not be readily available for many EMs.

It is also hard to choose between different empirical models such as SVAR, VECM, event studies, and panel frameworks to draw policy implications. A comparison of the results from different models, and perhaps methodologies like Bayesian model averaging, could be employed to get a comprehensive overview of cross-border spillovers from country-specific policies.

Given this state of the art, it might not be wise to use the analysis as anything more than a basis of discussion to rate policies. Instead, many policies will fall in the orange zone, with much of the discussion about how further adjustments can take them well and truly into the green zone. Experience—and postmortem analysis—may indicate some policies should truly have been classified red. Over time, analysis plus experience can allow a sharper rating of policies.

HOW TO PROCEED?

The next crucial questions are: Who should assess spillovers? What would be an appropriate forum to discuss spillover effects from specific policies and the ratings of these policies? How should we proceed?

A Group of Eminent Academics

Given the constraints and political difficulties under which international organizations operate, it may be appropriate to start with a group of eminent academics with reasonable representation across the globe and have them assess the spillovers and grade policies.

International Meetings

Perhaps the next step would be an agreement to discuss policies and their international spillover effects at meetings such as those of the IMF Board, the International Monetary and Financial Committee, the Bank for International Settlements, and the G20. The discussion would be based on background papers, which would be commissioned from both traditional sources like the IMF and nontraditional sources like the group of academics and EM central banks.

These papers would attempt to isolate the nature of spillovers as well as their magnitude and attempt a preliminary classification of policy actions. Almost surely, there will be a lot of fuzziness about which color to attribute to a wide range of recent policies. But discussion can help participants understand both how the policies could be classified if we had better models and data and how the models and data gathering can be improved.

Country Responsibilities before Formal Rules

When policies are being discussed so as to get better understanding, no policies that affect the international monetary system should be off the table. Importantly, simply denoting a policy with the label "monetary" should not give it an automatic free pass because it falls under the central bank's domestic mandate. What will be important is not the policy maker's mandate, professed intent, or instruments, but actual channels of transmission and outcomes, including spillovers.

Policy makers will respond to the background papers by stating and explaining their policy actions, attempting to persuade the international community that they fall in the green and orange zones.

International Conference

As the international community builds understanding on what constitutes sensible rules of the game and how to label policies in that context, perhaps an international conference may be warranted to see how the community's understanding of beneficial rules can be implemented. At that time, a discussion of how a central bank's international responsibilities fit in with its domestic mandate may be warranted. While recognizing the political difficulty of altering any central bank's mandate, the conference will have to deliberate on how international responsibilities can be woven into existing mandates. It will have to decide whether a new international agreement along the lines of Bretton Woods is needed or whether much can be accomplished by small changes in the Fund's Articles of Agreement, accompanied by corresponding changes in mandates of country authorities.

Role of the Fund

What role would the Fund play? The obligations of members and the authority of the Fund are derived from the Articles of Agreement. Section 1 of Article IV makes clear that IMF members are under general obligation "to collaborate with other members of the Fund to assure orderly exchange arrangements and to promote a stable system of exchange rates." The meaning of "general obligation" is unclear in the Articles but could be "relied upon as a basis for the Fund to call on its members to take specific actions or to refrain from taking specific actions" (IMF 2006). Article IV further states, "In particular, each member shall . . . (iii) avoid manipulating exchange rates or the international monetary system in order to prevent effective balance of payments adjustment or to gain unfair competitive advantage over other members . . ." Furthermore, the Principles for the Guidance of Members' Exchange Rate Policies (originally 1977, amended in 2007) note, "Members should take into account in their intervention policies the interests of other members, including those in whose currency they intervene."

Although the Articles of Agreement or the Principles do not define "manipulation" in any detail, IMF (2007) narrows the scope of manipulation by noting that "manipulation of the exchange rate is only carried through policies that are targeted at—and actually affect—the level of exchange rate. Moreover, manipulation may cause the exchange rate to move or may prevent such movement."

In practice, it may be difficult to determine if a policy is targeted at attaining a level of exchange rate. Direct policy actions such as intervention in the foreign exchange market or indirect policies such as monetary, fiscal, and trade policies or regulations of capital movements, regardless of the intent or purpose, can also affect the level of the exchange rate and can be interpreted as "manipulation." The interpretation of the Articles of Agreement could perhaps be broadened in scope to include a wider range of policies which can primarily have effects on the exchange rates, and therefore beggar-thy-neighbor consequences.

While the Articles of Agreement include members' obligations in relation to exchange rate policies, global financial stability implications of country-specific policies are not touched upon anywhere in the Articles. Members' obligations are considered only in relation to domestic growth objectives. For example, based on the Articles, a country with a weak economy can pursue loose monetary policies to stimulate output and employment. Despite the implications of such policies for financial stability in other countries, the country would argue that its policies are in line with Article IV, Section 1(i) which allows each member to "direct its economic and financial policies toward the objective of fostering orderly economic growth with reasonable price stability . . ." More generally, the Fund's Articles may need altering based on the discussion of the rules of the game.

Moreover, although broader surveillance by the Fund of its members' exchange rate policies and other policies with significant financial sector spillovers (and perhaps public statements about such policies) can have signaling effects, countries are not obligated to follow Fund advice unless in a program. The more pertinent question, therefore, might be: What can the Fund really do once its executive board determines that a particular country is in violation of its obligations under the new rules of the game? An optimistic view is that the clear focus on the downsides of the particular country's actions for the rest of the world will lead to political and economic pressures from around the world that make the country cease and desist. The clearer the eventual rules of the game, the more likely this outcome will be. Realistically, though, the world's experience with moral suasion (or name and shame) as a way to get countries to behave has, at best, been mixed. Regardless, we are so far from agreed rules that contemplating enforcement at this point seems premature.

CONCLUSIONS

As this paper suggests, there is much that needs to be pinned down on the international spillovers from domestic policies, especially as regards the international monetary system. Given the undoubted importance of cross-border trade and capital flows and the disruptions created by financial market volatility, it does seem an important issue to discuss. Nevertheless, with economic analysis of these issues at an early stage, it is unlikely we will get strong policy prescriptions soon, let alone international agreement on them, especially given that a number of country authorities—like central banks—have explicit domestic mandates.

This paper therefore suggests a period of focused discussion, first outside international meetings and then within international meetings. There can be no more important issue to understand and discuss than the international spillovers of domestic policies. Such a discussion need not take place in an environment of finger-pointing and defensiveness, but as an attempt to understand what can be reasonable, and not overly intrusive, rules of conduct.

As consensus builds on the rules of conduct, we can contemplate the next step of whether to codify them through international agreement and we can see how the articles of agreement of multilateral watchdogs like the IMF will have to be altered and how country authorities will interpret or alter domestic mandates to incorporate international responsibilities.

Obviously, any attempt to strengthen international rules in the current environment where countries are growing increasingly nationalistic, and turning away from international responsibilities, could be seen as optimistic at best and naïve at worst. We must, however, keep in mind two developments that make reform urgent. First, the increase in cross-border flows makes the world ever more integrated. Second, the world is becoming multipolar. The system worked in the past despite the absence of rules because it had one hegemon, the United States, which broadly influenced behavior in the system. As the economic world becomes more multipolar, and as rising powers reject the current system as well as the past understanding of rules as overly favorable to the dominant powers of the past, the risk of conflict over behavior increases. With no single hegemon to police the system, it will probably work better if there are broadly accepted rules that bind every large player. This paper is an attempt to start the dialogue toward reaching consensus on an acceptable set of rules.

References

Aasveit, Knut A., Hilde C. Bjørnland, and Leif Anders Thorsrud. 2013. "What Drives Oil Prices? Emerging versus Developed Economies." Norges Bank Working Paper no. 2012/11, May 7.

Akinci, Ozge, and Albert Queralto. 2018. "Balance Sheets, Exchange Rates, and International Monetary Spillovers." Working paper, Federal Reserve Bank of New York, June.

Avdjiev, Stefan, Catherine Koch, and Hyun Song Shin. 2018. "Exchange Rates and the Transmission of Global Liquidity." BIS Working Paper, March.

Bagwell, Kyle, and Robert W. Staiger. 2002. "The Economics of the World Trading System." Cambridge, MA: MIT Press.

Baskaya, Yusuf Soner, Julian di Giovanni, Sebnem Kalemli-Ozcan, and Mehmet Fatih Ulu. 2017. "International Spillovers and Local Credit Cycles." NBER Working Paper no. 23149.

Bernanke, Ben S. 2015. "Federal Reserve Policy in an International Context." Paper presented at the sixteenth Jacques Polak Annual Research Conference, Washington, DC, November 5–6.

Bodenstein, Martin, Christopher J. Erceg, and Luca Guerrieri. 2009. "The Effects of Foreign Shocks When Interest Rates Are at Zero." International Finance Discussion Papers no. 983, October 28.

Borio, Claudio. 2014, "The International Monetary and Financial System: Its Achilles Heel and What to Do About It." BIS Working Paper no. 456, August 31.

Borio, Claudio, and Piti Disyatat. 2009. "Unconventional Monetary Policies: An Appraisal." BIS Working Paper.

Calvo, Guillermo A., and Carmen M. Reinhart. 2000. "Fear of Floating." NBER Working Paper no. 7993, November.

Cashin, Paul, Kamiar Mohaddes, and Mehdi Raissi. 2012. "The Differential Effects of Oil Demand and Supply Shocks on the Global Economy." IMF Working Paper no. 12/253, October 23.

Chen, Qianying, Andrew Filardo, Dong He, and Feng Zhu. 2015. "Financial Crisis, US Unconventional Monetary Policy and International Spillovers." BIS Working Paper no. 494, March 16.

de Blas, Beatriz, and Katheryn Russ. 2010. "Understanding Markups in the Open Economy under Bertrand Competition." NBER Working Paper no. 16587.

Dees, Stephane, Filippo di Mauro, M. Hashem Pesaran, and L.Vanessa Smith. 2007. "Exploring the International Linkages of the Euro Area: A Global VAR Analysis." *Journal of Applied Econometrics* 22, no. 1 (March 14): 1–38.

Diamond, Douglas, Yunchi Hu, and Raghuram Rajan. 2017. "Pledgeability, Industry Liquidity, and Financing Cycles." Working paper, University of Chicago, November.

Eichengreen, Barry, Mohamed El-Erian, Arminio Fraga, Takatoshi Ito, Jean Pisani-Ferry, Eswar Prasad, Raghuram Rajan, Maria Ramos, Carmen Reinhart, Hélène Rey, Dani Rodrik, Kenneth Rogoff, Hyun Song Shin, Andres Velasco, Beatrice Weder di Mauro, and Yongding Yu. 2011. "Rethinking Central Banking." Brookings Institution, September 13.

Erceg, Christopher J., and Jesper Linde. 2011. "Asymmetric Shocks in a Currency Union with Monetary and Fiscal Handcuffs, vol. 7." Chicago: University of Chicago Press, 95–136.

Feenstra, Robert C., Gary G. Hamilton, and Eun Mie Lim. 2002. "Chaebol and Catastrophe: A New View of the Korean Business Groups and Their Role in the Financial Crisis." *Asian Economic Papers* 1, no. 2 (Spring): 1–45.

Forbes, Kristin J., and Roberto Rigobon. 2002. "No Contagion, Only Interdependence: Measuring Stock Market Co-movements," *Journal of Finance* 57, no. 5 (October): 2223–61.

Fujiwara, Ippel, Nao Sudo, and Yuki Teranishi. 2010. "The Zero Lower Bound and Monetary Policy in a Global Economy: A Simple Analytical Investigation." *International Journal of Central Banking* 1 (March): 103–34.

Haberis, Alex, and Anna Lipinska. 2012. "International Policy Spillovers at the Zero Lower Bound." Finance and Economics Discussion Series 2012-23. Federal Reserve Board, Washington, DC.

Hofmann, Boris, and Előd Takáts. 2015. "International Monetary Spillovers." BIS Quarterly Review, September.

IMF. 2006. "Article IV of the Fund's Articles of Agreement: An Overview of the Legal Framework."

IMF. 2007. "Review of the 1977 Decision—Proposal for a New Decision and Public Information Notice." Washington, DC.

IMF. 2014. "IMF Spillover Report" (blog). International Monetary Fund. Washington, DC.

IMF. 2015. "IMF Spillover Report" (blog). International Monetary Fund. Washington, DC.

Kamin, Steven B. 2016. "Cross Border Spillovers from Monetary Policy." Presentation for the 2016 PBoC-FRBNY Joint Symposium, Hangzhou, Zhejiang, China, March 15.

Morais, Bernardo, Jose-Luis Peydro, and Claudia Ruiz Ortega. 2015. "The International Bank Lending Channel of Monetary Policy Rates and QE: Credit Supply, Reach-for-Yield, and Real Effects." Board of Governors of the Federal Reserve System.

Ostry, Jonathan, and Atish Ghosh. 2013. "Obstacles to International Policy Coordination, and How to Overcome Them." IMF Staff Discussion Note, December.

Pesaran, M. Hashem, Til Schuermann, and Scott M.Weiner. 2004. "Modeling Regional Interdependencies using a Global Error-correcting Macroeconometric Model." *Journal of Business & Economic Statistics* 22, no. 2: 129–62.

Rajan, Raghuram. 2013. "A Step in the Dark: Unconventional Monetary Policy after the Crisis." Andrew Crockett Memorial Lecture, Bank for International Settlements, Basel, Switzerland, June 23. Accessed September 8, 2018, http://faculty.chicagobooth.edu/raghuram.rajan/speeches/AGM%2020133 %20Andrew%20Crockett%20Memorial%20Lecture%20Raghuram%20Rajan 1.pdf.

Rajan, Raghuman. 2014. "Competitive Monetary Easing: Is it Yesterday Once More?" Speech at Brookings Institution, Washington, DC, April 2014. Accessed September 8, 2018, http://faculty.chicagobooth.edu/raghuram.rajan /speeches/Competitive%20Monetary%20Easing%20Is%20it%20Yesterday %20Once%20More%20%20Brookings%20Institution.pdf.

Rey, Hélène. 2013. "Dilemma Not Trilemma: The Global Financial Cycle and Monetary Policy Independence." Paper presented at the twenty-fifth Federal Reserve Bank of Kansas City Annual Economic Policy Symposium, Jackson Hole, WY, August.

Rey, Hélène. 2014. "The International Credit Channel and Monetary Autonomy." Mundell-Fleming Lecture, International Monetary Fund, Washington, DC, November 13.

Rigobon, Roberto, and Brian Sack. 2003. "Measuring the Response of Monetary Policy to the Stock Market." *Quarterly Journal of Economics* 118: 639-69.

Shin, Hyun Song. 2016. "The Bank/Capital Markets Nexus Goes Global." Speech given at the London School of Economics and Political Science, November 15.

Taylor, John B. 2017. "Ideas and Institutions in Monetary Policy Making." Karl Brunner Distinguished Lecture, Swiss National Bank, Zurich, September 21.

Yue, Vivian Z., and Leslie Shen. 2011. "International Spillovers on Government Bond Yields: Are We All in the Same Boat?" Federal Reserve Bank of New York, mimeo, August 1.

APPENDIX

The new rules could be based on the effects of specific policies on the weighted average of welfares of individual countries. Countries' populations could potentially be used as weights.

Assume there are 2 countries: X and Y, and 2 time periods: 1 and 2. X takes a policy action in period 1. The effect of X's policy on global welfare can be specified as follows:

(1) $$dW = a * dW(x) + (1 - a) * dW(y)$$

(2) $$dW(x) = dW_1(x) + dW_2(x)$$

(3) $$dW(y) = dW_1(y) + dW_2(y)$$

$dW_k(x)$, and $dW_k(y)$ denote the effect of X's policy on welfare of countries X and Y in period k, where $k = 1, 2$.

Below we consider some principles which could allow policy makers and relevant authorities to grade policies as green, red, or orange.

Case 1. X's policy action is rated green

If $dW(x) > 0$, $dW(y) > 0$, and $dW > 0$, such a policy would clearly be desirable and should be rated green. Conventional monetary policy could fall in this category, as it would raise output in the home economy and create demand for exports from the foreign economy.

Next, take the case when there are temporary negative spillovers for Y such that $dW_1(y) < 0$. The policy, however, through its effect on home economy growth and demand for foreign goods, can provide offsetting positive spillovers to Y in period 2, such that $dW_2(y) > 0$. There may be temporary negative effects for Y through increased volatility in period 1 such that $dW_1(y) < 0$. But $dW(y) = dW_1(y) + dW_2(y) > 0$.

In this case, the policy could also be rated green. This would be the case if the policy, e.g., an unconventional monetary policy, acts as a booster shot and can jump-start a large home economy and create significant positive spillovers for foreign economies through a large increase in the demand for their exports.

Case 2. X's policy action is rated red

If $dW(x) < 0$, $dW(y) < 0$, and $dW < 0$, such a policy would clearly be undesirable and should be rated red.

Next, take the case when $dW(x) > 0$, but the magnitude of $dW(x)$ is small, such that the positive spillover effects for Y through higher growth and increased demand for export are weak and the negative effect through increased volatility in Y dominates. $dW_1(y) < 0$, $dW_2(y) > 0$ but small in magnitude, such that $dW(y) = dW_1(y) + dW_2(y) < 0$. In this case, the policy could also be rated red.

This would be the case if, for example, unconventional monetary policy actions lead to a weak recovery in X and only small positive effects on exports to Y but large capital inflows and asset price bubbles in Y. In this case, the policy could also be rated red. Global welfare would decrease with this policy.

Case 3. X's policy action is rated orange

Assume a policy action is such that $dW(x) > 0$, but $dW_1(y) < 0$, $dW_2(y) < 0$, and $dW(y) < 0$ i.e., although there may be large positive effects in X, there are sustained negative effects in Y. In this case, even if $dW = dW(x) + dW(y) > 0$, such a policy could belong to the orange category. For example, conventional monetary policies in X to raise growth could fall in the orange category if X and Y are at a stage of financial cycle where low interest rates resulting from loose monetary policies could lead to significant financial stability risks in X and Y. Even though the large positive effect in X could dominate any financial stability risks in X, that would not be the case in Y, which would experience sustained negative spillovers. Such a policy would be rated orange.

Finally, take three examples of policies that could be graded based on the above rules. The three examples are described below.

1. Country X depreciates its exchange rate vis-à-vis Y or prevents appreciation using direct intervention; 3 countries: X, Y, and Z, 2 periods 1 and 2.

Period 1: X gains as a depreciation of its exchange rate makes its exports more competitive. Y loses due to cheap imports from X which affect domestic output and employment; a third country— say Z—also loses as demand switches away from Z toward X.

Period 2: Growth in X increases demand for exports from Y and/ or Z. Y and Z benefit.

If the elasticity of growth with respect to exchange rates is very high in X, such that it gives a booster shot to X, and also leads to a large increase in demand for exports from Y and Z, this policy could be rated green. If, however, there are supply constraints in X, which leads to a very weak recovery in X, and a small increase in exports from Y and Z, then the beggar-thy-neighbor effects in Y and Z would dominate. Therefore, this policy could be rated red. It could be rated orange if there are sustained beggar-thy-neighbor effects in Y and Z; even if global welfare improves due to a large increase in output in X, the sustained negative effects in Y and Z would put this policy in the orange category.

2. Country X uses more subtle or indirect policies (e.g., conventional/unconventional monetary policies) which also affect the

exchange rate. The effect on global welfare of these policies could be estimated in a similar way as in the case of direct exchange rate policies.

3. Country X uses policies which lead to a depreciation of the exchange rate in X, but which are also associated with large capital inflows into Y and Z, and could have implications for financial stability in Y and Z and therefore on global financial stability. The change in global welfare would comprise two components in this case: change in trade balance and change in financial stability. Financial stability could be measured by a summary measure such as credit growth. The change in trade balance and financial stability would first be converted into an index between 0 and 1, before they are summed up.

More precisely, the effect of X's policy on global welfare in period could be specified as follows:

$$dW = a * dW(x) + b * dW(y) + (1 - a - b) * dW(z)$$

$$dW(n) = dITB(n) + dICG(n)$$

where $n = x, y, z$. *ITB* and *ICG* denote the index of trade balance and credit growth, respectively. The policy could then be graded based on the same principles as discussed in Case 1.

ISSUES FOR DISCUSSION

There are several issues that may need to be considered in order to grade policies in the case of the three examples described above. Some of these issues are described below:

How do we deal with undervaluation versus depreciation? Large depreciations could have "beggar-thy-neighbor" effects, even if the exchange rate is not "undervalued" vis-à-vis some benchmark. Moreover, the determination of the benchmark itself is not straightforward.

How do we take into account the fact that Y and Z could use other policies (e.g., loosening of monetary policy) to compensate for the loss in exports and welfare in period 1? Should we evaluate the global welfare effects from X's policies, ceteris paribus, or should we take into account the effects of "retaliatory" policies? As discussed above, the spillover effects could be based on Y and Z's welfare if the policy was not undertaken versus Y and Z's welfare after the policy is initiated and it responds.

How should we measure exchange rate depreciation? The real effective exchange rate (REER)? Should the measure of REER take into account the increasing importance of global value chains? A depreciation of the exchange rate would give a lower boost to exports and welfare for countries whose exports use imported intermediates intensively.

Should we use a composite measure of financial stability rather than credit growth?

Should we use a simple sum of trade balance and credit growth or a weighted sum? Weights could depend on country characteristics.

DISCUSSANT REMARKS

Thomas J. Sargent

There are many interesting things to discuss in the paper and in Raghu's talk. I would change the title to "Equilibrium International Monetary Policies" for reasons I learned from my late Hoover colleague George Stigler and that I want to describe here. One beautiful thing about this paper is the struggle between Raghu and his coauthor that surfaces in diverse sections of the paper. It is an old intellectual battle that I want to elaborate. George Stigler said, "A war can ravage half a continent and raise no new issues in economic theory." Many of the issues that are discussed in this paper have been with us a long time. I want to talk about these in light of contributions by my late Hoover colleagues Milton Friedman and George Stigler, my present Hoover colleague John Taylor, and also a one-time good friend of Herbert Hoover.

Start with Milton Friedman. Friedman emphasized the importance of distinguishing between temporary and permanent actions. Friedman is famous for stressing the limits of monetary policy. His 1967 presidential address to the American Economic Association surprised many people who had perceived Friedman to be someone who thought monetary policy was very powerful. In his presidential address, Friedman denied that. He asserted that monetary policy could have at most temporary, variable, and hard-to-predict effects on real variables, including every real variable in sight: output, unemployment, real interest rates, and real exchange rates. He said that the most monetary policy could accomplish—and only a particular monetary policy, namely a systematic, predictable, and permanent monetary policy—was to affect inflation rates and price levels in predictable ways. But such a policy couldn't affect real variables like output, unemployment, or real interest rates for long or in ways that we could understand.

Friedman also said that rules were better than discretion, continuing a tradition dating back to the framers of our Constitution. Also in common with one theme of Rajan's paper, Friedman confessed and professed ignorance of macroeconomic structures. Friedman's work displayed a persistent ambivalence toward formal quantitative analysis based on expected utility and control theory. With L. J. Savage, Friedman wrote one of the key papers about expected utility in economic analysis. But Friedman refused to use expected utility when he did quantitative macroeconomic analysis. He said that he didn't know enough about the structure of the economy to employ expected utility for macroeconomic analysis, this despite the fact that Friedman was a great econometrician and statistician. Friedman said that distributed lags were long and variable (although he never quite said exactly what that meant). As a consequence, Friedman was very cautious in using his empirical findings. This same caution stemming from model specification doubts is a theme of Rajan's paper too.

But research progresses. After Friedman, research technologies improved. Things became more rigorous. Intellectual children of Friedman arrived with rational expectations wings (or horns). Rational expectations theory has a rigor and discipline that brought a tight operational sense in which distributed lags would be variable (because they depend on government policy functions). And rational expectations brought restrictions and discipline on our theories of beliefs. Big players here were Lucas, Ned Prescott, John Taylor, and Lars Hansen.

This brings me to the notion of equilibrium strategies—a key component of Rajan's paper. This concept can be thought of as extending and formalizing Friedman's notions of permanent versus temporary actions, as well as conveying a tighter and more convincing formulation of the idea that rules are better than discretion. Another key idea brought by recent technical advances in the Chicago/Hoover tradition is Lars Hansen's work on robustness.

That work formalizes Friedman's ideas about not trusting models and adjusting decisions in light of that distrust. What do you do when you don't trust your model? And what do you do when there is a set of models out there, all of which you distrust? What should you do? How should you make policy? There are really interesting remarks in Rajan's paper about how to manage such distrust. Actually, I'll just read it: "We make the case that models reflect the policy biases of those devising them." That's a deep and profound remark that we should talk more about. I'm not going to talk more about it here, but that could be the subject of another conference about policy making and robustness to model doubts.

In another Hoover tradition, please allow me now to talk about some monetary history. I offer these words in the spirit of Stigler's remark. Stigler didn't make that remark about wars ravaging half a continent out of the blue. He knew a lot of history. In reading Rajan's paper, it is natural to recall a sweep of monetary history. After World War I, in the 1920s, Great Britain, with great difficulty, set up a gold exchange standard based on the pound. In that system, the UK pound functioned as an international reserve currency for much of Europe and beyond. That lasted from 1921 to 1931. It collapsed in 1931 after some big shocks that we're still struggling to understand. After 1931, until 1939 or 1945, there were exchange rate disorders and enhanced trade barriers. Those exchange rate disorders and enhanced trade barriers were correlated and were probably mutually influencing each other. There followed huge shocks to the fiscal backings of many currencies during World War II. That set the stage for the United States dollar to replace the British pound as reserve currency. That was what Bretton Woods confirmed by setting up a gold exchange standard centered in Washington, a fixed exchange rate based on the US dollar. It prevailed from '44 to '71. Lurking underneath all of these things are price-level politics driven by debt deflation theories and realities, both domestically and internationally. Why is the price level important? Here is an impolite and politically incorrect answer in the form of an old Fed insider saying what you can say in the hallway but never in public: *the job of monetary policy is to make bad loans into good loans.* And how do you do that? You redistribute from creditors to debtors by manipulating the price level. That trick is as old as the hills.

Monetary history is full of examples of conflicts of interest both within and across countries. A curious witness to these conflicts is how Robert Skidelsky changed the title of the third volume of his biography of John Maynard Keynes. The original British title was *Fighting for Britain, 1937–46.* Fighting for Britain against whom? The United States. The book was about Keynes representing British interests against the United States in struggling over which country was going to pay more financially for the war. Who was going to bear the fiscal burden? Whose soldiers were going to die? Keynes lost argument after argument to the Americans. The publishers thought that they could not sell books with Skidelsky's UK title in the United States, so they changed it to *Fighting for Freedom.*

I conclude by showing you a message that was written in the depths of the Great Depression by someone who had been a very good friend of Herbert Hoover, actually someone who wanted Herbert Hoover to be president when they were friends during World War I. The document that I want to show you was written in '33, a time when Milton Friedman was in high school or junior high school and hadn't written the economics I described earlier. Please read the words carefully. The author said, "I would regard it as a catastrophe amounting to a world tragedy, if this conference called to bring about a real and permanent financial stability and greater prosperity, should in advance of any serious effort to consider these broader problems, allow itself to be diverted by a proposal of purely artificial and temporary experiments affecting monetary exchange rates of a few nations only."

(The following is especially for Mike Bordo and Ned Prescott, who love history too.) The writer of the following words had a sense of humor, so don't miss the pun: "The world would not long be lulled by the *specious* fallacy." (The author is talking against the background of a long history of specie standards.)

Herbert Hoover's (former) friend proceeds to say, "The sound internal economic system of a nation is a greater factor of its well-being than the price of its currency in changing the terms of currencies of other nations." The author is saying that it's not temporary exchange rate stabilizations, it's fundamentals. This sounds like a Hoover Institution economist. What are the fundamentals required to render things healthy? Reduced costs of government. Government revenues sufficient to cover government financial obligations including servicing government debts. The government budget constraint is front and center. Government debt is a tax anticipation certificate. That's what this author is saying. He goes on to say: "Let me be frank in saying that the United States seeks the kind of dollar which a generation from now will have the same purchasing and debt-paying power as the dollar value we will hope to attain in the near future." The author declares that he is not merely an inflation targeter. He's a price-level targeter. The author's key advisers were price-level targeters too. The author goes on to say, "That objective means more to the good of other nations than a fixed ratio for a month or two in terms of the pound or franc." The author is talking about permanent strategies, not temporary actions. He is talking this way when Milton Friedman is still a schoolboy and before John Taylor was born.

Who was the author I have quoted? It is Franklin D. Roosevelt. And the text is Roosevelt's notorious "bombshell message" in which he torpedoed the so-called London Financial Conference. He said, "Our broad purpose is the permanent stabilization of every nation's currency." Then he said, "The restoration of world trade is an important factor, but here also temporary exchange fixing is not the answer." What's striking about these passages is Roosevelt's emphasis on fundamentals. The so-called bombshell message is badly maligned in many history books, but read it for yourself. The reasoning is sound and timely today.

Let me just close by asking: What do we make of all this? First, the issues that Roosevelt raised were widely talked about within and across countries back in '33; we're still talking about them today. This brings me back to the quote from Stigler with which I started. Let me tell you a story about George Stigler and Milton Friedman that will take us to a question that underlies Rajan's paper. The question is: Are prevailing government policies equilibrium objects? Being equilibrium objects means that they're determined by people pursuing their best interests within a coherent system in which each person's decision rule influences other persons' constraints. There's a beautiful theme or struggle that runs through Rajan's paper, and it's a very old theme. Raghu takes both sides of this argument. Maybe the struggle is between the two coauthors of Raghu's paper but it is probably actually also inside both authors. The struggle goes back to Walter Bagehot. There's a passage in *Lombard Street* in which Bagehot pits evolution against purposeful institutional design. Bagehot was writing about the British banking system. He contrasted the existing British system with what he said a well-designed system would actually be. He outlines an ideal system based on competitive banks with no lender of last resort and remarks that it would be a very different system than the existing one. Bagehot then asks: Would I recommend immediately adopting the well-designed system? Surprisingly, he says no. His reason is that the existing system had evolved out of a long process that rendered it stable and resistant to changes. Bagehot says that would-be reformers are whistling in the wind. Bagehot says we have to accept the institutions that history has given us.

Despite the main theme and the recommendations in Rajan's paper, his talk reveals that he appreciates Bagehot's position. I quote Rajan verbatim: "We are prisoners of our institutions. Take the world as it is, not as you want it." Rajan said that, but he didn't put it in his slides or his paper. So there's a wonderful struggle, which I think is beautiful, and it shows how daunting and enduring the problem is.

Rajan is not the first person to have this struggle, so I'm going to conclude with this story about George Stigler and Milton Friedman. This unfolded at a small dinner I attended at the Hoover Institution. Friedman and Stigler were old friends since their graduate school days. George Stigler was a person who thought along with Rajan that we are prisoners of our institutions. We should study them but accept that they're equilibrium institutions. Forget about trying to change them. That's what Stigler thought and Friedman, of course, knew that. At that dinner, Stigler said, "Milton, do you consult for business firms?" Friedman said, "No, I never consult." Stigler asked, "Why?" Friedman said, "I have nothing valuable to tell a business firm. Business firms are doing the best they can. They optimize. They know much more than I do, so they're well run." Whereupon Stigler asked, "Okay, Milton, then why on Earth are you always trying to tell governments what to do?"

GENERAL DISCUSSION

JOHN COCHRANE: That was great. I'm going to abuse my rights as
moderator to get the questions going. If I can think of one thing
that distinguishes the two views I just heard, it would be the
answer to this question: Japan has been for twenty-five years
at 0 percent interest rates, very slight deflation, and slow growth.
Raghu talked about things Japan could do to jump-start its way
out of this apparently monetary malaise. Tom said that monetary policy doesn't have permanent effects on output, so whatever growth disappointments Japan has had are not monetary.
So has Japan been living the Friedman rule, optimal monetary
policy, 0 percent rates, and slight deflation, for twenty-five years,
and its problems are real? Or are Japan's problems monetary?
And if so, do monetary difficulties really last twenty-five years,
most of them with very low unemployment?

RAGHU RAJAN: On that, I think I would agree with the thrust of your
question. Japan, if any, has real problems rather than monetary
problems. In fact, if you look at Japan's growth, given the shrink-
age of the labor force in recent years, it's pretty good. It's pretty
reasonable. And to some extent that gets at my point, which is
even if monetary policy has very limited effects, the fact that
there's some goal you want to achieve makes you push very
hard on something which has very little influence to the point
that you risk political disruption, which has serious economic
effects. That really is the thrust of my point, that you may not
have much in the effects on real activity through all that you're
doing, but because of actual or perceived effects elsewhere,
there is a political reaction. You know, that fantastic quote about
Roosevelt—well, one of the things that emerged from his action
at that conference, is that the conference broke up. And to some
extent you had the entire thirties, where there was great suspi-
cion of each other during that period, and to some extent, the

Bretton Woods. However much you may complain about the fixed exchange rate system, etc., at least there was a system that people respected. And all I'm arguing is that it may be time— fully respecting that we know very little—it may be time to start thinking about whether we need a system, whatever that system will be, and whether the current system is enough.

And to Tom Sargent's point about equilibria, yeah, of course equilibria are a result of evolution, but part of that evolution is debate.

JOHN COCHRANE: You are part of that evolution.

MICHAEL BORDO: I have a very simple question. If every country followed a monetary rule, like the Taylor Rule, then why do you need coordination?

RAGHU RAJAN: I'm not advocating coordination. In fact, I'm saying there really is no need for it. And I'm advocating something less constrained than John. I'm advocating limits to whatever you do so that certain policies that have large spillover effects may be ruled out, and within that range, do whatever you want. Now John is going one step further and saying, forget those policies, but within the range of allowable policies, I want something like a Taylor Rule. I haven't got to where John is, but that could be something that people agree to. So, I'm not advocating by any means, in fact I was ridiculing the statement that we call each other and find out what's optimal for you. But that's what I'd do.

SEBASTIAN EDWARDS: One of the points that was made—and I'd like to get the reaction both from Raghu and from Tom—was pursuing price-level targeting as opposed to inflation targeting. And that connects very well with Tom's comments. As he pointed out, what FDR wanted to do—partially based on Irving Fisher's proposal of a "compensated dollar"—was to target the price level; bring prices back to their 1926 level. This was tried in the thirties by Sweden. So the question for Raghu is whether it would make a difference, in your view, in terms of policy coordination if we would switch mostly to price-level targeting as opposed to inflation targeting.

And the second point I want to make very briefly is related to what Tom said about how little we know about certain relations. In fact, in 1933, until three days before or four days before the "bombshell" that FDR wrote, people thought that he was for coordinating and stabilizing the exchanges. And there is a beautiful—I encourage you to look at it—clip on the Internet where we see Raymond Moley, the economic adviser, going to visit FDR on the Amberjack (he's sailing on his yacht) to get instructions on what to do in London. And what FDR tells him is, go and stabilize the exchanges. And then, no one knows who he talks to, and completely changes his views, and decides that stabilizing the dollar is the wrong policy. And so, which model the policy maker sides with may make a huge difference, I think, and that is something which should be taken into account, I believe, in your view, Raghu.

RAGHU RAJAN: I leave the bulk of the response on price-level targeting to Tom. My own sense is that how the public's expectations of inflation gets formed is another area we know very little about. My worry is some of our models seem to suggest that once we shift to a different objective, those expectations get formed fairly quickly, and follow this new objective, and that solves a lot of problems. And my worry was always: How do I get even a simple message across to the public? I found it very, very hard. So, I'm not sure it's so easy to change those expectations, which makes a lot of difference in how effective price-level targeting will be. And whether there are various versions of it, how you can convey the import of what to expect to the public may be more difficult. But I'll leave the broader response to Tom.

THOMAS SARGENT: There's a skeleton in the closet about coordination, namely, John Kareken and Neil Wallace's *Quarterly Journal of Economics* paper in the early eighties challenging Milton

Friedman's view that markets do a good job of setting exchange rates. Under plausible conditions about demands for money, Kareken and Wallace showed that exchange rates are indeterminant. Their reasoning was basically the same reasoning that tells us that markets alone can't determine the exchange rate between nickels and dimes and that is why a government has to set that exchange rate. In a class of models with fiat currencies, there's room for only one fiat currency in the world; with multiple currencies there's a continuum of equilibrium exchange rates. Kareken and Wallace infer from this situation that monetary authorities across countries must coordinate implicitly or explicitly. The Kareken-Wallace analysis haunts all monetary models of the exchange rate. Models break exchange rate indeterminacy in somewhat dirty ways, often by doing implausible or unnatural, strange things with money in utility functions of agents residing in different countries. For example, I'm an American, so I love dollars but not pounds. You're British, so you love pounds, not dollars. Assumptions like that, or similar ones for cash-in-advance constraints, are used to break exchange rate indeterminacy. So if those devices are fragile, the force for coordination comes out. And that's all in a flexible price model. In a sticky price model, forces for coordination are in many ways even stronger.

GITA GOPINATH: The point that both of you raised, I guess Tom raised more so, is that we just don't understand how monetary policy affects real variables. There are kind of long lags, so it's unclear. But there's another transmission that's unclear, which is the impact of monetary policy on exchange rates. We've been playing with these models for a long time, and usually with these models, if you put any kind of monetary variable on the right-hand side to explain exchange rate behavior it does poorly at forecasting it. So this then leads to the question, especially for the dollar, the euro, the Japanese yen, it's very hard to pinpoint and say, "This particular appreciation has to do with monetary policy and not something else." So, given that we live in that world, how are we going to measure what it means to say, "Okay, now this is expenditure switching-driven policy rather than increasing overall demand?" And so, what are your thoughts on that?

RAGHU RAJAN: Well, I'm going to refer you to John Taylor, who sort of shows a little more of an effect of these unconventional policies and balance sheet measures on exchange rates. But I agree completely with you that different studies show different degrees that these policies can affect exchange rates. And I think that there are issues over what horizon—is it temporary, permanent, etc.? So, I don't want to stake all of this on: Does it actually have an effect? I think it is enough to have a perception of having an effect. Because the reaction of other central banks sometimes relies on that perception. I would argue that during this post-crisis episode, some central banks—I won't name them—have been taken kicking and screaming into quantitative easing. They didn't want to do it, but others were doing it, and they were being accused of not doing the right thing.

And so, to the extent that there's a perception, it could have an effect on policy. Now if the policies are irrelevant, they don't make a difference. But I think the policies do have an effect on, for example, capital flows and the effects elsewhere, and they have an effect on the political discussion. Oh, you're initiating a currency war . . . or not. The discussions have been relatively mild. But as we get into the realm of populist nationalism, I think these can get stronger, which is why some clarity about what each one is trying to do and some respect for the limits of that might be useful.

THOMAS SARGENT: I think what you said was really important about how uncertain we are about important dimensions. A message that is a big part of John Taylor and Volcker Wieland's work is that just because we don't know everything, doesn't mean we don't know anything. Characterizing uncertainty in terms of probability distributions of outcomes is a most important part of our jobs.

PAUL TUCKER: Raghu, it seems to me—both today and since you've first raised this—that you're really talking about monetary politics rather than monetary economics. And I'm sympathetic to that, in that when Ben Bernanke and others in the Fed responded to you and Brazil in the way they did, I can remember thinking, "Oh, they may not have noticed that the world is changing, with India and others becoming powerful players in global politics." But if one does think of it through the lens of monetary politics, it seems to me that there are some challenges to the prescriptions you make. So, your red line was: if a policy measure has a small effect at home, meaning a small economic effect, but nasty effects abroad, then the policy maker shouldn't do it. But what if the small economic effect at home has a big political effect at home, in terms of, say, sustaining political stability? Sometimes, it's necessary for macroeconomic policy makers to do things that will demonstrate to the country that they're trying, in order to underpin the broader system and consent in the system of government. My challenge to you, then, is that in a sense I would—I'm going to overstate it—drop the economics in presenting your concern and instead think about it purely in terms of monetary politics, and then explore the different dimensions of the monetary politics. That, it seems to me, whether you do it or I do it, it's eventually going to be done, because the shifts in the geopolitical order are going to have implications for the international monetary and financial system. And they are as likely to be designed in state departments as they are in treasury departments, and much more likely in either of those than in central banks.

RAGHU RAJAN: Great point. I couldn't agree with you more. I mean the specific example you raised is to my mind what has driven in some countries the extent of accommodation, that we need to be seen to be doing something, given the broad sense that nothing else is going on and that the establishment has given up on people like us. I have to agree that monetary politics has been a central feature here, and it works on both sides of the border.

JOHN COCHRANE: If I can push back, Raghu, "we" doesn't have to be the central bank. I do notice a great deal of central bank aggrandizement here. There's nothing "we" can do that actually works, but we need to show that we are "doing something." Maybe central banks should leave ineffective or symbolic actions to the Treasury or the president.

RAGHU RAJAN: So, I don't want to be seen as a wuss agreeing with every comment, but I agree with that also, which is that central banks have also taken upon themselves too much by arguing that they're the only game in town. And in fact, by limiting themselves, it may actually allow others to feel that sense of responsibility and take up more. So, again, I think this is why I'm saying these are complicated issues that need to be examined more closely. And it may be that rules might work in taking off some of the responsibility. I've done what I could—at this point, I've run into the rules, so you guys take over. That could work.

CHAPTER TWO

Dollar Dominance in Trade and Finance

Gita Gopinath

According to the major paradigm in international macroeconomics, namely the Mundell-Fleming paradigm (Mundell 1963; Fleming 1962), the importance of a country's currency in international trade is tied closely to its share in world trade. This is because each country is assumed to export its goods in its own currency. That is, if we consider trade among the United States, India, and Japan, the assumption is that all exports from the United States are invoiced in dollars, all exports from Japan are invoiced in yen, and all exports from India are invoiced in rupees. Further, because the paradigm assumes that prices are sticky in the exporter's currency, exchange rate fluctuations across countries affect their bilateral terms of trade, defined as the ratio of the at-the-dock price of imports to that of exports. Specifically, a depreciation of the nominal exchange rate is associated with a depreciation of the terms of trade that is an increase in relative price of imports relative to exports. These exchange rate-driven fluctuations in the terms of trade are a central mechanism of Milton Friedman's argument for the optimality of flexible exchange rates—and for the perennial complaint among countries that their trading partners manipulate their exchange rates and engage in "currency wars" to raise their competitiveness in international markets.

Besides these assumptions on trade, modern New Keynesian incarnations of the Mundell-Fleming and other major paradigms typically assume that international financial markets are complete in that a full set of Arrow-Debreu securities are traded and there are no financial frictions.[1] With this assumption, made mostly for modeling convenience (unlike those for trade), the currency of denomination of financial assets has no meaningful role.

In the following sections I describe briefly how reality is very different from these assumptions with regards to international trade and finance and how the dollar dominates both spaces with important real consequences. Further, summarizing Gopinath and Stein (2018a), I explain how the world can end up with a single dominant currency (the dollar) despite the existence of other potential dominant currencies (the euro). The argument in Gopinath and Stein (2018a) emphasizes the complementarity that exists between a currency's role as a unit of account for invoicing decisions and its role as a safe store of value.

SOME FACTS ON DOLLAR DOMINANCE

Trade

As stated previously, the Mundell-Fleming paradigm assumes that every country invoices its exports in its own currency, the so-called producer currency pricing paradigm. A second alternative paradigm as spelled out in Betts and Devereux (2000) and Devereux and Engel (2003) assumes instead that every country invoices its exports in the destination currency, the so-called local currency pricing paradigm. Both these assumptions do not pass the smell test, as studies of trade invoicing reveal the overwhelming preponderance of dollar invoicing in international trade. In my Jackson Hole Symposium paper (Gopinath 2015), I report statistics on trade invoicing for a sample of forty-three countries. These countries represent 55 percent of world imports and 57 percent of world

---

1. An alternative to a full set of Arrow-Debreu securities is to parameterize a model such that terms of trade changes alone provide full insurance.

FIGURE 2.1.1. Dollar Dominance in World Trade: Aggregate
Source: Gopinath 2015

exports. I document that the dollar's share as an invoicing currency is 4.7 times its share in world imports and 3.1 times its share in world exports, as depicted in figure 2.1.1. Consequently, there is neither producer currency pricing nor local currency pricing, but mainly dollar pricing. To highlight how special the role of the dollar is, it is useful to contrast this with the share of the other major global currency, the euro, in trade. The euro's share as an invoicing currency in world exports is 1.2 times the share of euro country exports. In other words, while some non-euro countries invoice exports in euros, this is of a much smaller magnitude than the use of dollars.

Figure 2.1.2 provides a more detailed breakdown by plotting for each country the share of its imports invoiced in dollars (black bar) next to the share of its imports from the United States (gray bar). Under the Mundell-Fleming paradigm, these two bars should have the same height. On the contrary, the dollar's share in invoicing outstrips its share in the country's imports. In the case of India, 86 percent of its imports are invoiced in dollars while only 5 percent of India's imports originate in the United States. Similarly, 86 percent of India's exports are invoiced in dollars while only 15 percent of India's exports are to the United States. It is interesting to

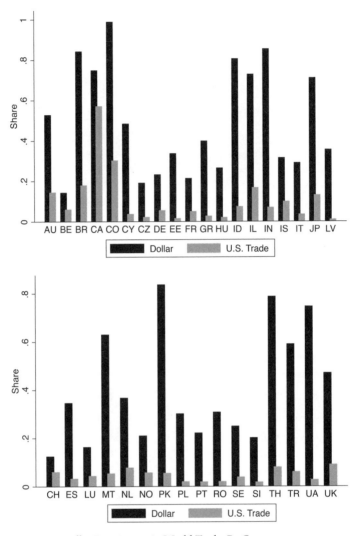

FIGURE 2.1.2. Dollar Dominance in World Trade: By Country
Source: Gopinath 2015

note that even in the case of Japan and the United Kingdom, whose currencies are reserve currencies, only 40 percent of exports in the case of Japan and 51 percent in the case of the United Kingdom are invoiced in their own currency. The real exception here is the United States, with 93 percent of its imports and 97 percent of its exports invoiced in its own currency. I also emphasize that this heavy dollar invoicing is not just about commodity prices like oil prices or copper prices that are denominated in dollars, but applies to a much wider set of goods.

Just because exporters quote a price in dollars does not by itself imply that these dollar prices are sticky. In a series of papers with coauthors, I document that dollar stickiness in the short run is indeed a feature of non-commodity prices in international trade (Gopinath and Rigobon 2008; Gopinath, Itskhoki, and Rigobon 2010; Casas et al. 2017; Boz, Gopinath, and Plagborg-Møller 2017a). These findings are summarized in my definition of an international price system characterized by two key features. First, the overwhelming share of world trade is priced/invoiced in a small set of currencies, with the dollar the dominant currency. Second, international prices *in their currency of invoicing* are not very sensitive to exchange rates at horizons of up to two years.

Consistent with the evidence of sticky dollar pricing, Boz, Gopinath, and Plagborg-Møller (2017b) find no evidence of the comovement between nominal exchange rates and the terms of trade that is a central piece of the Mundell-Fleming paradigm. Using a newly constructed data set of harmonized (non-commodity) annual bilateral import and export unit value and volume indices for fifty-five countries covering 91 percent of world trade for the period 1989–2015, Boz, Gopinath, and Plagborg-Møller (2017b) estimate that a 1 percent depreciation of the bilateral exchange rate is associated with only a 0.8 percent depreciation of the bilateral terms of trade (in the year of the depreciation), with a confidence interval of 0.04, 0.13. As a reference, the producer currency pricing paradigms would predict a value close to 1, while the local currency pricing paradigms would predict a value close to −1. This finding is consistent with the fact that prices in international trade are sticky in a dominant currency, which is overwhelmingly the dollar.

Dominance in Asset Markets

Contrary to the complete markets assumption in standard New Keynesian models, it is well recognized that markets are incomplete and the dollar is heavily used in international financial transactions. In the case of emerging markets, it has been long recognized that they rely heavily on foreign currency borrowing and that, too, in dollars, a phenomenon referred to as "original sin" (Eichengreen and Hausmann 2005). Figure 2.1.3 from Bräuning and Ivashina (2017) reports statistics on syndicated cross-border loans from 1990 Q1 through 2016 Q3. As the currency breakdown of loans reveals, the dollar is overwhelmingly the currency of choice. The euro, on the other hand, has a significant share mainly for emerging Europe and developed countries. Indeed, the dollar liabilities of non-US banks, which are on the order of $10 trillion,

FIGURE 2.1.3. Dollar Dominance in World Finance

Geographic Region	# Borrowers	# Loans	Currency Breakdown of Loans		
			USD	EUR	Other
Emerging Africa (incl. Middle East)	944	1,902	92%	5%	3%
Emerging Asia and Pacific	3,955	7,618	87%	1%	12%
Emerging Europe	1,259	3,379	76%	20%	4%
Emerging Americas	1,431	2,661	97%	0%	3%
Developed Countries	26,118	59,887	61%	24%	14%

(Source: Bräuning and Ivashina, 2017)

Note: The statistics are based on syndicated cross-border loans from 1990:Q1 through 2016:Q3. Country groups are based on the BIS classification. Offshore centers are excluded from the sample.

are roughly comparable in magnitude to those of US banks (Shin 2012; Ivashina, Scharfstein, and Stein 2015). According to Bank for International Settlements (BIS) locational banking statistics, 62 percent of the foreign currency local liabilities of banks are denominated in dollars.

A consequence of dollarization of world finance is that firms outside of the United States often suffer a balance sheet (currency) mismatch problem. This is because dollar borrowing in many cases is done by firms that do not have corresponding dollar revenues, so that these firms end up with a currency mismatch and can be harmed by dollar appreciation as established by Aguiar (2005), Du and Schreger (2014), and Kalemli-Ozcan, Kamil, and Villegas-Sanchez (2016).

Dominance in Central Bank Reserves

According to the IMF's COFER (Currency Composition of Official Foreign Exchange Reserves) data base, out of $10 trillion of reserves (2017 Q4), for which it has data on currency composition, the share in dollars is 63 percent, followed by the euro at 20 percent. As argued in Obstfeld, Shambaugh, and Taylor (2010), these high levels of reserves reflect not only trade considerations but also the desire of central banks to be the lender of last resort to their banking systems.

Dollar "Exorbitant Privilege"

Last, it is often noted that the dollar enjoys an "exorbitant privilege" in world markets in that US dollar risk-free assets generally pay lower expected returns (net of exchange rate movements) than the risk-free assets of most other currencies. That is, there is a violation of uncovered interest parity (UIP) that favors the dollar as a cheap funding currency (Gilmore and Hayashi 2011; Hassan 2013).

These facts on dollar dominance in the spaces of trade, finance, and central bank reserves lead to a natural question of what gives rise to such dominance, which I turn to in the next section.

WHAT MAKES A CURRENCY DOMINANT?

There exist several explanations for why a single currency may dominate in trade invoicing (Engel 2006; Gopinath, Itskhoki, and Rigobon 2010) and separately for why it may dominate in safe assets (Hassan 2013; Gourinchas and Rey 2010; He, Krishnamurthy, and Milbradt 2016; Farhi and Maggiori 2018). However, there exists no unifying explanation for dominance in both trade and finance. It cannot be just sheer coincidence that the dollar dominates in multiple spaces. It is precisely this joint dominance that we explore in Gopinath and Stein (2018a). We are motivated here by the historical evidence on the emergence of dominant currencies best summarized in a quote by Eichengreen (2010): "Experience suggests that the logical sequencing of steps in internationalizing a currency is: first, encouraging its use in invoicing and settling trade; second, encouraging its use in private financial transactions; third, encouraging its use by central banks and governments as a form in which to hold private reserves."

The mechanism in Gopinath and Stein (2018a) can be explained using the heuristic of figure 2.1.4. Start from the top-left box in

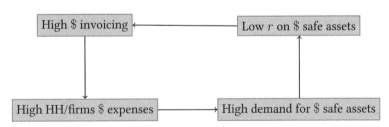

FIGURE 2.1.4. Making of a Dominant Currency
Source: Author.

figure 2.1.4. Suppose there is high dollar invoicing in trade so that importing households and firms in emerging markets have predictable spending in dollar terms (a predictability that arises from the stability of dollar prices), in addition to predictable spending on local goods invoiced in local currency (bottom-left box). Given the volatility in exchange rates, this gives rise to a demand for dollar safe assets in addition to local currency safe assets. This safety has to do not just with getting rid of nominal (default) risk but importantly of getting rid of real consumption risk. That is, by holding a safe dollar deposit, emerging market importers can guarantee themselves a predictable level of consumption of imported goods. The demand for these dollar safe assets is then increasing in the share of expenditure devoted to imported goods invoiced in dollars. The preference for safe assets in dollars and in local currency makes these assets more expensive (that is, they have a higher price) relative to risky assets. In addition, there is the possibility of a violation in uncovered interest parity across safe dollar and safe local currency assets. The particular form of this violation depends also on the supply of safe assets.

Among the suppliers of dollar safe assets are the US Treasury and US banks and firms that can "tranche" their dollar earnings to produce safe claims. These sources of supply are what one would describe as natural sources of dollar safe assets. However, if the demand for dollar safe assets exceeds this supply, emerging market (EM) banks and firms need to be drawn in to create safe assets. These emerging banks and firms have a comparative disadvantage in producing such safe assets, given that their projects pay out in local currency. That is, to produce safe assets the bank needs to ensure that, even in the worst-case realization of the projects, the bank has sufficient funds to repay. In the case of local currency safe assets, this would require that, even in the worst-case scenario for payoffs of the local currency projects, banks can repay their liabilities. However, to create dollar safe assets it must be that in

addition the bank is able to repay in the worst-case realization of
the exchange rate, that is, in the event of a currency crisis. This
makes it costlier for EM banks to produce dollar safe claims as
opposed to local currency safe claims. So in this case the only
reason they will do so is if it is cheaper for the bank to borrow
in dollars. Consequently, in equilibrium when the marginal sup-
plier of the dollar safe asset is an EM bank or firm with a currency
mismatch it must be that uncovered interest parity is violated and
dollar safe assets pay a lower interest rate as compared to local currency safe assets (box in the upper right-hand corner).

Now suppose that some emerging market projects produce
goods that are for export to other emerging markets and a decision needs to be made whether to invoice exports in dollars or in
the producer's currency. The upside to invoicing in dollars is that
it generates the collateral needed to be able to borrow cheaply in
dollars. This benefit has to be weighed against the cost of earning
revenues in dollars when the ultimate shareholders are domestic
EM households whose consumption basket is tilted toward local
currency goods. Given this trade-off, if the interest rate on dollar
borrowing is sufficiently low, exporters will choose to invoice in
dollars. Unlike previous explanations for why firms invoice exports
in dollars that have to do with the curvature of the demand they
face and the particulars of their cost function, our (complementary) explanation has everything to do with finance. Exports are
invoiced in dollars because doing so makes it cheaper to finance
projects given the lower interest rates on dollar borrowing.

A possible alternative to invoicing in dollars might be to invoice
in home currency and swap that for a dollar payout using a financial
hedging instrument. Presumably, this should provide the equivalent collateral to be able to borrow cheaply in dollars. Our argument for why invoicing is chosen over financial hedging is because
of the evidence that the latter is more expensive. As explained in the
paper, the agency risks associated with trade are smaller than those

associated with financial hedging and consequently it is less costly for the exporter to invoice in dollars. This is supported by empirical evidence that hedging is indeed costly and has negative spillovers to investment (Rampini and Viswanathan 2010; Rampini, Viswanathan, and Vuillemey 2017, among others).

Finally, the loop is closed by recognizing that the choice of EM exporters to invoice in dollars affects the consumption share of EM households and firms that is invoiced in dollars. This then amplifies the safe asset demand in dollars which reinforces the initial demand for dollar safe assets, lowers interest rates on such assets, and in turn rationalizes the decision of exporters to invoice in dollars. The argument therefore goes as follows: Why do exporters invoice in dollars? Because it is cheaper to finance in dollars. Why is it cheaper to finance in dollars? Because exporters invoice in dollars. This two-way feedback can entrench the dollar as the global currency of choice, even when other countries are roughly similar to the United States in terms of economic fundamentals.

Size matters in becoming a global currency. That is, for the two-way feedback mechanism to work it must be that the country is significant in world imports alongside exporting in its own currency. The United States exports in dollars and it is a significant fraction of world trade. As to why the dollar and not the euro, Gopinath and Stein (2018a) appeal to history selecting the dollar as the dominant currency, as it was dominant well before the birth of the euro in 1999. Even if the combined GDP of countries that use the euro is a close second to the United States, the historical dominance of the dollar preserves its position.

Given that central banks play the role of lenders of last resort, the dollarization of banking in emerging markets leads to the dollarization of central banks' reserves as explained in Gopinath and Stein (2018b). In the event of a banking crisis, the central bank is expected to step in to bail out holders of safe deposits. It can do this either by saving *ex ante* in the form of dollar reserves or by taxing *ex post.* Because crises are associated with large currency devaluations, there is a benefit to accumulating dollar reserves *ex ante* so as to minimize the cost of taxation *ex post.* This is why, despite the fact that dollar reserve accumulation is associated with a negative "carry" in that the central bank borrows at a higher interest rate in local currency as compared to what it earns in dollar safe assets, it is optimal to hold dollar reserves, and this is increasing in the share of the country's banking that is dollarized.

I conclude by briefly discussing the Chinese renminbi and crypto-currencies. China in recent years is following closely the recipe of internationalization outlined in the Eichengreen quote. Through a concerted policy push, the renminbi's share as a settlement currency in China's trade has grown from 0 percent in 2010 to 25 percent in 2015. These are still early days and the global adoption of the renminbi will require full convertibility of the renminbi, capital account liberalization, and stability of and trust in Chinese financial institutions and central bank policy, all of which can take time. As our model highlights, a country like the United States can retain its dominant position for much longer after it has lost the lead in global trade, but it is important to keep in mind that when the switch begins the process can be quite rapid because of the complementarity between trade invoicing and safe asset demand. As for the potential of crypto-currencies such as bitcoin to acquire dominance, my view is that given that such currencies in their current form serve neither as a unit of account nor as a cheap transaction technology, but primarily as a highly risky store of value, the prospect that they will dominate seems remote.

References

Aguiar, Mark. 2005. "Investment, Devaluation, and Foreign Currency Exposure: The Case of Mexico." *Journal of Development Economics* 78, no. 1: 95–113.

Betts, Caroline, and Michael Devereux. 2000. "Exchange Rate Dynamics in a Model of Pricing-to-Market." *Journal of International Economics* 50, no.1: 215–44.

Boz, Emine, Gita Gopinath, and Mikkel Plagborg-Møller. 2017a. "Global Trade and the Dollar." Technical report, mimeo. Harvard University.

Boz, Emine, Gita Gopinath, and Mikkel Plagborg-Møller. 2017b. "Global Trade and the Dollar." Working paper.

Bräuning, Falk, and Victoria Ivashina. 2017. "Monetary Policy and Global Banking." NBER Working Paper Series 23316, March.

Casas, Camila, Federico J. Díez, Gita Gopinath, and Pierre-Olivier Gourinchas. 2017. "Dominant Currency Paradigm: A New Model for Small Open Economies." IMF Working Paper no. 17/264, November.

Devereux, Michael, and Charles Engel. 2003. "Monetary Policy in the Open Economy Revisited: Price Setting And Exchange Rate Flexibility." *Review of Economic Studies* 70 (October): 765–84.

Du, Wenxin, and Jesse Schreger. 2014. "Sovereign Risk, Currency Risk, and Corporate Balance Sheets." Working paper, Harvard University OpenScholar.

Eichengreen, Barry. (2010). "The Renminbi as an International Currency." Policy paper.

Eichengreen, Barry, and Ricardo Hausmann. 2005. *Other People's Money: Debt Denomination and Financial Instability in Emerging Market Economies.* Chicago: University of Chicago Press.

Engel, Charles. 2006. "Equivalence Results for Optimal Pass-Through, Optimal Indexing to Exchange Rates, and Optimal Choice of Currency for Export Pricing." *Journal of the European Economic Association* 4, no. 6 (December): 1249–60.

Farhi, Emmanuel, and Matteo Maggiori. 2018. "A Model of the International Monetary System." *Quarterly Journal of Economics* 133, no. 1 (February): 295–355.

Fleming, J. Marcus. 1962. "Domestic Financial Policies under Fixed and under Floating Exchange Rates." *Staff Papers (International Monetary Fund)* 9, no. 3 (November): 369–80.

Gilmore, Stephen, and Fumio Hayashi. 2011. "Emerging Market Currency Excess Returns." *American Economic Journal: Macroeconomics* 3, no. 4 (October): 85–111.

Gopinath, Gita. 2015. "The International Price System." In *Jackson Hole Symposium* 27. Federal Reserve Bank of Kansas City.

Gopinath, Gita, Oleg Itskhoki, and Roberto Rigobon. 2010. "Currency Choice and Exchange Rate Pass-through." *American Economic Review* 100, no. 1 (March): 304–36.

Gopinath, Gita, and Roberto Rigobon. 2008. "Sticky Borders." *Quarterly Journal of Economics* 123, no. 2 (May): 531–75.

Gopinath, Gita, and Jeremy C. Stein. 2018a. "Banking, Trade, and the Making of a Dominant Currency." NBER Working Paper no. 24485, March 28.

Gopinath, Gita, and Jeremy C. Stein. 2018b. "Trade Invoicing, Bank Funding, and Central Bank Reserve Holdings." *American Economic Review Papers and Proceedings* 108: 542–46.

Gourinchas, Pierre-Olivier, Hélène Rey, and Nicolas Govillot. 2010. "Exorbitant Privilege and Exorbitant Duty." IMES Discussion Paper Series 2010-E-20.

Hassan, Tarek A. 2013. "Country Size, Currency Unions, and International Asset Returns." *Journal of Finance* 68, no. 6 (December): 2269–2308.

He, Zhiguo, Arvind Krishnamurthy, and Konstantin Milbradt. 2016. "A Model of Safe Asset Determination." NBER Working Paper no. 22271, May.

Ivashina, Victoria, David S. Scharfstein, and Jeremy C. Stein. 2015. "Dollar Funding and the Lending Behavior of Global Banks." *Quarterly Journal of Economics* 130, no. 3: 1241–81.

Kalemli-Ozcan, Sebnem, Herman Kamil, and Carolina Villegas-Sanchez. 2016. "What Hinders Investment in the Aftermath of Financial Crises: Insolvent Firms or Illiquid Banks?" *Review of Economics and Statistics* 98, no. 4 (October): 756–69.

Mundell, Robert A. 1963. "Capital Mobility and Stabilization Policy under Fixed and Flexible Exchange Rates." *Canadian Journal of Economics and Political Science* 29, no. 4 (November): 475–85.

Obstfeld, Maurice, Jay C. Shambaugh, and Alan M. Taylor. 2010. "Financial Stability, the Trilemma, and International Reserves." *American Economic Journal: Macroeconomics* 2, no. 2 (April): 57–94.

Rampini, Adriano A., and Siva Viswanathan. 2010. "Collateral, Risk Management, and the Distribution of Debt Capacity." *Journal of Finance* 65, no. 6 (December): 2293–2322.

Rampini, Adriano A., Siva Viswanathan, and Guillaume Vuillemey. 2017. "Risk Management in Financial Institutions." Working paper.

Shin, Hyun Song. 2012. "Global Banking Glut and Loan Risk Premium." *IMF Economic Review* 60, no. 2: 155–92.

DISCUSSANT REMARKS

Adrien Auclert

This paper begins with a set of five apparently disconnected facts about the global role of the dollar.

The first fact is the importance of the dollar in global trade invoicing. Consider the paper's figure 2.1.2, reproduced from Gita's 2015 Jackson Hole paper (Gopinath 2015). The figure plots, for a set of countries, the share of imports invoiced in dollars, relative to the share of imports that actually come from the United States. As is apparent, virtually every country invoices a lot more of its imports in dollars than it actually buys from the United States—a sharp contrast to the Mundell-Fleming paradigm in which the imports from any given country are always invoiced in that country's currency. This and other related facts from Gopinath (2015) have prompted an important conversation in the international finance community on the causes and the consequences of this large role of the dollar in trade invoicing and, more broadly, about the role of the dollar as this dominant currency. This paper provides answers to some of these questions.

It turns out that trade invoicing is not the only place where the dollar plays an outsize role. Fact 2 is that it also plays an important role in denominating the deposits of non-US banks. Fact 3 is that it also plays an outsize role in denominating the liabilities of non-US corporations.

The dollar's importance in international finance does not stop there. Fact 4 is that US dollar borrowing is typically cheaper, in the sense that there are systematic uncovered interest rate parity (UIP) violations that favor the dollar as a borrowing currency. Fact 5 is that corporate balance sheets are also currency-mismatched, in the sense that their assets are not as heavily skewed toward the dollar as their liabilities.

This paper proposes, for the first time, a unified and elegant theory connecting these five sets of facts. It then derives potential implications for the euro or the renminbi going forward. How likely is it that these currencies will replace the dollar as a dominant currency one day, in the sense of these five facts?

The model has two key ingredients. By far the most important ingredient is the assumption that the US dollar is a unit of account for assets and liabilities, *including* trade payables and trade receivables—the former is a liability for importers, the latter an asset for exporters. When prices are sticky in the invoicing currency, the liabilities of importers and the assets of exporters are not indexed to the exchange rate. This creates a motive for asset-liability management: firms want to match the currency denomination of their assets to that of their liabilities. Banks intermediate this desire. This explains facts 1–3.

The model's second key ingredient is that the US dollar is a safe store of value. As a result, in-equilibrium dollar funding is cheap (fact 4), creating an incentive for currency mismatch in balance sheets (fact 5).

The argument is summarized in figure 2.2.1. Consider any country other than the United States—say an emerging market country. Imagine that that country's importers are invoiced in dollars. Their

FIGURE 2.2.1. The Model's Causal Chain from Dollar Invoicing of Imports to Dollar Invoicing of Exports.
Source: Author.

trade payables are therefore dollar liabilities, generating an incentive for them to hold dollar deposits so as to match the denomination of their liabilities and their assets. This demand for dollar deposits puts pressure on dollar interest rates, leading local banks to issue such deposits. Moreover, low interest rates on dollar loans lead *exporters* to want to borrow in dollars, so that bank assets are also in dollars. Next, given that exporters have dollar liabilities, they also want to match these to their assets, encouraging them to invoice in dollars (in the model, they maintain some currency mismatch, but this is not essential). These non-US exporters now have *their* exports invoiced in dollars, in turn affecting other countries in a self-reinforcing loop. This idea is at the heart of the paper's model.[1] In fact, the mechanism is so strong that it can lead to a situation of multiple equilibria, in which the dollar's role in trade and banking becomes self-reinforcing.

The paper raises one key question: why doesn't the world just dollarize? The paper does not explicitly model the benefits of flexible exchange rates. If indeed there is such a strong incentive to match the currency of assets, liabilities, and trade invoices, there is a case for dollarizing everywhere.

Interestingly, a large literature in the sixties and seventies, the optimal currency area literature (Mundell 1961; McKinnon 1963; Kenen 1969), took the opposite approach: it was mostly modeling the *costs* of having the same currency, while leaving the benefits unmodeled. To me, Gita's paper provides a crisp example of the benefit side of the currency union—it allows importers, exporters, and banks to reduce the exchange rate risk on their balance sheets. One interesting avenue for research would be to explore these costs and these benefits jointly inside the same paper.

As I mentioned earlier, the paper generates multiple equilibria because of these large complementarities between the dollar

---

1. See Doepke and Schneider (2017) for a similar formulation.

denomination of imports and exports. Interpreting history along these lines, the paper argues that we can think of the US dollar's replacement of the pound as the dominant currency as a switch from one equilibrium to another. In principle, going forward, we might see the equilibrium switch again, with the euro or the renminbi becoming the new dominant currency. But what this static model misses is that existing assets and liabilities have long maturities. So in a sense, the anchor of history is likely extremely strong—it would take a really long time for all assets and liabilities to be redenominated in any new currency, and the staggered nature of contracts makes such a coordination very large to imagine.

As I have argued, the main assumption of the paper is that the US dollar plays a role as a unit of account. But there's also this role as a store of value, which in the model generates UIP violations. Consider a simplified model where savers are valuing dollars directly in their utility and can choose to consume either today or tomorrow. In this model, these savers are risk-neutral and they can save in the form of either domestic deposits or dollar deposits. To do the latter, they swap their current domestic deposits for dollars today and then have to bring them back tomorrow at tomorrow's exchange rate. This model generates a UIP violation (or an exorbitant privilege), because there is a direct benefit from holding the dollar over holding the swap, which depresses dollar interest rates in equilibrium.

This explanation for UIP is complementary to typical risk-based explanations, in which investors are worried about the exchange rate risk and the dollar commands lower equilibrium rates of return because it appreciates in bad times and so provides a good hedge. In this typical view, UIP violations emerge naturally, while covered interest rate parity (CIP) holds as a result of no arbitrage conditions—something that appears to be true in the data, except in the recent period since the financial crisis. The argument in the paper is that CIP should still hold when dollars are valued in the consumer's utility. This relies on the assumption that consumers who swap a dollar forward aren't just as happy holding the dollar directly, which is a fairly extreme assumption. If the paper made the alternative assumption in which investors do get the dollar benefits from having swapped dollars ahead of time, the model could be used to explain the cross-currency basis that we've seen open up since 2008.

My final point is on testing the theory. The paper tests one particular cross-country prediction, which is that countries that have larger invoicing shares in dollars to begin with also tend to have larger dollar deposits as a share of total denomination of deposits issued by their banks. But the theory provides many micro-level predictions beyond this important cross-country prediction. As an example, importers in the model that have large invoicing in dollars should also hold many more deposits in dollars. And banks whose clients are importers with larger exposures (those who have more invoices) should also issue more dollar loans. Exporters who choose to invoice in dollars will also tend to borrow in US dollars, and so on. I think it would be really nice to test these many predictions directly in matched bank-firm data.

To conclude, this is a novel and coherent framework that links the prominent role of the dollar in both trade invoicing and banking. The main assumption of the paper is that dollar invoicing creates an asset-liability management motive for firms, which triggers a causal chain from import invoicing to export invoicing via cheap funding. My view is that, in this story, the role of the dollar as a unit of account is much more important than its role as a safe store of value. More broadly, I am certain that there will be many more papers on this fascinating topic, so that it would be nice to flesh out the particular testable implications of this model of dollar dominance relative to explanations already in the literature.

References

Doepke, Matthias, and Martin Schneider. 2017. "Money as a Unit of Account." *Econometrica* 85, no. 5: 1537–74. https://doi: 10.3982/ECTA11963.

Gopinath, Gita. 2015. "The International Price System." Working Paper no. 21644, National Bureau of Economic Research, October. https://doi.org/10.3386 /w21646.

Kenen, Peter. 1969. "The Theory of Optimum Currency Areas: An Eclectic View." In *Monetary Problems of the International Economy*, edited by Robert A. Mundell and Alexander K. Swoboda. Chicago: Chicago University Press.

McKinnon, Ronald I. 1963. "Optimum Currency Areas." *American Economic Review* 53, no. 4 (September): 717–25.

Mundell, Robert A. 1961. "A Theory of Optimum Currency Areas." *American Economic Review* 51, no. 4 (September): 657–65.

GENERAL DISCUSSION

GITA GOPINATH: The question was, why doesn't the whole world dollarize? In our setup, we have assumed exogenous. Like you said, there's a whole bunch of goods that you buy domestically, that have a price in local currency, and have a local sticky currency price. So if we introduced a monetary authority into this model, then given this assumption that we live in a world where there's a whole bunch of goods that are priced in your own local currency, you would have reasons why you would not want to fully dollarize, because then you'd give up independent monetary policy. And independent monetary policy would be valuable, because you would get still the right relative price adjustment in terms of your traded and your non-traded goods. So you're fully aware of all of this.

And so, since there is an existing literature on what the costs are of giving up monetary policy flexibility, we focused here on just the other part of it. But clearly, I think the next step if we want to tie this into the bigger question of monetary policy, I think we need to do more on it.

The CIP violation is a bit of a quaint thing, and it shows up once in a while in the middle of a financial crisis. I think the phenomenon you're talking about is more general and shows up all the time. It's why we didn't focus on it.

So the theory of testing at the micro level, I think that's a very good idea. But I think the first-order thinking about being a dominant currency is that, unfortunately, this is like one observation for a country. So if you think of Argentina, all firms would export in dollars, all firms would import in dollars, the banking sector is dollarized. And so, there's not interesting within-firm variation. But that said, I think you could think of other countries, Switzerland, for instance, where you have a mix of three currencies—the euro, the dollar, and the Swiss franc—and see whether you have interesting variation over there.

MICHAEL BORDO: If I look at the history of the international monetary system, there's a reason why the pound emerged as the dominant currency in the nineteenth century and the dollar in the twentieth century. It is based on the deep fundamentals of the rule of law and property rights, etc., which led to the development of deep financial markets and sound institutions, as well as another factor, which is global economic and political power. I am not discounting the invoicing story but I believe that these deeper fundamentals are a very important part of an explanation of how a dominant currency evolved. And it seems to me very questionable whether China could acquire this position until they satisfy these preconditions.

GITA GOPINATH: I completely agree that the rule of law and property rights are important, which is why in the model, when we talk about the emergence of a dominant currency, we compare the US dollar and the euro, where we think there's similarities there between the institutions and central bank credibility and all of that. In fact, one of the very crucial variables there that's in the model is the extent to which the renminbi would depreciate if things go terribly wrong. And if you feel that this is a central banking environment where you can't have that much credibility associated with it, then it's going to take a much longer time for the renminbi to come in there. You need full convertibility. You need stronger financial institutions, and all of those matter. But what I find quite interesting is the fact that the recipe book, the way that they're going about internationalizing the renminbi, is very much in the style of the way it happened previously with the dollar and then previously with the pound.

JUHI DHAWAN: If I could offer a couple of comments from what we're seeing in the marketplace. One, earlier this year, China launched a futures oil contract priced in yuan. This seems to signal a move away from dollars toward renminbi. While, obviously, current share of such contracts in the energy market is low, it will be interesting to follow to see how it gains traction over time. Two, while I completely agree with comments made earlier, that the rule of law and the importance of sound institutions is critical in determining which currency dominates as a reserve currency, it is also important to consider the money flows under way in financial markets. Sticking with China, the country has stated that its foreign exchange reserves have peaked and, further, the central bank has adopted a basket of currencies to stabilize its exchange rate against, rather than just the dollar. Again, this may be indicative of the possibility of a break from prior recent history on the dominance of the US dollar. Monitoring real asset purchases and financial flows at a time of transition of monetary policy in multiple large countries of the world seems to be more important than ever.

GITA GOPINATH: I agree with you. So this other paper that I mentioned, that I have with Jeremy Stein on central bank reserves, there's another argument for why there might be gains to coordination, which Raghu didn't bring up. But in this environment, where central banks are trying to kind of recognize the fact that they have a dollarized banking system, and that helps with having dollar reserves, because in case of a crisis you can come in and bail out your banks as opposed to taxing heavily, that gives rise to this externality, which is that this huge demand for dollar reserves is driving down interest rates in dollars. And those lower interest rates in dollars are then further encouraging the domestic banking sector to dollarize. So we certainly have an argument for why there's excess reserve accumulation by central banks, which is then feeding into the problem.

ROBERT HALL: You should extend this very interesting line of research to other standards. First of all, we have one worldwide standard for keeping time. This standard is used everywhere. For weights and measures, all the rest of the world uses the metric system, except the US. But the US has had to accede to the metric system. For example, you need to have metric wrenches to work on any car today. But America's adherence to English weights and measures puts the US at a disadvantage. The Carter administration decreed under Article I of the Constitution that we had to use the metric system, but the Reagan administration, recognizing how unpopular it was, changed it back. So we're still suffering from becoming a minority in the world in the case of standards for weights and measures. England, of course, doesn't use English weights and measures anymore, but the US does. So a similar line of analysis would apply to these issues, in addition to the standards for quoting prices considered in the paper.

MICHAEL MELVIN: I was struck by the bar chart on the fraction of trade from the US and the fraction of imports denominated in dollars, and certain commodities are dollar-based globally, right? So to what extent can you explain that wedge by oil imports? There wasn't enough time to sort out the different bars, but it may not be so much freedom of choice by the importer as it's just given.

GITA GOPINATH: So to the simple question of how much of this is basically a bunch of countries importing commodities that have a dollar price traded on an exchange, is a flexible price . . . For the countries where we are able to make the distinction, where we take out commodities and keep the rest, these pictures look very similar. So it's not the case. Now we don't have data for every single country in the world that can do that breakdown, but for all countries that I've looked at, where we could actually tell those two apart, it's still overwhelmingly the dollar.

ROBERT HELLER: Certainly in Silicon Valley, we talk all day long about network effects. Isn't the dollar's dominance similar to network effects? The dollar almost took over the world, and it's very difficult for a second competitor to come up and to compete with the currency once it's dominant, just simply because of network effects.

GITA GOPINATH: Yes, I think you're right. This is going into the details of how the network gets kind of an argument. There's no network specifically here, but this is an argument of why you would want everybody to end up holding the dollar, even though they're doing this in a very decentralized way. And this is coming from the low interest rates and the trade invoicing, which are just feeding on one another. Now there could be other kinds of explanations, which are based on kind of global supply chains, that I have my liabilities that I owe to another seller to me, and if that's going to be a dollar liability, I'd like to receive payment in dollars, so those other channels are also in there, which we haven't fleshed out, but that also can kind of enhance this argument that you inferred.

JIM DORN: I think it's true that the renminbi is being international-ized as you pointed out, but it's not yet a safe-haven currency, as Eswar Prasad pointed out in his recent book [*Gaining Currency: The Rise of the Renminbi*]. I also think that one of the main things going on in China right now with Xi Jinping is the huge crackdown on the free flow of information. China needs a free market in ideas to have an international global currency that's widely accepted.

GITA GOPINATH: To some extent, I can agree, yes.

JOHN SMYTH: Thank you for your research. It's very useful and appli-cable at my job at JP Morgan. I wanted to see if you've seen any flow-through in terms of lowering the cost to borrow, because if you've got dollar deposits, and you're transacting mostly in dol-lars, your cost to borrow is less. Given that the European Central Bank has been on a bond-buying spree, and it costs less for a junk bond issuer in Europe, in Italy, to borrow, than it does our US government, have you seen any flow-through to the euro as a currency gaining traction because it's cheaper now to borrow in Europe than it is here?

GITA GOPINATH: That's a good point. What we've taken as completely neutral in the model is monetary policy. So the way I think of what's happening in the euro area relative to the US right now is we have these differential monetary policy stances which show up in these different borrowing rates. We're going to have to see how this plays out. It's too early to tell. The simple answer is I haven't seen anything about it since the divergence in interest rates has happened in terms of invoicing and other things from the euro area. But what I do know, and this is what we're just seeing kind of very casually in terms of correlations, is the fact that there was the US crisis, and then post the crisis in the euro area, where there was a real concern about whether the euro would actually exist as a currency, and you actually saw a decline in euros in the banking system, in euro liabilities, and you see a decline in euro trade invoicing, in both.

I feel our paper is about saying, okay, 80 percent of our trade is in dollars, and then there are movements and movements around it. I worry about 80 percent less about the movement, but there seems to be some co-movement between the two.

JOHN COCHRANE: This question may end with more humor than substance. Here in the Silicon Valley, right now, everybody is abuzz over blockchain. That's just about every new venture capital project. There is a vision that a global electronic currency, if it could be made to have a stable value and many other problems fixed, would allow exactly Bob's weights and measures, a stable price standard immune from everything we talked about in the first session—governments deciding they need currency controls, capital controls, and, if we run into debt crises, inflations and expropriations. In the chaos, there is a vision afoot of a nongovernment currency potentially taking over as the international standard. You likely have a "blockchain comment" ready, and it would be good to hear it.

GITA GOPINATH: At the time I presented this paper, it was not blockchain. It was, "Do you think bitcoin could be the next dollar?" And my answer to that is, *no*. It's terrible for transaction purposes, and it doesn't serve that purpose at all. And the bottom line is I don't think this is not going to be an unregulated enterprise. If it turns out that there is another currency out there that's basically taking over the power of the US central bank, I just don't think that that will exist. And here you and I might differ. I actually do think monetary policy has some positive effects, and so the idea that there's a finite supply of these coins, that brings me back to the old problems of the gold standard, and I do like the idea of someone having control over the amount of this that's floating around, and so again, this is all new technology. I don't want to say that there's no space in which it might exist. But it's not something I'm going to start writing a paper about.

ANDREW LEVIN: I'd like to flag a connection to the previous session, where Raghu Rajan talked about international responsibility and Paul Tucker highlighted political realities. And this paper shows that there are clear political and economic benefits to having a reserve currency, i.e., the US has an "exorbitant privilege." Those benefits provide a motive for the Congress and the Treasury and the Federal Reserve to take responsibility for assuring the continuing role of the US dollar as a reserve currency, and that could provide an impetus for addressing the international political issues.

PAUL TUCKER: I wanted to add to that question, please. So when you were talking about the transition from sterling-based invoicing to dollar-based invoicing, I wondered to what extent you thought about how the world coordinated on that switch happening, and to what extent it required acquiescence by the UK.

This strikes me as tremendously important in terms of framing the issues around any future change. It seems to me obvious that the US one day acquiescing in renminbi invoicing becoming a dominant thing isn't quite the same thing at all as London acquiescing in the switch to dollars, as the security relationship is profoundly different.

The other suggestion I wanted to make about the next phase of this work, when you introduce monetary policy, is not to think about monetary policy in the normal way we do (in terms of stabilizing the path of aggregate demand and so on). Rather, think about it as providing liquidity on demand in your own currency. A few years ago I suggested to Janet Yellen and some others that far from being rather restrictive about providing swap lines against other currencies, instead, as international use of the renminbi grows, it's plausible that we will see the US authorities and the Chinese authorities positively marketing swap lines as a way of underpinning invoicing in their currency and assets denominated in their currency being regarded as the safe asset. That strikes me as kind of an important part of the monetary politics we potentially face in the coming decades, which has nothing to do with stabilizing nominal demand at home.

GITA GOPINATH: I agree with everything you said.

GEORGE SHULTZ: Here's the problem. Right now, we have gigantic debt, huge deficits, and rising interest rates, so there is a compounding process: the burden of the debt rises, the deficit rises, the debt rises, the burden rises, and so on. It is totally out of control, but no one is paying the slightest attention to it. Meanwhile, people are buying things from the US with US dollars, but they're beginning to wonder if the dollar is going to be worth anything. My great friend Sam Nunn, who was a senator and legendary chairman of the Senate Military Affairs Committee, is good at telling jokes. I saw him the other day and said, "Sam, tell me a joke." He said, "Washington, DC."

Things are out of hand. What's going to happen?

GITA GOPINATH: I can't agree more. I think you're right. The US already has a debt problem. If it's going to blow that up even more, it's going to flag concerns. The question is whether there is a viable alternative there. Initially, at some point, the euro seemed viable, and then you had the euro crises, and now there's going to be another period of wait and watch. In the case of the renminbi, I think the Chinese government is pushing very hard to internationalize it, but at the same time they're worried about the volatility of their exchange rates. So if anything, for now they've actually put more controls on capital flows. So in the absence of a very easy alternative, I don't know how long this process will take, but clearly none of what's going on right now helps.

SYMPOSIUM ON

Capital Flows, the IMF's Institutional View and Alternatives

Introduction

George P. Shultz

John Taylor asked me to chair this session. He knows that I'm an outsider, so he gave me permission to make a few remarks from the perspective of an outsider on the topic here: capital controls and the IMF.

First of all, I spent about twelve years on the faculty at the University of Chicago, where one of my great friends was George Stigler. He and I were golfing buddies. George's office was across the hall from mine, and Milton was often there, so I got to know Milton and George, and I listened to them. They were out of my league—but still, I absorbed some ideas: for example, the marketplace is pretty good at sorting things out.

When I was secretary of labor, I was looking at changing our view of emergency disputes, discrimination in the workplace, and so on. One of my most interesting experiences was managing for the president the desegregation of schools in the South. That was a fascinating thing to do.

Then, all of the sudden, I'm the first director of the Office of Management and Budget. So suddenly it's a different world of taxes, revenues, and the like. When I arrive, I find that there's a big financial company called Penn Central that has badly mismanaged its affairs and is about to go bankrupt. Arthur Burns, chairman of the Fed, thought that if that happened, it would be a severe blow to the financial system. I thought it was a mistake; maybe it was the Milton and George in me. But as I'm arguing with Arthur, half of me is thinking, "What is a lousy labor economist doing arguing with Arthur Burns about financial markets?" All of the sudden, in comes a man named Bryce Harlow, one of the smartest, savviest political advisers ever in Washington. Bryce says, "Mr. President, the Penn Central, in its infinite wisdom, has just hired your old law firm to represent them in this matter. Under these circumstances, you can't touch this with a ten-foot pole." So there was no bailout, and what happened? The financial markets were strengthened. Yes, there was some kerfuffle, but everybody had to look at their hole card and say, "Hey, we'd better get straightened out because they're not going to bail us out," so it improved matters. It made an impact.

Before long, my friend Paul Volcker tells me there's going to be a run on the bank. I asked, "What do you mean?" He says, "There are more dollars out there than there is gold at Fort Knox. We're going to have to close the gold window." That led to a dramatic set of announcements by President Nixon of his new economic policy. I told him, "You'd better be careful, Mr. President, because that's what Lenin called his policy. It may not work." I thought it was a bad policy—wage and price controls, and so on—but I lost that battle.

At any rate, the exchange rate system at that point was in a total mess. John Connally was secretary of the Treasury. They negotiated something called the Smithsonian Agreement, which didn't work. So I asked the Treasury people, "What is your plan?" They said, "It's a secret." When, all of a sudden, I become secretary of the Treasury and I ask, "Okay, what is your plan?" they say, "We don't have one." I said, "Okay, I thought that was the case."

So we had to work on this problem, and I thought, going back to my Chicago days, that a floating exchange rate was the best answer.

Paul Volcker said, "Well, the Europeans and the Japanese want a par value system." I thought about that, and I called Milton, and we had a long series of telephone conversations. We decided on a program that was a floating exchange rate system in the clothing of a par value system. It was pretty neat. We worked on that, and I think as things evolved, it was a sort of sloppy, managed float, so here we are.

But then, a couple of decades or so ago, the IMF gets involved in countries that are in bad shape, and it bails them out. I'm thinking, "Hey, Penn Central: same old idea, same problem. The IMF is out of its jurisdiction. It's supposed to be about exchange rates." I wrote an article with Walt Wriston, who was head of Citicorp, and Bill Simon, who was my successor, saying that the IMF was way out of line and we ought to just get rid of it. Of course, nobody took that seriously.

At any rate, I now see that the IMF is worrying about capital flows, and I say, "Wait a minute, it's the same old problem. The problem isn't capital flows; the problem is the central banks creating more money than is useful in their own countries, and it's slopping around." So let's get it straight.

I have a suggestion. I've been to the bank fund meetings and they're lots of fun. The clan gathers. Why is it? Because both the IMF and the bank have money. But thinking about money is the wrong mindset for the IMF because it was put into place originally as a result of the currency manipulation and the protectionism during the Great Depression, and it was supposed to worry about the currencies. So it seems to me that the IMF is the other side of the coin of the trading system. The meeting should be between the WTO and the IMF. So my suggestion is: let the banks have monetary meetings. The structure of the meetings will get the IMF to think about its basic job, which is the trading system.

CHAPTER THREE

MANAGING CAPITAL FLOWS: TOWARD A POLICY MAKER'S VADE MECUM

Jonathan D. Ostry

The work I will present in this session began nearly a decade ago, in 2009, as capital flows to emerging market economies (EMEs) were rebounding and policy makers were beginning to think about how they might respond. The issue seemed particularly relevant given that some EMEs, particularly in Eastern Europe, had recently experienced a capital inflows-induced boom-bust cycle of epic proportions. Initially, the thought was that coming up with a coherent policy framework—taking account of the recipient countries' interests as well as the multilateral repercussions—could be done swiftly, given that managing EME capital-flow boom-bust cycles was hardly a new issue. And, of course, there was a long history of advice to draw on, as well as the accumulated wisdom from the academic literature.

Not to overly caricature, but my sense of the prevailing view in official circles and much of academia at the time was that EMEs should simply allow their currencies to appreciate in the face of capital inflows (appreciation being a market-driven force that naturally would dampen inflows) and tighten fiscal policy if there was a risk of economic overheating. Foreign exchange market intervention was recommended only to counter very short-term market volatility (sometimes referred to as "disorderly market conditions"); as for capital controls, they were to be eschewed pretty much without exception.

The views expressed are those of the author and should not be attributed to the IMF. This contribution draws on my co-authored book *Taming the Tide of Capital Flows* (MIT Press, 2017).

In thinking afresh about these issues, it seemed logical not to foreclose the use of any policy instrument without a solid rationale for doing so. In that context, policy makers have at their disposal potentially five tools: monetary and exchange rate policies; fiscal policy; macroprudential measures; and capital controls. There did not seem strong grounds a priori to exclude their use nor to rank them in a normative fashion. In a sense, this was the main point of the first paper I draw on in today's presentation (Ostry et al. 2010)—a point that proved highly controversial when it was made because it recognized that capital controls on inflows *might* have a legitimate place in the policy maker's toolkit.

I also draw on a second paper (Ostry et al. 2011a) whose insight was that, in open economies, many prudential measures—for example, those limiting foreign currency exposures—are economically equivalent to capital inflow controls. For example, higher reserve requirements on banks' liabilities in foreign currency, while legally not a capital control insofar as the measure applies equally to deposits of residents and nonresidents, would have the same impact on capital flows as a capital inflow control if the foreign currency liabilities of banks are to nonresidents. This is an important insight because, in practice, the policy community has blessed macroprudential tools almost as strongly as it has shunned measures that discriminate according to residency (capital controls). In fact, both nondiscriminatory and discriminatory measures can make meaningful contributions to financial stability: the salient issue is which type of measure is better targeted to the financial-stability risk at hand (if the risk is from flighty foreign investors rather than residents, a capital control indeed might have more traction).

THE INSTITUTIONAL VIEW

These two papers sparked intense debate and controversy when they were issued, both within the Fund and outside. Meanwhile,

EMEs continued to be deluged with foreign capital and began experimenting with a variety of policy responses—including capital controls—to deal with the macroeconomic and financial-stability consequences of capital flows. At the IMF's Executive Board, the issue of policy responses to capital flows—especially the role of capital controls and prudential measures that could act like them— became highly contentious. This led IMF staff to prepare a series of Board papers to inform our policy advice. In 2011, the IMF's governing body, the IMFC, called on the Fund to advance "work on a comprehensive, flexible, and balanced approach for the management of capital flows." Building on earlier Fund policy papers, analytical work, and the Board discussions, the Institutional View (IV) was developed and adopted in November 2012.

The IV sought a common ground among the diverse views on capital flows. Its intention was to provide a framework which ensures that policy advice provided to Fund member countries on capital flow management is "consistent, even-handed, flexible, and takes into account country circumstances." The IV does not cheerlead countries to fully open their capital accounts, in marked contrast to the IMF position in the mid-1990s when it sought jurisdiction over these issues. It recognizes in particular that "there is no presumption that full liberalization is an appropriate goal for all countries at all times" and that, while capital flows can bring great benefits to countries, openness likewise carries substantial risks.

The IV envisages a role for macroeconomic policies—including foreign exchange intervention—as well as capital controls and related prudential measures (collectively referred to as capital flow management measures, or CFMs) in managing capital flows under certain circumstances. What are those circumstances? When confronted with an inflow *surge*, the IV proposes a role for CFMs when macroeconomic policy space is limited, when it takes time to pull other policy levers (or for those policies to have an effect), and when there are risks to financial stability. Importantly, for financial-stability purposes, the IV envisages that CFMs can be maintained *over the longer term*, provided that "no less discriminatory measure is available that is effective." For outflow episodes, the IV advises that CFMs could be used temporarily in crisis situations or when crisis is imminent.

With respect to foreign exchange market intervention (FXI), the IV suggests that in the face of inflows, the currency should be allowed to appreciate provided it is not already overvalued, but that reserves may be accumulated when overvaluation becomes a problem provided the country isn't already over-reserved according to the Fund's prudential metrics. For outflow episodes, the IMF staff operational guidance note suggests that FXI could be appropriate when exchange rate changes are contributing to disorderly market conditions, provided that such intervention does not cause reserves to fall to inadequate levels as determined by appropriate metrics.

ROLE OF UNWANTED PUSH FACTORS

Of course, there was an important conjunctural element that added force to the arguments that capital inflow receiving countries should have latitude to adopt policies that could insulate them against the macroeconomic and financial-stability risks induced by volatile capital flows. From the EME perspective, inflow surges were largely an unwanted spillover from advanced-economy monetary policies. The fear that the "monetary tsunami" could easily reverse was very much on their minds—they had lived through this many times before, as the long history of boom-bust cycles (surges and crashes), going back decades, amply demonstrates. The Brazilian finance minister at the time echoed what was on the minds of many policy makers, namely that the inflationary and currency-overvaluation consequences of inflows legitimated "self-defense" measures, as EME countries had no say over the monetary policy decisions of the countries at the epicenter of the global crisis. But the point being made was not specific to the conjuncture of quantitative easing, given that EMEs had been faced with similar challenges for decades in the past.

Giving EME policy makers greater latitude to deal with the problems inflicted by advanced-economy (AE) monetary policy would have been less of an issue if AE policy makers took greater account of the financial spillovers from their policies. This was a theme of remarks made by Reserve Bank of India Governor Rajan back in 2014—and repeated at today's conference—in calling on "large-country central banks . . . to internalize more of the spillovers from the policies in their mandate." But those central banks did not buy the argument, with Fed Chair Ben Bernanke arguing instead that any adverse repercussions on EMEs through capital flows were more than offset by favorable growth spillovers through trade. While coordination or global rules to constrain large-country policies whose "negative emissions" loomed large was debated (see Blanchard and Ostry 2013; Ostry and Ghosh 2016), they failed to gain traction.

MANAGING INFLOW SURGES

There is convincing evidence that surges and crashes of capital flows are influenced to an important degree by common global factors, such as advanced-economy (especially US) interest rates, global investors' risk aversion, and commodity prices (Ghosh, Ostry, and Qureshi 2016). While capital flows can help finance much-needed investment and can help to smooth consumption for credit-constrained individuals, *surges* give rise to special concerns, including rising macroeconomic and financial-stability vulnerabilities. On the macroeconomic side, the issues are economic overheating, depending on the type of inflow (Blanchard et al. 2016), currency appreciation, and credit booms. On the financial-stability side, worries include maturity and currency mismatches on balance sheets, sometimes manifest in FX-denominated credit booms.

Widening macro and financial vulnerabilities in turn amplify crisis risk in EMEs, with surges increasing the likelihood of crisis (relative to more normal inflows) fourfold. *How* countries manage the surge period turns out to be a powerful determinant of whether a crisis or a dignified end to the surge ensues. Successful strategies, the evidence shows, include using the toolkits at policy makers' disposal to ensure that vulnerabilities remain contained during the surge period. Indeed, a natural mapping of targets and instruments exists, with monetary policy targeted to overheating concerns; FX intervention to mitigate over-appreciation of the currency; and prudential tools applied to financial-stability risks. Capital controls may serve to underpin the effectiveness of these orthodox measures or they may be used in a more structural manner to foster a safer mix of inflows (e.g., by discouraging carry trades).

The latter point is related to the prudential theory of capital controls which argues that full financial integration may not be a desirable end-goal for emerging market countries when distortions or externalities mean that the assumptions of a first-best competitive equilibrium are violated. In the presence of imperfect information, for example, free capital mobility may amplify existing distortions, encourage moral hazard and excessive risk-taking, and expose countries to contagion and herding effects. Modern incarnations of this line of thinking encompass formal models in which capital controls (or, equivalently in many of these models, macroprudential measures) act as a Pigouvian tax against excessive inflows to attain the constrained optimum. The tax is an *ex ante* measure, akin to a Tobin tax designed to prevent excessive inflows, which then mitigates the impact of subsequent outflows more effectively than direct measures to stop outflows when reversals occur.

ASSESSING THE EFFECTIVENESS
OF CAPITAL CONTROLS

While some structural measures to curtail especially risky flows may be desirable, much of the recent debate has been about the use of cyclically varying measures and the degree to which they have traction. A problem with a number of the studies on the effectiveness of these measures is that they are unclear about the policy objective against which the measures are being assessed. Some studies, for example, find that capital controls have little effect in reducing the overall volume of inflows and their associated consequences (e.g., currency appreciation or overheating) and from this conclude that capital controls are ineffective. But if the goal is to shift the composition of inflows so the country ends up with a less risky external-liability structure, and if the studies find that controls are successful against this objective, then controls might be viewed as having traction against an established objective.

Empirical studies need to confront a number of difficulties in evaluating the effectiveness of capital controls, including creating the counterfactual and contending with the fundamental identification problem whereby countries tend to impose controls precisely when they face large inflows. This reality yields a spurious positive correlation between inflow controls and inflows and tends to bias estimates of the effectiveness of controls in reducing the aggregate volume of flows toward zero. There is indeed a voluminous literature on the effectiveness of controls, which tends to find more favorable evidence in favor of compositional effects than on aggregate-volume effects. Some researchers have undertaken meta-studies that comprehensively review the empirical literature on capital-control effectiveness. The general finding is that inflow controls tend to make monetary policy more independent and are successful in altering the composition of flows. My own work

(Ostry et al. 2011b; Ostry et al. 2012) exploits the natural experiment afforded by the global financial crisis and finds that countries that had capital controls (or currency-based prudential regulations that mimic them) in place in the run-up to the crisis tended to be more resilient (i.e., experience smaller output declines) during the crisis. Aside from this, my work also suggests that prudential capital controls acted to reduce financial-stability risks (manifest, for example, in high levels of FX lending by the domestic banking system).

TAKEAWAYS

To sum up, boom-bust cycles in cross-border capital flows are nothing new. They happened during the late nineteenth-century golden era of financial globalization, they were present in the interwar period, and they reemerged in the decades following World War II as capital account restrictions were dismantled and private capital flows resumed. But views about managing capital flows have swung markedly over this period—from the laissez-faire attitude of the nineteenth century, to the structural controls envisaged under Bretton Woods, to the free market principles and Washington Consensus of the 1980s and 1990s, to the recent reevaluation in light of the global financial crisis.

It is clear, however, that many advanced economies used restrictions on capital inflows for prudential purposes until the 1980s. For emerging market countries, the lesson from history and from the academic literature is that capital flows can bring myriad benefits but fully unfettered flows may not be optimal, and measures to manage inflows form a legitimate part of the policy toolkit. When and how such measures should be used, and how they fit with other (monetary, exchange rate, and macroprudential) policies, is what I have tried to sketch in these few pages, and more fully in the book on which they draw.

References

Blanchard, Olivier, Jonathan D. Ostry, and Atish Ghosh. 2013. "Overcoming the Obstacles to International Macro Policy Coordination is Hard." *VoxEU*, December 20.

Blanchard, Olivier, Jonathan D. Ostry, Atish R. Ghosh, and Marcos Chamon. 2016. "Capital Flows: Expansionary or Contractionary?" *American Economic Review* 106, no. 5 (May): 565–69.

Ghosh, Atish R., Jonathan D. Ostry, and Mahvash S. Qureshi. 2016. "When Do Capital Inflow Surges End in Tears?" *American Economic Review* 106, no. 5 (May): 581–85.

Ghosh, Atish R., Jonathan D. Ostry, and Mahvash S. Qureshi. 2017. *Taming the Tide of Capital Flows.* MIT Press.

Ostry, Jonathan D., Marcos Chamon, Atish R. Ghosh, and Mahvash Qureshi. 2012. "Tools for Managing Financial-Stability Risks from Capital Inflows." *Journal of International Economics* 88, no. 2: 40–21.

Ostry, Jonathan D., and Atish R. Ghosh. 2016. "On the Obstacles to International Policy Coordination." *Journal of International Money and Finance* 67: 25–40.

Ostry, Jonathan D., Atish R. Ghosh, Marcos Chamon, and Mahvash Qureshi. 2011b. "Capital Controls: When and Why?" *IMF Economic Review* 59, no. 3 (August): 562–80.

Ostry, Jonathan D., Atish R. Ghosh, Karl Habermeier, Marcos Chamon, Mahvash S. Qureshi, and Dennis B. S. Reinhardt. 2010. "Capital Inflows: The Role of Controls." IMF Staff Position Note No. 4, International Monetary Fund.

Ostry, Jonathan D., Atish R. Ghosh, Karl F. Habermeier, Luc Laeven, Marcos Chamon, Mahvash Qureshi, and Annamaria Kokenyne. 2011a. "Managing Capital Flows: What Tools to Use?" IMF Staff Discussion Note No. 6, International Monetary Fund.

CHAPTER FOUR

THE IMF'S INSTITUTIONAL VIEW: A CRITIQUE

Sebastian Edwards

Thank you, first of all, to John Taylor and John Cochrane for inviting me. And it's always a pleasure to be here at Hoover and in particular to be at this conference, which has become a big tradition and an opportunity to meet old friends.

I don't have a PowerPoint. And I do have a new book as well, but I'm not going to advertise it. [Laughter] And I am going to follow the instructions that were given to us on the panel, which is to talk about the International Monetary Fund's Institutional View. I do have some comments on what Jonathan said outside the sphere of the Institutional View and I will address those if I have time toward the end of my presentation.

The IMF's Institutional View on capital flows management, which is a euphemism, of course, for capital controls, is provided in two documents. If you read who were the authors of those documents, the intersection between the 2012 and the 2016 documents is one person, and that's Jonathan Ostry. So that makes him the perfect person to talk about the Institutional View. I must as a way of disclosure say that Jonathan and I are coauthors and we've known each other for a very, very long time. I was a visiting scholar at the IMF when he arrived as a young economist, just graduated from Chicago, where I think he wrote his thesis under the guidance of Assaf Razin. So the IMF Institutional Views are two papers, one from 2012 and one from 2016.

The two IMF documents that capture and summarize the IMF Institutional View are extremely well written and very, very carefully done. And a very large number of people participated in preparing them. There is something in the papers for everyone. If I were to be a little provocative, just a little, and sort of label or title this session, one possible title would be, "When Did the IMF Lose its Groove?" Or, "When Did the IMF Become a Really Boring Institution?" I remember a conference that Rudi Dornbusch and I organized in Seoul, South Korea. The local institution was the KDI and Jung Sun Park was the key person there. It was about capital controls. It was twenty-five years ago. There was a huge debate throughout the conference between the IMF representative at the conference and one of the participants, where the IMF was absolutely clear in stating that capital controls were *never* good. We talked about the dynamics of liberalization, and in that context someone asked: What about sequencing of reforms? And the IMF said, no sequencing. They should be lifted immediately. What about maybe relaxing them gradually? Not gradual at all, we were told. They should be abolished very fast. So who were these two people? On the IMF side was Manuel Guitian, whom some of you may remember, who was number two to David Finch. If David had been there, he'd have had exactly the same view. And on the other side, none other than Bob Mundell. So, if you have the IMF being more in favor of capital mobility than Bob Mundell, you know that it is really out there. And that was the old time—not any longer. As the Institutional View documents clearly show, the IMF now hedges its position. It argues that there are a number—many, indeed—of circumstances when capital controls may be warranted.

Indeed, what the two papers do is give you a little bit about everything, and as I said: Capital controls? Well, sometimes yes, sometimes no; it depends on this, it depends on that; it is good sometimes, you should really look at the long term and maybe without capital controls. But during his presentation Jonathan several times said it's structural, not cyclical. That means that, well, maybe even in the very, very long run, since the structure doesn't really change, maybe we should still have capital controls.

Let me just focus on what the papers say. In what follows, I will focus on the most recent document, the one from 2016. The first thing that I think is quite remarkable, and it connects with the first session, is how little we know about the models, about the effects, even about the policies. The 2016 IMF paper has a very interesting table, which is table 2 on page 31. And what that table says is how many capital flow management measures were taken between the years 2013 and 2016, and it's about 900 of them. Then they classify them in four categories: control on portfolio investment, control on derivatives, control on direct investment, and differentiated reserve requirements on capital flows. And then there is a fifth category, which is "other." Well, about 70 percent of the measures are under "other." So, although one of the IMF's tasks is to analyze the nature of controls, it has found it difficult to classify them. We don't even have a very good view of what are the policies or measures that we're talking about.

The second point that I think is interesting is made in paragraph 50 and, again, it relates to the point made in the first session of this conference. The paper says: we really don't know much about how effective capital controls on inflows are. And it says: we need better assessment of the effectiveness of capital controls. This is an ongoing issue, and I think that's a very important point. The main aspect of this issue, of course—this refers to capital controls on inflows—is that they are never taken as a sole measure, they are never taken on their own. They're always part of a package. One of the lessons that I learned from Rudi Dornbusch is that when you're older than fifty, it's not really good taste to talk too much about your own work. I'm going to break that golden rule and talk a little bit about my work. A few years ago I did a paper with Roberto Rigobon from MIT about the effectiveness of the Chilean capital controls. What we found out is that they were effective, but the effectiveness was really the accompanying policy, which was a band for the exchange rate. And the band dictated that every time the peso tried to break through the band, the band was widened. So it was a flexible, very pragmatic band that had a very low degree of credibility. But sometimes it was binding, while other times it wasn't. So we really could not tell at first how effective the controls themselves were. And then we found out that the controls on inflows weren't really that effective; the effectiveness really came from the intervention in the foreign exchange market.

The two papers refer repeatedly to the sequencing of policy. But the sequencing discussion is concentrated and deals exclusively with the sequencing of capital controls. They start by saying, *first you have to liberalize FDI inflows. Then you have to liberalize FDI outflows, and only slowly, long-term bonds, and so on and so forth.* I would have liked to have had a broader discussion of sequencing involving other markets. In particular, when it comes to emerging markets, the interaction between capital markets and the labor markets, it is essential. Jim Heckman did quite a bit of work many years ago trying to measure the degree of distortions in labor markets in the emerging markets. The interaction between labor market constraints, which are gigantic, and the financial sector is something one should take into account when discussing the sequencing of policy.

Another issue that I would have liked to see more deeply treated by the IMF is the whole question of moral hazard. Of course, the term appears in both reports, and Jonathan did mention it in his presentation. But I don't think that it is discussed strongly enough. The question, of course, is: How differently are policy makers going to behave if they have the option of saying, at any time, "Well, the IMF allows us to use capital controls"? A number of examples from Latin America indicated, quite clearly, that the extent of moral hazard is deeply affected by the institutional setup. For instance, there is a huge difference between Chile, which has a completely independent central bank, and Brazil, where it is not independent but sort of well behaved, and Venezuela, where it is not independent and it is very badly behaved.

Let me move into a different topic which appears repeatedly in the two official papers that summarize the IMF's Institutional View. Both documents are replete with the notion: *you should do this if the currency is not overvalued.* Or, *you should do that if the degree of overvaluation is large.*

But it turns out that we don't really know very well how to recognize real exchange rate misalignment. In spite of the fact that the IMF spends thousands of men- and women-hours per year on its models on exchange rate overvaluation, we have made very, very little progress on that issue. If you analyze carefully what investment banks do regarding trying to determine whether a currency is out of line or whether it responds to fundamentals, you will conclude that the models are very crude. We are doing almost exactly the same thing that we were doing twenty-five years ago. Very little progress has happened, and the paper proceeds as if we have good, powerful models to understand misalignment. But the truth is that we don't.

The two documents that summarize the Institutional View deal in detail with the so-called originator countries. This is related to the very interesting paper presented earlier by Raghu Rajan on the responsibility of central bankers in advanced countries with regard to their policies' impact on the emerging nations. I think that the notion that central banks in the advanced nations will take into account how their own policies will affect emerging countries is pure wishful thinking. Historically it has not happened, and unless we are talking about major systemic crisis it is very unlikely to happen in the future. Let's think of what happened just one day before this conference. Our good friend Freddy Sturzenegger, the governor of the central bank of Argentina, raised the policy rate by 700 basis points. The policy rate in Argentina now is 40 percent. And the inflation rate is 22 percent. So you just do the math. What's the real policy rate in Argentina? Can you imagine that Jay Powell and the FOMC are going to think twice about raising the Federal Funds Rate because poor Freddy is under a lot of pressure in Buenos Aires? It's not going to happen. And I can go and tell you many stories from history. When Miguel Mancera —and John Taylor knows this—came and talked to Alan Greenspan in 1994 because the *tesobonos* were being sold like crazy in Mexico as a response to the Federal Reserve raising rates, Greenspan said, "I'm sorry. Mexico is not one of the regional Feds. I don't care what's going on there. My job is to worry about inflationary pressures in the United States." Now, to be fair, the Treasury then responded by using the stabilization fund, although Congress didn't like that. The stabilization fund was created in 1934, after the devaluation of the dollar. Larry Summers used it and helped Mexico, and Mexico paid every penny back. So the "originator countries" discussion— I think it's nice, but I think it's really not very realistic.

Something else I found missing . . . and I know that it's easy to ask for more in a paper that is already quite comprehensive. But since it doesn't cost me anything to ask for more, I will do it. I think there should be a greater discussion on the benefits of free capital mobility and pension funds management. If you look at the countries that have funded pension systems—and I go back to Chile, for instance—you will find out that the extremely good rate of return obtained by these funds was related to the ability to diversify internationally and move capital in and out of the country easily.

So to end let me mention three countries—only three, since I already talked about Argentina. The first one is my own country of origin, Chile. As Jonathan pointed out during his presentation, the IMF's decision to write about the Institutional View started in 2009 with the global financial crisis. Country after country after country would come to the IMF and say, "Should we do what Chile did and impose controls on inflows?" Or, "Could we follow in Chile's steps?" Or, "What do you have to say about the Chilean experience?" And the IMF would say at first in the 1990s, "Well, we don't know." And the ministers in a bind would come back and say, "But Chile does it, and it's worked very finely." So Chile, I think, is a case that we have to talk more about. And one good reason to talk about Chile is that the country got rid of controls in 2000 and since then the economy has worked perfectly fine. And not only that, it continues to be the number one country in Latin America, it continues to be the country everyone looks at, and it continues to be one where in terms of policy one looks and tries to follow. So here we have a case of the poster child of capital controls, getting rid of them and opting for capital mobility, and yet the IMF does not deal with that case in the two main documents about the Institutional View.

The second country I want to mention is Venezuela. That, of course, is an obvious case where capital controls on outflows don't work because they are imposed without any supporting policy. But a question is: When Venezuela comes in, what is the IMF going to tell it? Don't get rid of the controls? Get rid of them very fast? So that is a question I think is very important. There are Venezuelas out there that are coming and urgently need to know what to do about capital controls in the short run, in the middle run, and in the longer run.

The other country I want to mention is Iceland. Iceland had controls on outflows. They were opposed by almost everyone. They were criticized, and Iceland has recovered from its gigantic 2008 crisis in a very beautiful way. It's been growing at 6 percent. Inflation is almost nonexistent and there are 1,318 people unemployed in Iceland. But Iceland still has controls on outflows. Should they keep them? I don't think so. But there is a question there: Maybe it's an exception? Structurally, it's a small country. It really has only four types of exports. And I think that every indication is that in the longer run Iceland should have no capital controls. Of course, there should be concerns about macrostability, but that can be achieved with other policies, macroprudential policies.

Let me finish with one point that is not in the papers, but that Jonathan made during his presentation, and that's the connection between crises, social conditions, and capital flows. If you look at Latin American crises during in the last twenty years, you will find that they were all quite different from each other. Some crisis countries had very significant capital controls. Chile in 1982 is a good example. Unemployment ended up being 32 percent. And there was a dictatorship that contained social pressure at a certain level. Mexico '82 also happened in the presence of significant capital controls. Mexico '93 is another case of a crisis with nontrivial capital controls. Brazil '98, once again a crisis in a country with fairly stiff capital controls. So the notion that they were capital-controlled did not mean that the crisis didn't happen.

Now, of course, there were crises without capital controls, Uruguay and Argentina, and John Taylor was very much involved in trying to solve the Uruguayan crisis. What is very interesting is that after those two crises, which were very similar, Argentina reverted to very tight controls on everything. And it imposed a haircut of 75 percent on debt holders. Uruguay, with the assistance of the IMF and the Treasury—Anne Krueger and John Taylor were involved there—very quickly recovered, enacted very temporary measures, and the haircut was only 7 percent.

My bottom line is that I missed a stronger prescription from the IMF. The prescription that I would like to hear from the IMF is that emerging countries should generally aim toward having no controls. Of course, there may be dangers getting there, but we will help you deal with those problems.

CHAPTER FIVE

Capital Flows, the IMF's Institutional View, and an Alternative

John B. Taylor

In these remarks, I first review the IMF's recently developed Institutional View on the use of capital controls. I then list a number of concerns I have with this view and outline an alternative approach to the international monetary and financial system.

THE IMF'S INSTITUTIONAL VIEW

The International Monetary Fund put forth its Institutional View in November 2012, when it published the document "The Liberalization and Management of Capital Flows: An Institutional View" (IMF 2012).[1] This was several years after the global financial crisis and the Great Recession of 2007–09. As Blanchard and Ostry (2012) explained in an op-ed at the time, the document brought together much work at the IMF, including that by Ostry et al. (2010) and Ostry et al. (2011). More recent IMF reports (2016a, 2016b) review the experience with the Institutional View over the years since 2012.

The book *Taming the Tide of Capital Flows: A Policy Guide*, by Ghosh, Ostry, and Qureshi (2017) provides an excellent and

---

1. The document was prepared by a team that included Jonathan Ostry, Atish Ghosh, and Mahvash Qureshi from the IMF's Research Department and was approved by Olivier Blanchard (economic counselor and director of the Research Department), Sean Hagan, Siddharth Tiwari, and José Viñals.

detailed summary of the origins of the Institutional View and the rationale for resulting policies.[2]

Around 2010, several countries were "re-imposing capital controls to stem inflows in the wake of historically unprecedented accommodative monetary policies of the US Federal Reserve (later joined by the European Central Bank and the Bank of Japan). Capital controls, a long-forgotten subject in academia and a taboo among mainstream policy circles, were back in the limelight" (p. 5). "After a remarkable internal effort at consensus building" at the IMF during which many papers were written and seminars were held, a "compromise was hammered out" in the form of the "Institutional View" document (p. 64).

The "Institutional View" argues that "there is no presumption that full liberalization is an appropriate goal for all countries at all times" but rather that "capital controls could be maintained over the longer term" (p. 64) and that "capital controls form a legitimate part of the policy toolkit" (p. 6). To be sure, there is still some mention of the long-held view that "cross-border capital flows to emerging markets have the potential to bring several benefits." But what is new about the Institutional View is that "capital flows require active policy management," which includes "controlling their volume and composition directly using capital account restrictions" (p. 8).

The "Institutional View" document (IMF 2012) defines key terms and gives examples. For example, the annex entitled "Capital Flow Management Measures: Terminology" states, "For the purposes of the institutional view, the term capital flow management measures (CFMs) is used to refer to measures that are designed to limit capital flows." CFMs thus include "capital controls" that "discriminate on the basis of residency" and macroprudential policies that differentiate on the basis of currency (p. 40). But other mac-

---

2. The quotes and page numbers in the next two paragraphs are from Ghosh, Ostry, and Qureshi (2017).

roprudential measures, such as changes in the loan to value ratio, are not considered CFMs.

The distinction between capital flow management measures and macroprudential measures (MPMs) is important as stressed in IMF (2013): "CFMs are designed to limit capital flows. Macroprudential measures are prudential tools that are designed to limit systemic vulnerabilities. This can include vulnerabilities associated with capital inflows and exposure of the financial system to exchange rate shocks. While there can therefore be overlap, macroprudential measures do not seek to affect the strength of capital flows or the exchange rate per se."

Nevertheless, CFMs and MPMs are often responding to the same forces. For example, a very low interest rate abroad may lead to an outflow of capital from abroad and an inflow of capital to the home country, an example of a "push" factor from abroad.[3] If monetary policy makers, concerned about an appreciation of their currency, respond with lower interest rates at home, they risk an unwanted housing boom at home. To combat this, they may decrease the required loan-to-value ratio in housing (an MPM but not a CFM). Alternatively, policy makers may leave interest rates alone and impose capital controls on inflows (a CFM) to prevent capital from seeking the higher return and driving up the exchange rate. Thus, CFMs and MPMs are alternative ways of responding to the same push factor from abroad. As I discuss later, both CFMs and MPMs may be inferior to other policy actions, including actions abroad which do not cause a capital outflow.

The best way to understand the scope of actions that constitute the IMF's Institutional View is to examine a list of capital flow management measures. As part of recent research on the impact of CFMs on such variables as exchange rates, capital flows, and interest rates, a paper by Forbes, Fratzscher, and Straub (2015) provides

---

3. See Cerutti, Claessens, and Puy (2015) for further discussion of such push factors.

such a list of capital flow management measures which the IMF has in mind. Here is the list:

Capital controls

- Quantitative limits on foreign ownership of domestic companies' assets
- Quantitative limits on borrowing from abroad
- Limits on ability to borrow from offshore entities
- Restrictions on purchase of foreign assets, including foreign deposits
- Special licensing on FDI and other financial transactions
- Minimum stay requirements for new capital inflows
- Taxes on capital inflows
- Reserve requirements on inflows of capital (e.g., unremunerated reserve requirements)

Macroprudential measures

- Reporting requirements and limitations on maturity structure of liabilities and assets
- Restrictions on off-balance-sheet activities and derivatives contracts
- Limits on asset acquisition
- Limits on banks' FX positions
- Limits on banks' lending in FX
- Asset classification and provisioning rules
- Taxes on FX transactions
- Capital requirements on FX assets
- Differential reserve requirements on liabilities in local and FX currencies

To be sure, an action such as a change in the loan-to-value ratio is a macroprudential measure that is not also a capital flow management measure.

It is also useful to understand the connection between the OECD (Organisation for Economic Co-operation and Development) Code of Liberalization of Capital Movements and the IMF's Institutional View. According to the OECD (2015): "The IMF uses its Institutional View on capital flow liberalisation and management for providing advice and assessments when required for surveillance, but the Institutional View does not alter Fund members' rights and obligations under the IMF Articles of Agreement or other international agreements." In contrast, "The OECD Code is an international agreement among governments on rules of conduct for capital flow measures."

CONCERNS

The primary motive underlying the recent interest in capital flow management is the increase in capital flow volatility and exchange rate volatility in recent years. This increase is clearly demonstrated in the research reported in Ghosh, Ostry, and Qureshi (2017) and is also found in research by Rey (2013), Bruno and Shin (2015), Carstens (2015), Taylor (2016), and Coeuré (2017).

There is some debate about the reasons for this increased volatility, but the main explanation offered by Ghosh, Ostry, and Qureshi (2017) is that "capital surges into emerging markets—and stops surging—largely because of global factors outside the countries' control, with US monetary conditions notable among them" (p. 415). Similarly, Fratzscher, Lo Duca, and Straub (2016) find that "QE increased the pro-cyclicality of flows outside the US, in particular, into emerging market equities." Rey (2013) and Taylor (2013) came to similar conclusions about the role of monetary policy in the advanced countries.

However, having recognized that the source of the increased volatility of capital flows is the advanced country central banks, the Institutional View effectively takes these actions as given and proceeds to develop a toolkit for emerging market economies to use to limit the flows into and out of their countries. As explained by Ghosh, Ostry, and Qureshi (2017), "We have mostly concentrated on the unilateral response of emerging market countries, given the reality that they are mostly on their own." Perhaps this is the tack they have taken because, as they note, the reality was that the Fed, as they quote then chairman Ben Bernanke, "countered such arguments vehemently," saying that the policies "left emerging markets better off." Bernanke (2013) argued that capital controls should be considered, perhaps as in the Institutional View, saying, "Nevertheless, the International Monetary Fund has suggested that, in carefully circumscribed circumstances, capital controls may be a useful tool." While Blanchard (2016) found that monetary policy in advanced economies has had spillover effects on emerging market economies, he viewed capital controls as "a more natural instrument" for achieving macroeconomic and financial stability.

In any case, my first concern with the Institutional View is that it does not endeavor to address the main cause of the problem—which is the push by policy actions in the advanced countries. Efforts should be made to deal with that issue in any reasonable international reform. Mishra and Rajan (2018), for example, argue that the advanced countries' central banks should avoid—be given a no-go red light for—unconventional monetary policies with large spillover effects. In my view, outright coordination is not necessary to achieve this international outcome, as I explain in the next section.

A second concern is the harm caused by using, in on-again, off-again fashion, a package of uncertain discretionary interventions such as those on the list above, which the IMF staff may suggest to emerging market countries under the banner of the Institutional View. A surprise turning-down of capital controls—especially with the threat of reimposition—can cause as much uncertainty as a surprise turning-up of controls. There are clear analogies with the danger of discretion versus rules in fiscal and monetary policy. To be sure, there are disagreements among economists on the rules-versus-discretion issue. But in practice, the CFMs under the Institutional View are discretionary rather than rule-like policies.

A third concern is that research by Forbes (2007) and others shows that CFMs have uncertain effects, often do not work, and can have harmful effects by cutting off useful lending to emerging markets. Edwards (1999) considered the evidence from Chile and other countries. He concluded that controls on outflows are easily circumvented, although controls on inflows gave the Chilean monetary authorities a better ability to change the domestic interest rate. Calvo, Leiderman, and Reinhart (1996) note that capital flows can be rerouted around controls perhaps through "under-invoicing of exports" or "over-invoicing of imports." Forbes, Fratzscher, and Straub (2015) found that "most CFMs do not significantly affect" exchange rates, capital flows, interest-rate differentials, inflation, equity indices, and different volatilities. One exception is that removing controls on capital outflows may reduce real exchange rate appreciation. They found that certain CFMs "can be effective in accomplishing specific goals—but most popular measures are not 'good for' accomplishing their stated aims."

It is possible to incorporate formally the effect of capital flow management measures (such as capital controls or currency-based prudential measures) in macroeconomic models, say by adding a term to a capital flow equation as in Ghosh, Ostry, and Qureshi (2017, 164). But the coefficients of such equations are very uncertain, and the quantitative impact of the CFMs is thus largely impossible to estimate accurately when computing impacts by differentiating with respect to the capital control term. Moreover, to properly assess CFMs, it would be necessary to perform a rules-based analysis of the impact of capital controls in which systematic dynamic properties and expectations are taken account of.

A fourth concern is about side effects of attempts to evade the controls. Edwards (1999) found evidence that "controls on capital outflows have resulted in corruption, as investors try to move their monies to a 'safe haven.' Moreover, once controls are in place, the authorities usually fail to implement a credible and effective adjustment program . . . There is also evidence suggesting that controls on capital outflows may give a false sense of security, encouraging complacent and careless behavior on behalf of policymakers and market participants."

A fifth concern is the possible negative spillover to international trade policies. Interventions into capital markets, including capital restrictions, often go together with interventions in good markets, including tariffs and quotas, although some argue that they can be separated as was once the subject of a debate (Bhagwati and Taylor 2003). With the current heightened tensions over trade policy, there are understandable concerns about trade wars. But there is an inconsistency about arguing against restrictions in goods markets while at the same time arguing for restrictions in capital markets.

A sixth concern is the possible slippery slope between CFMs and other restrictions on investment—including fixed investment—which are imposed for competitive reasons, such as to gain firm ownership or rights over intellectual property. Most would say that an open trading system would avoid such restriction on investment. But in some political contexts it is difficult to advocate CFM limits on so-called "hot money" while saying this does not apply to other forms of capital flows.

AN ALTERNATIVE APPROACH

The first plank of an alternative approach would be a normalization of monetary policy in the advanced countries along with a departure from unconventional balance sheet policy and a move toward more rules-based monetary policies. At the least, it would be useful to list key ways to reduce the "push" factors in the advanced countries, rather than simply taking them as given and focusing on interventionist actions in the emerging market economies. See Cerutti, Claessens, and Puy (2015) for examples. The rules-based reform suggested by Mishra and Rajan (2018) would try to avoid monetary policies with large negative spillover effects. More generally, a rules-based reform of the international monetary system would lead to greater economic and financial stability and less volatile capital flows as shown in Taylor (1985, 2016, 2018). The best way to achieve a rules-based international monetary system is to put in place a rules-based system in each country. It would be the job of each central bank to choose its monetary policy rule and what it reacts to. In this respect, it is encouraging that speeches, publications, appointments, and actions at the Federal Reserve during the past year and a half are consistent with being on such a path to normalization. This paves the way to an international normalization.

A second plank would be a commitment to a principle that liberalization of capital flows is an appropriate goal for the world economy. Of course, we all recognize that we are not in a world of open capital markets now, that a transition will take time, and that, during the transition, controls may sometimes be needed as a stopgap measure. As Edwards (1999) explained: "Controls on capital movements should be lifted carefully and gradually, but—and this is the important point—they should eventually be lifted." As discussed above, this goal is not now part of the Institutional View, which would have capital flow management measures continue into perpetuity. Nor is it part of the OECD's interpretation of the IMF's Institutional View. According to the OECD (2015), "The OECD shares the IMF Institutional View that there is no presumption that full liberalization is an appropriate goal for all countries at all times."

A third plank would be the adoption of reforms in individual countries that make markets more resilient to capital flows and thus pave the way toward this goal. If there were agreement reached on the first and second planks, then it would be easier to develop reform recommendations and implement them with these other planks in mind. This could involve gradual and permanent phaseouts of capital flow restrictions. The emphasis would be placed on creating a credible, well-functioning, market-based, flexible exchange rate system for countries that are not part of currency areas.

CONCLUSION

In these remarks, I first described the IMF's Institutional View consisting of capital flow management measures designed to restrict the flow of capital across international borders. I reviewed how this approach evolved in the past five years to become an integral part of the international monetary system, as viewed by the IMF, largely in response to increased capital flow volatility which in turn can be traced to policies in the advanced countries. I listed concerns with the use of such measures, including that they may lead to more restrictions on international trade and investment. Finally, I proposed an alternative approach based on three planks: a more rules-based international monetary system, a long-term goal of liberalized capital flows, and country reforms to make the financial system more resilient.

References

Bernanke, Ben. 2013. "Monetary Policy and the Global Economy." Speech to the London School of Economics, March 25.

Bhagwati, Jagdish, and John B. Taylor. 2003. "Trade Agreements and Capital Controls." Debate at the American Enterprise Institute, moderated by Claude Barfield, August 11. Accessed August 12, 2018. https://www.c-span.org/video /?177757-1/trade-agreements.

Blanchard, Olivier. 2016. "Currency Wars, Coordination, and Capital Controls." NBER Working Paper no. 22388, July. Accessed August 12, 2018. http://www.nber.org/papers/w22388.

Blanchard, Olivier, and Jonathan D. Ostry. 2012. "The Multilateral Approach to Capital Controls." VOX CEPR's Policy Portal, December 11.

Bruno, Valentina, and Hyun Song Shin. 2015. "Capital Flows and the Risk-Taking Channel of Monetary Policy." *Journal of Monetary Economics* 71: 119–32.

Calvo, Guillermo, Leonardo Leiderman, and Carmen Reinhart. 1996. "Inflows of Capital to Developing Countries in the 1990s." *Journal of Economic Perspectives* 10, no. 2 (Spring): 123–39.

Carstens, Agustin. 2015. "Challenges for Emerging Economies in the Face of Unconventional Monetary Policies in Advanced Economies." Stavros Niarchos Foundation Lecture, Peterson Institute for International Economics, Washington, DC, April 20.

Cerutti, Eugenio, Stijn Claessens, and Damien Puy. 2015. "Push Factors and Capital Flows to Emerging Markets: Why Knowing Your Lender Matters More Than Fundamentals." IMF Working Paper no. 15/127, June.

Coeuré, Benoît. 2017. "The International Dimension of the ECB's Asset Purchase Programme." Speech at the Foreign Exchange Contact Group Meeting, Frankfurt, Germany, July 11.

Edwards, Sebastian. 1999. "How Effective are Capital Controls?" *Journal of Economic Perspectives* 13, no. 4 (Fall): 65–84.

Forbes, Kristin. 2007. "The Microeconomic Evidence on Capital Controls: No Free Lunch." In *Capital Controls and Capital Flows in Emerging Economies: Policies, Practices, and Consequences,* edited by Sebastian Edwards, 171–202. Chicago: University of Chicago Press.

Forbes, Kristin, Marcel Fratzscher, and Roland Straub. 2015. "Capital Flow Management Measures: What Are They Good For?" *Journal of International Economics* 96: S76–97.

Fratzscher, Marcel, Marco Lo Duca, and Roland Straub. 2016. "On the International Spillovers of US Quantitative Easing." *Economic Journal* 128, no. 608 (February): 330–77.

Ghosh, Atish R., Jonathan D. Ostry, and Mahvash S. Qureshi. 2017. *Taming the Tide of Capital Flows.* Cambridge, MA: MIT Press.

IMF (International Monetary Fund). 2012. "The Liberalization and Management of Capital Flows: An Institutional View." Policy paper, November 14.

IMF. 2013. "Key Aspects of Macroprudential Policy." Policy paper, June 10.

IMF. 2016a "Capital Flows—Review of Experience with the Institutional View." Policy paper, November 7.

IMF. 2016b. "IMF Executive Board Discusses Review of Experience with the Institutional View on the Liberalization and Management of Capital Flows." News release no. 16/573, December 20.

Magud, Nicolas E., Carmen Reinhart, and Kenneth Rogoff. 2007. "Capital Controls: Myth and Reality—A Portfolio Balance Approach to Capital Controls." Federal Reserve Bank of San Francisco, Working Paper no. 2007-31, May.

Mishra, Prachi, and Raghuram Rajan. 2018. "Rules of the Monetary Game." Paper presented at Currencies, Capital, and Central Bank Balances policy conference, Hoover Institution, Stanford University, Stanford, CA, May 4.

OECD (Organisation for Economic Co-operation and Development). 2015. "The OECD'S Approach to Capital Flow Management Measures Used with a Macro-Prudential Intent." Report to G20 finance ministers, Washington, DC, April 16–17. Accessed August 16, 2018. http://www.oecd.org/daf/inv/investment-policy/G20-OECD-Code-Report-2015.pdf.

Ostry, Jonathan D., Atish R. Ghosh, Karl F. Habermeier, Marcos Chamon, Mahvash S. Qureshi, and Dennis B. S. Reinhardt. 2010. "Capital Inflows: The Role of Controls." IMF staff position note, February 19.

Ostry, Jonathan D., Atish R. Ghosh, Karl Habermeier, Luc Laeven, Marcos Chamon, Mahvash S. Qureshi, and Annamaria Kokenyne. 2011. "Managing Capital Inflows: What Tools to Use?" IMF Staff Discussion Note, April 5.

Rey, Hélène. 2013. "Dilemma not Trilemma: The Global Financial Cycle and Monetary Policy Independence." Paper presented at the Global Dimensions of Unconventional Monetary Policy Conference, Federal Reserve Bank of Kansas City, Jackson Hole, WY, August 24.

Taylor, John B. 1985. "International Coordination in the Design of Macroeconomic Policy Rules." *European Economic Review* 28, nos. 1–2 (June–July): 53–81.

Taylor, John B. 2013. "International Monetary Policy Coordination: Past, Present and Future." BIS Working Paper no. 437, December.

Taylor, John B. 2016. "A Rules-Based Cooperatively-Managed International Monetary System for the Future." In *International Monetary Cooperation: Lessons from the Plaza Accord after Thirty Years*, edited by C. Fred Bergsten and Russell Green, 217–36. Washington, DC: Peterson Institute for International Economics.

Taylor, John B. 2018. "Toward a Rules-Based International Monetary System." *Cato Journal* 38, no. 2 (Spring/Summer): 347–59.

GENERAL DISCUSSION

GEORGE SHULTZ: We have a few minutes for questions.

ROBERT HALL: John Taylor and Secretary Shultz opined here that modern central banking is a disturbing influence in the world capital market. I'd like to argue against that. A modern central bank borrows in the open capital market. The Fed funds itself today in the short-term debt market by issuing bank reserves. It uses those funds to buy more securities. So, it's indistinguishable from a hedge fund executing a carry trade. The Fed borrows short-term to fund a portfolio of about six-year average maturity. There is no meaningful sense that these transactions create money in modern central banking. The Fed isn't creating money when it borrows from banks. There's no sense in which central banks are somehow expanding anything. All they're doing is buying one kind of fixed-income asset and funding that by issuing fixed-income claims.

So, why do we worry? The Fed cannot have any net effect in debt markets. It's just exchanging one type of debt for another. And that's what all kinds of financial institutions do. There's nothing special about what central banks do. The only thing special about central banks is that their obligations serve as the definition of the monetary unit. It's not disturbing world capital markets. It's not issuing money. It's not increasing liquidity. It's not doing any of those things. It's just borrowing at market rates in one market and buying securities in a very closely related market. It can't have much effect. Instead of having the Fed borrow short-term and buy longer-term, it would be equivalent for the Treasury just to issue short-term in the first place.

JOHN TAYLOR: I disagree completely that the balance sheet part of monetary policy doesn't have any effect. Just because you're issuing reserves to finance the purchases of certain things doesn't mean the short-term interest rate or other financial variables, including exchange rates, don't change. It's not true theoretically that such monetary policy actions do not have any effect, and it's not true empirically.

ROBERT HALL: No, the number that the Fed picks, that is highly influential, is the rate on reserves, which is how it controls interest rates in dollar-denominated securities. And that's part of its exercise in determining the value of the monetary unit, and that's centrally important. But that's what's special. But it's not sloshing money around. It's changing the return that it's paying and locking dollar interest rates into the Taylor Rule, or whatever policy rule they're using. That's totally influential, and that's subject to all of the things that we normally think about.

But the idea that there's a special effect in the capital markets from this intervention is what I'm arguing against. There are very important effects if they decide that we need more inflation or less inflation and change the interest rate. The important thing that the Federal Open Market Committee does every six weeks is determine the interest rate.

JOHN COCHRANE: I want to come back to capital controls. Central banking discussions tend to slip into euphemistic language for rather brutal policies. Governments don't control "capital flows," they control people. A capital control is the same as a trade restriction. The government may say, "Bob Hall, you may not buy steel from a Japanese producer." A capital control is, "Bob Hall, you may not borrow from a Japanese bank. You've got to borrow from my favorite bank here." Capital controls are financial repression, and really a financial expropriation.

I think Jonathan has basically stated a theorem, which I agree with, in that the "thens" follow from the "ifs." A planner could achieve wonderful things with capital and all sorts of other controls. But the planner would need to be omniscient. The planner needs to know the difference between a bubble and a boom. He or she has to be able to tell a supply surge from a demand pull, to tell a glut from a proper supply response, an imbalance from a change, an overvaluation from a proper enthusiasm.

JOHN COCHRANE: The planner has to be apolitical. The planner has to not funnel money to domestic banks because he or she is trying to prop up the domestic banks or his or her cronies. The planner has to understand all the effects of a policy. Jonathan went so far as to say central banks should start worrying about inequality. Maybe China shouldn't have opened up so much because they got unequal. They opened up, they got unequal as well as stupendously better off.

That such a hypothetical planner could do wonderful things is true. That central bank staffs like to write optimal policy papers that dream of such competent technocratic dirigisme is true. But is it really wise to go to the central bank of Argentina in its current troubles, armed with the theorem that an omniscient, apolitical, disinterested central planner could do wonderful things? That seems to me very dangerous advice—and this danger seems to be the core of the disagreement before us.

JONATHAN OSTRY: John, I don't assume, and the Fund doesn't assume, omniscience. But your point about informational requirements of policy making could be made about any number of economic policies, and not just capital controls. So I'm really not sure why you are singling out the informational challenges for implementing capital controls especially. I am also not sure why you and others on the panel have more doubts about the effectiveness of capital controls than about the effectiveness of other policy instruments—such as macroprudential tools— which seem to command broader support in this room. If we need humility about instrument effectiveness in managing the financial-stability risks arising from volatile capital flows, I think the humility is warranted for both types of instrument: capital controls and macroprudential tools.

Just to clarify a point that John Taylor made about the need to say more about the role of source countries, let me just make two factual points there. There is an entire series of papers that lead up to the IMF's Institutional View, while this panel has focused on only two of them (the ones from 2012 and 2016). There is a separate paper, that was discussed at the IMF's board a few years back, and that deals explicitly with the role of source countries (an issue that Keynes and White thought was essential to confront when they spoke about "managing both ends" of the capital flow transaction). Unfortunately, we haven't had a chance to talk about the issues in today's panel, though Raghu came closest to touching on them this morning.

JOHN TAYLOR: In making my point that not much is said about source countries, I referred to, and quoted extensively from, your 2017 book with Atish Ghosh and Mahvash Qureshi; the book incorporates the views and research in the papers in that series. Don't forget the book.

JONATHAN OSTRY: On the book, I need to reiterate that there's a sharp line between the book and the IMF's position as laid out in the board paper for the Institutional View. I did not spin the book today as being about the IV (quite the contrary), and the IV, of course, predates the book by several years (although the analytical frame for the IV is based on the thinking in the staff papers and journal articles I coauthored, that are cited in the book). I was careful in delineating at the outset of my talk that I was basing it largely on my book, rather than on the IV paper.

Coming back to the role of source countries, I should mention that, apart from the work for the IV, there was a separate initiative around the same time, undertaken by the IMF, in relation to what is known as the Integrated Surveillance Decision. The ISD sought to deal with the issue of spillovers from the policies of large players in the international monetary system, but it only got so far. What the international community was prepared to endorse in the ISD was simply that, if there are two policies that have roughly the same domestic benefit, but differ in terms of their spillover, the Fund would ask the country to choose the policy that exerts the smaller adverse spillover. This is quite some distance from the rules of the road that Raghu mentioned this morning and indeed that I talked about in an earlier paper of mine published some years ago.

I just want to respond to Sebastian on the issue of counter-cyclical fiscal policy in emerging market countries. The statements in my presentation were not normative, they were positive. They were in the vein that emerging market countries have not made much use of countercyclical fiscal policy to respond to capital inflow surges. This is what the data we've collected show. This says nothing about whether they should have used this instrument more. Certainly, the received wisdom is that they should have. And that's why it's all the more puzzling to us that they have not.

PART II

CHAPTER SIX

Monetary Policy with a Layered Payment System

Monika Piazzesi and Martin Schneider

This chapter considers the transmission of monetary policy in a modern monetary economy. It builds on Piazzesi and Schneider (2017), who introduce a model of a payment system with two layers. In an end user layer, households and firms pay for their purchases of goods and securities with inside money provided by financial intermediaries. Monetary policy operates in a different layer, the bank layer: the central bank controls the interest rate on an instrument that is traded almost exclusively by intermediaries. This is true whether the central bank targets an interbank rate such as the US federal funds rate or whether it sets the interest rate on reserves—households and firms directly hold neither interbank loans nor reserves.

The key departure from standard models of monetary policy is that different assets are not perfect substitutes. Rates of returns on different assets are therefore not equated in equilibrium. This feature shuts down the standard channel by which changes in a policy rate are transmitted to other interest rates. Under the standard transmission mechanism, the central bank is assumed to have direct control over interest rates that guide households' and firms' intertemporal decisions such as savings, investment, and price setting.

In a layered payment system, monetary policy instead works by changing banks' incentives to produce inside money. Inside money is valued for its liquidity—it earns a convenience yield. It is not a perfect substitute for other assets since the convenience yield declines with the quantity of inside money that is available: end users tend to hold more money when it is cheaper to do so. In a layered payment system, reserves and interbank loans—which are essential for producing liquid inside money—similarly earn a convenience yield. Banks hold more of these assets if it is cheaper to do so. Equilibrium equates *total* returns on all assets: rate of return plus convenience yields.

Three important policy implications follow. First, interest rate policy tends to be weaker than what standard models predict. While the central bank can set the interest rate on, say, reserves, the total return on reserves also includes the convenience yield, which depends in turn on spending as well as the quantity of reserves. The convenience yield generates a wedge between the reserve rate and the rate on other, less liquid assets. This wedge moves around with the state of the economy and can change even if policy does not. Second, by affecting the convenience yield, the quantity of reserves can work as a separate policy tool. Finally, financial structure matters: the convenience yields on interbank loans and reserves depend on the role of these instruments in the payment system.

As a concrete example, this paper considers monetary tightening starting from a situation of abundant reserves, which describes the current regime in the United States as well as several other developed countries. In this regime, the spread between the interest rate on reserves and that on other short safe debt is negligible. Central banks currently discuss two possibilities. The first option is to raise the interest rate on reserves but keep the quantity of reserves sufficiently large so that reserves remain abundant, as the US Federal Reserve has done in recent years. Short safe interest rates would continue to rise together with the interest rate on reserves. The second option is for the central bank to further sell off securities for reserves, eventually shrinking the quantity of reserves to the point where a spread between the interbank rate and the reserve rate emerges.

With a layered payment system, these two options for tightening have different effects on inflation and interest rates. An open market sale of securities changes the mix of collateral assets that banks use to back inside money. In particular, the policy reduces the quantity of the most liquid such asset: reserves. As long as reserves are abundant and the securities sold are similar in quality to reserves, the sale has no effect. A sufficiently large sale, however, makes liquidity scarce for banks. The interest rate on other short safe debt rises relative to the interest rate on reserves. The resulting spread makes it more costly to produce inside money and induces banks to issue less inside money.

In contrast, an increase in the interest rate on reserves increases the rate of return that banks earn on the safest form of collateral, namely short safe debt. In response, banks optimally increase their holdings of such collateral relative to the amount of inside money they issue. If the quantity of reserves available to the banking system is unchanged, banks optimally reduce their issuance of inside money. The contraction of money in this case works only through the money multiplier, not by changing the monetary base. Of course, it is possible to change the quantity of reserves as well. In fact, with a layered payment system, monetary policy can no longer be summarized by a single interest rate but must take into account the quantity of collateral available to banks.

Since the two policies affect different margins of banks' decision making, different features of financial structure matter for assessing their impact. The effects of an open market sale depend on liquidity management in the banking system as a whole. More efficient netting arrangements, for example, economize on reserves and imply that a larger open market sale is required to induce scarcity. Once reserves are scarce, the structure of the interbank market determines the banking system's demand for reserves. The effects of a higher interest on reserves depend on the nature of other collateral that can be used to back inside money. Since a higher reserve rate reduces the money multiplier, it benefits the holders of nominal assets such as long-term fixed rate mortgages. If banks hold nominal assets, their balance sheets strengthen and they reduce their issuance of inside money by less, leading to a weaker policy impact.

The remainder of this chapter provides more details on the key mechanism. We first provide background on recent policy changes and their treatment in the literature, then sketch the model, and then discuss policy with a layered payment system. We focus throughout on the behavior of intermediaries. Details on how the mechanism can be embedded into macroeconomic models are included in related papers. Piazzesi and Schneider (2017) embed the banking sector described here into a flexible price model, whereas Piazzesi, Rogers, and Schneider (2018) consider a New Keynesian model with sticky prices. Lenel, Piazzesi, and Schneider (2018) provide evidence on the connection between bank balance sheets, portfolio risk, and interest rate spreads.

BACKGROUND

In recent years, central banks around the world have massively expanded the supply of reserves. In many countries, monetary easing has made reserves *abundant*: there is no longer a spread between the interest rate on reserves and interest rates on short safe debt that provides the same payoff as reserves, such as overnight interbank loans. In a regime with abundant reserves (also referred to as a "floor" system), the central bank changes the stance of policy directly by altering the interest rate on reserves.

This new regime stands in sharp contrast to the typical policy environment before the global financial crisis when reserves were *scarce*: the spread between overnight and reserve rates was positive and large. For example, the US federal funds rate for overnight interbank loans averaged 5.66 percent between 1955 and 2008, much higher than the reserve rate of zero. In a traditional scarce reserves regime (or "corridor system"), the central bank targets the overnight interbank rate and its trading desk adjusts the supply of reserves with this goal in mind.

It is important to distinguish between abundance of reserves and the so-called "zero lower bound" on interest rates. It is true that many central banks initially made reserves abundant at a time when the interest rate on reserves was in fact zero. The first data points about the new regime thus featured zero (or very low) reserve rates as well as overnight rates. This was only a coincidence, however: more recently, reserves have been abundant also at positive or negative levels of interest rates.

For example, in the wake of recent monetary tightening in the United States, the interest rate on reserves and the federal funds rate have been rising virtually in lockstep. Reserves thus remain abundant at rates that are substantially above zero. At the same time, the euro area experience has shown that there is no lower bound at zero. Indeed, in recent years, the negative Eonia (euro overnight index average) rate has been closely tracking the similarly negative ECB (European Central Bank) deposit facility rate.

Many central banks now face the question of whether reserves should remain abundant in the long run or whether they should reduce the supply of reserves so as to move back to scarcity. It is clear that the choice of regime affects how the payment system works. For example, banks manage liquidity differently when overnight borrowing is costly relative to reserves. What is less well understood is how the policy regime affects the transmission of monetary policy to the macroeconomy and, in particular, how monetary tightening affects inflation.

Standard models of monetary policy do not distinguish between scarce and abundant reserve regimes. Indeed, in the New Keynesian framework, the focus is on a single interest rate controlled by the central bank that adopts the Taylor rule (Taylor 1993; see Woodford 2003 or Galí 2015 for textbook treatments). That interest rate also serves as a benchmark rate for all intertemporal decisions in the economy, such as investment and hiring. In other words, by controlling the policy rate, the central bank controls the entire yield curve as well as firms' cost of capital.

The key assumption underlying New Keynesian analysis is that financial markets treat all assets as perfect substitutes. In particular, there is nothing special about short safe debt such as reserves or overnight credit: much like other assets, short safe debt is valued only for its rate of return and not, say, for its liquidity or its quality as collateral. As a result, the transmission of monetary policy is very powerful and the stance of policy can be summarized by the policy rate alone. How the policy rate is changed in practice is a detail of the economy's "plumbing" that is not relevant for policy transmission.

Much recent analysis of the zero lower bound applies the same logic to a world in which nominal rates are bounded below by zero and prices are rigid, so that all real rates of return hit a lower bound. The bound on the nominal interest rate is often motivated by the presence of currency—the idea is that if nominal rates on reserves or deposits were negative, then banks or end users would exchange it one-for-one for currency. This approach to thinking about recent events cannot handle the fact that interest rates on both reserves and deposits have been negative. Moreover, it does not make a distinction between abundance of reserves and low interest rates.

A MODEL OF PAYMENTS IN A MODERN ECONOMY

The framework developed by Piazzesi and Schneider (2017) provides a different perspective on monetary policy transmission. It starts from two simple observations on fixed-income markets. First, central bank interest rate policy does not directly affect rates of return on assets held by households and firms. Instead, whether the central bank targets an overnight interbank rate or varies the interest rate on reserves, it targets an instrument held directly only by banks or other intermediaries that provide payment services such as money market mutual funds.

The second observation is that interest rates on short safe instruments targeted by central banks are different from other rates that guide the decisions of households and firms. The short safe instruments that are held by nonbanks are typically "inside money" provided by banks or money market mutual funds and earn interest rates—such as deposit rates—that are lower than the short safe rates earned by banks on instruments such as short government bonds. The longer term instruments that are relevant for, say, investment decisions tend to earn higher interest rates than the short safe rates earned by banks.

Piazzesi and Schneider (2017) provide a simple model that is consistent with both observations. The model describes a layered payment system typical of modern economies: in an *end user layer*, households, firms, and institutional investors pay for goods and securities with inside money provided by intermediaries ("banks," for short). In the *bank layer*, banks handle end users' payment instructions and pay each other in central bank money. There is no currency in the model. The idea is that currency is used for a small share of transactions and is held mostly abroad and in the informal sector.

The banking sector in the model adds value because it provides a technology for payments. End users like inside money ("deposits," for short) because it provides liquidity that is convenient for trading goods and securities. The liquidity benefit of deposits explains why end users are willing to hold them even at low interest rates. In order to provide liquidity benefits, banks face financial frictions. First, end users require that deposits be backed by sufficient collateral—that is, banks hold assets of sufficient quality. Second,

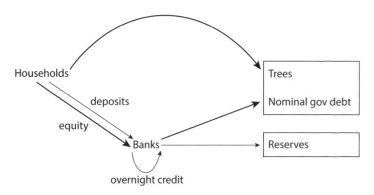

FIGURE 6.1.1. Ownership of Assets with a Layered Payment System

end users' payment instructions generate deposit flows between banks, which require liquidity management. Banks can handle deposit flows by holding reserves or borrowing in the interbank market.

The basic structure of asset ownership is illustrated in figure 6.1.1. Households can invest in three different assets that are in nonzero net supply: reserves, nominal government debt, and "trees" that are other claims on output. Households can invest in assets either directly or through banks. Banks are competitive firms that issue deposits and equity. Since households own bank shares and banks maximize shareholder value, households also decide banks' capital structure and investment. In particular, they decide to what extent trees and debt are held through the banking system as opposed to directly. At the same time, reserves can be held only via banks, reflecting the current regulatory environment in most countries. There is also an interbank market where banks make short-term loans to each other.

In a frictionless world, all asset positions—indicated by arrows in figure 6.1.1—would be indeterminate, all assets would be perfect substitutes, and all rates of return would be equal, at least after risk adjustment. To make predictions about positions, we thus introduce financial frictions. Assets that help overcome frictions are then valuable beyond simply their rate of return: they convey liquidity or collateral benefits that decline with the quantity of assets available. The presence of liquidity and collateral benefits accounts for spreads between different interest rates. Since benefits decline with quantity, trade-offs between spreads and quantities generate determinate optimal positions.

The first friction is that it is costly to exchange assets for goods, and this cost is smaller for deposits. Since deposits thus facilitate the purchase of goods, households value them for their liquidity and not only for their rate of return. As a result, the model predicts a spread between deposits and other assets such as bank equity that reflects the liquidity benefit of deposits. We emphasize that this spread is always positive: even when reserves are abundant so reserves are no longer more liquid for banks than other short debt, it remains the case that deposits are more liquid for households than any other debt. This property of the model is important to match the behavior of spreads in the data.

COSTLY LEVERAGE

The second friction is that bank leverage is costly. In particular, there is a resource cost per unit of debt of the bank that is decreasing in the *collateral ratio* of the bank, defined as weighted assets divided by debt (deposits plus interbank borrowing), or the inverse of leverage. The interpretation is that a bank has to make some effort to convince depositors (or regulators) that it is sound. This is less costly if the bank has lower leverage or its assets are of higher quality (that is, they receive a higher weight in the collateral ratio). It is not necessary for these leverage costs to be large. What matters is that they decline with the collateral ratio and tend to zero as the collateral ratio increases—a bank that issues no debt has an infinite collateral ratio and pays no leverage cost.

Costly leverage leads to a number of key predictions. First, there is an optimal collateral ratio that trades off the spread between deposits and bank equity against the cost of leverage. Bank deposits are a cheap source of financing for banks because they provide a liquidity benefit to households and hence earn a lower rate of return than bank equity. For banks with low overall levels of debt, it is therefore cheaper to issue deposits than to raise equity. Since the first dollar of debt implies no leverage cost, it is always optimal to issue *some* deposits. The more deposits a bank issues, the lower its collateral ratio, which in turn increases its leverage cost. At the optimal collateral ratio, the marginal leverage cost is equated to the spread between the deposit rate and the bank's cost of capital, its rate of return on equity.

Costly leverage further implies that banks value assets as collateral and not only for their rate of return. When a bank invests a dollar in short safe debt, say, it knows that this not only contributes to its return on assets but also increases its collateral ratio and hence lowers its leverage cost. Banks are thus willing to hold short safe debt even if its rate of return is below the rate of return on bank equity. The model thus predicts a spread between safe short-term debt held by intermediaries that issue deposits and assets held directly by households that are valued only for their payoffs.

Moreover, the model predicts that the spread between short safe debt and other assets should be higher when bank balance sheets are weaker in the sense that collateral ratios are lower. Banks with low collateral ratios are willing to pay more for collateral. They bid up the price of short safe debt, which lowers the interest rates. This mechanism fits well with recent evidence: as the economy entered the financial crisis, bank balance sheets were weak and interest rates on short safe debt were low.

A final prediction of the model that follows from costly leverage is market segmentation: in equilibrium, short safe bonds are held only by banks and not directly by households. Given the spread between short bonds and other assets, banks that receive collateral benefits are happy to hold short safe bonds even at low rates of return. In contrast, households perceive these bonds to be too expensive and prefer not to hold them directly—they prefer other assets such as bank equity. This prediction is in line with observed positions: most short paper in the US economy is held by intermediaries, whereas the short-term assets held by households are predominantly deposits.

Summing up, we have now described the positions indicated by dark arrows in figure 6.1.1. Bank deposits are produced because they provide liquidity to households. Since leverage is costly, banks also issue equity and buy assets as collateral. Banks therefore buy short safe debt. They can buy short safe debt as well as trees. How many trees they buy in equilibrium is not essential for the argument here. In the full model in Piazzesi and Schneider (2017), banks compete for trees with other asset management firms and the allocation of trees depends on who has the better technology to invest in certain classes of trees.

LIQUIDITY MANAGEMENT

The final element of the model is bank liquidity management, represented by the light arrows at the bottom of figure 6.1.1. In order to capture the idea that reserves provide liquidity to banks, we assume that banks face liquidity shocks. The idea is that banks may experience deposit outflows as part of their provision of payment instruments: sometimes customers' payment instructions require wire transfers to other banks. We further assume that such transfers are subject to a liquidity constraint: banks must either wire reserves they already hold or access the overnight credit market to obtain additional reserves.

Banks thus manage liquidity with two tools: reserves and overnight credit. Since overnight credit is subject to the same leverage cost as deposits, it is always better to first exhaust reserves before turning to the overnight market. When do they have to borrow? We assume that liquidity shocks are proportional to deposits. The likelihood that banks must borrow overnight is then captured by a second key balance sheet ratio: the *liquidity ratio*, defined as their reserves divided by deposits. If a bank's liquidity ratio is low, then there is a good chance that deposit outflows require borrowing. At the other extreme, if the bank were to invest only in reserves, then it could for sure withstand any liquidity shock without borrowing.

What is the optimal liquidity ratio chosen by banks? It is determined again by trading off a spread against a nonpecuniary benefit. Banks value reserves for their liquidity: holding reserves allows them to avoid costly overnight borrowing in the event that they experience a large deposit outflow. This liquidity benefit is decreasing in the liquidity ratio: if the liquidity ratio is higher, the chance that banks must turn to costly borrowing declines. Under the reasonable assumption that liquidity shocks are bounded— that is, there is a largest outflow that is lower than 100 percent of deposits—there will be some threshold ratio such that the liquidity benefit reaches zero. If all conceivable outflows can be covered with existing reserves, any further dollar of reserves does not convey a liquidity benefit.

We therefore have two cases for the choice of liquidity ratio. If there is a positive spread between the interest rate on short safe debt and the interest rate on reserves, then there exists an optimal liquidity ratio such that the marginal liquidity benefit of the last dollar of reserves added to the balance sheet is exactly equal to the spread. We note that this optimal liquidity ratio depends on the bank's collateral ratio: a better collateralized bank finds it cheaper to borrow in the interbank market, and therefore perceives a lower marginal liquidity benefit of reserves. In the case with a positive spread, banks borrow in the interbank market if they experience a large enough liquidity shock. The second case occurs when the spread between the short rate and the reserve rate is zero. In this case, the bank chooses a liquidity ratio above the threshold where it never has to borrow and would be willing to hold additional reserves at zero spreads.

The optimal liquidity management by banks thus generates a demand for reserves. At high interest rates, banks choose high collateral ratios that make it cheap to borrow overnight from other banks. In this case, banks choose low liquidity ratios. At lower rates, banks choose lower collateral ratios at which it would be expensive to borrow overnight from other banks. In this case, banks choose higher liquidity ratios. The resulting inverse relationship between interest rates and demand for liquidity is much like a conventional "money demand function" for banks.

TWO EQUILIBRIA

Liquidity management and costly leverage together determine the optimal choice of each bank, which determines the liquidity ratio and collateral ratio. A key property of the model is that although we allow for heterogeneous banks that make a rich set of balance sheet choices, these banks choose the same liquidity ratio and collateral ratio, so that we can describe the behavior of the aggregate banking sector with these ratios. An equilibrium of the model requires optimal savings and portfolio choices by households, optimal balance sheet choices by banks, and market-clearing for goods and assets. This equilibrium is fully characterized by the behavior of the two aggregate banking ratios.

The equilibrium liquidity ratio determines whether the economy is in a regime with abundant or scarce reserves. In the regime with abundant reserves, banks have a high enough liquidity ratio that they do not have to borrow from each other. The equilibrium fed funds rate and the reserve rate are the same and all activity on the overnight interbank credit market ceases. After several rounds of quantitative easing, the United States has been in the abundant reserve regime after the financial crisis. Before the crisis, the United States was in a scarce reserves regime, where banks choose a low liquidity ratio and need to borrow from other banks if they are hit by large liquidity shocks. As a result, reserves are valued for their convenience, which creates a positive spread between the fed funds rate and the reserve rate.

TIGHTENING IN THE ABUNDANT RESERVE REGIME

There are two options for monetary policy to tighten. The first option is an open market sale of securities which changes the mix of collateral assets that banks use to back inside money. In particular, the policy reduces the quantity of reserves. As long as reserves are still abundant after the sale and the securities sold are similar in quality to reserves, the sale has no effect. A sufficiently large sale (for example, as in a large unwind of the Fed's portfolio), however, makes liquidity scarce for banks. The model predicts that the interest rate on other short safe debt rises relative to the interest rate on reserves. The resulting spread makes it more costly to produce inside money and induces banks to issue less inside money.

The second option is an increase in the interest rate on reserves. This policy increases the rate of return that banks earn on the safest form of collateral, namely short safe debt. In response, banks optimally increase their holdings of such collateral relative to the amount of inside money they issue. If the quantity of reserves available to the banking system is unchanged, banks optimally reduce their issuance of inside money. The contraction of money in this case works only through the money multiplier, not by changing the monetary base.

While both policies can lead to higher interest rates, they have opposite effects on the liquidity of the banking system. An open market sale reduces the aggregate liquidity ratio, whereas a higher reserve rate increases the liquidity ratio. Since these policies affect bank balance sheets differently, their effectiveness depends on financial structure in different ways. A key question for the effectiveness of an open market sale is how banks manage to operate with fewer reserves. If banks' liquidity management is highly efficient, an open market sale may not be able to increase interest rates because it may not be substantial enough to reach scarcity. For example, in an economy with few banks, many transactions are netted on the books of the same bank. Moreover, more efficient netting between financial institutions also reduces the need for reserves.

An important aspect for the effectiveness of changes in the reserve rate is the nature of other collateral that banks can use to back inside money. Since a higher reserve rate reduces the money multiplier, the policy tends to benefit the holders of nominal assets such as long-term fixed rate mortgages. If banks hold many nominal assets, their balance sheets strengthen in response to a higher reserve rate and they can reduce their issuance of inside money by less, leading to a weaker policy impact.

References

Galí, Jordi. 2015. *Monetary Policy, Inflation, and the Business Cycle*. Princeton, NJ: Princeton University Press.

Lenel, Moritz, Monika Piazzesi, and Martin Schneider. 2018. "The Short Rate Disconnect in a Monetary Economy." Working paper, Stanford University, Stanford, CA.

Piazzesi, Monika, Ciaran Rogers, and Martin Schneider. 2018. "Money and Banking in a New Keynesian Model." Working paper, Stanford University, Stanford, CA.

Piazzesi, Monika, and Martin Schneider. 2017. "Payments, Credit, and Asset Prices." Working paper, Stanford University, Stanford, CA.

Taylor, John B. 1993. "Discretion versus Policy Rules in Practice." Carnegie-Rochester Conference Series on Public Policy 39: 195–214.

Woodford, Michael. 2003. *Interest and Prices: Foundations of a Theory of Monetary Policy*. Princeton, NJ: Princeton University Press.

DISCUSSANT REMARKS

Oleg Itskhoki

This is an extremely meaty paper. It took me quite a while to work through it, and it was absolutely worthwhile. There were a lot of dimensions to the paper. I'm going to discuss just a few of them, but the paper definitely contains a lot more.

The idea of the paper is to build a detailed micro-model of how the monetary transmission works through the banking system, and then study the macroeconomic implications of this transmission mechanism. One can then use it to ask the question of the optimal aggregate liquidity management by the government. The model combines quite a few ingredients, and each of them appears simple and intuitive in partial equilibrium. Yet the paper's main contribution is in having all these individual ingredients work nicely together in general equilibrium. And it is very impressive how Monika and Martin can characterize the equilibrium outcomes in a tractable way.

The model is an endowment economy. The macro variables to be determined in equilibrium are consumption, inflation, and asset prices. The reason why consumption is not equal to output is because there are real collateral costs, and so consumption can differ across equilibria depending on how large are the aggregate collateral costs in the economy.

There are three types of agents: the households (consumers), the banks, and the government. There are multiple assets in the economy (deposits, reserves, short-term debt, bank equity, stock markets, etc.) and the paper characterizes equilibrium prices of all assets. Typically, one can characterize the prices of all assets either when they are all equivalent or when the markets are complete. Neither is the case in the present paper, and it is very impressive how all asset prices admit closed-form characterization in this rich equilibrium environment.

There are two types of frictions in the payment system: (a) a liquidity constraint (cash-in-advance) on both households and banks and (b) a collateral constraint (costly leverage) on both banks and the government. Therefore, there are a total of four constraints on three types of agents, and all of them are consequential. It is the intersection of these four constraints that creates the interesting equilibrium outcomes.

In the limiting case, the economy becomes a frictionless neoclassical economy where the constraints don't bind. I will refer to it as a Friedman-rule economy. The Friedman rule is more complex in this economy. It not only guarantees that money and bonds have the same rates of return, but in fact that all assets have the same returns, and agents are indifferent about their portfolio choices, and no constraints are binding. Away from the Friedman rule, the constraints are binding and the asset prices are different for different assets, and the allocation is not first best.

This is how the model works. First, consider the liquidity constraint on the household sector. In order to consume, the households need liquidity, and this liquidity is inside money, or deposits. In a conventional model, one needs to hold money, the reserves, in order to buy consumption. Here, one does not need money issued by the government to buy consumption. Instead, one uses deposits to finance consumption expenditure in each period. Therefore, the households need the deposits in order to pay for their consumption; hence, they are willing to take lower interest rates on their deposits relative to other assets, when the liquidity constraint is binding. As a result, the interest rate on deposits is lower than on the other assets, when the constraint is binding. In turn, this allows the banks to make profits using this gap in interest rates.

The banks pay back these profits to their stakeholders, the households. To summarize, the first sign that the liquidity constraints are binding is that the rate on deposits is lower than the interest rate on other assets, and the banks are making profits off the deposits.

The second friction is also a liquidity constraint, but now on the banks. The banks issue deposits and sometimes they need to quickly liquidate their positions. If people want their money back, the banks need to be able to pay them back on short notice. This is modeled as a random liquidity shock on the banks. In order to pay back, the banks need to have either reserves, which is the outside money issued by the government, or they can borrow in the interbank market. Because these funds are useful for the bank when liquidity constraints bind, the banks are willing to take lower interest rates on holding the reserves. If they hold bonds, they're also willing to hold them at a lower interest rate, as long as bonds provide liquidity (collateral) services.

This is not enough, however. The model also requires that the banks find it costly to hold too much of the reserves, as reserves are expensive and the banks need leverage to make profits. The banks face an exogenous real cost of leverage. As a result, there exists a collateral ratio—the ratio of liquid assets to liabilities—and the collateral costs decrease with the collateral ratio. If the banks have a lot of collateral, the leverage costs are low, but this means that the banks are not making the differential returns on assets and liabilities, and this creates a trade-off. The leverage costs are real costs, and they reduce the amount of output left for consumption in the economy. To summarize, the banks want to hold the reserves to relax both the collateral constraint and the liquidity constraint. However, holding reserves is costly, if the returns on reserves are low relative to the returns on other assets. The Friedman rule increases the quantity of reserves in the economy, making them cheap and abundant, increasing the return on reserves, until both the liquidity and the collateral constraints of the banks are fully relaxed and the economy approaches the first best.

What are the other assets? One can hold short-term bonds and the equity of the banks. But they are less effective as means of dealing with collateral and liquidity constraints, while reserves are most effective in relaxing both. Finally, why can't one get the high return on reserves? In principle, the government could provide a lot of reserves at no cost. But the problem is that the government also faces costs of leverage, and the leverage for the government is modelled as the size of the transactions in the economy relative to the size of the balance sheet of the government. Hence, the government also does not like to have a big balance sheet, and this is why it offers a limited quantity of reserves, making them scarce and expensive, and driving low the return on reserves. This is the reason why the Friedman rule is not achieved in this economy.

Taking into account that increasing the balance sheets of both banks and the government is costly, there exists an internal solution for the optimal quantity of liquidity in the economy, and the constraints are binding in equilibrium. In the internal solution, there is a differential return on different types of assets. The government can choose the interest rates on reserves, and it can choose the growth rate of the outside money (the reserves), and it can also choose the composition of its balance sheet, subject to the constraints. Therefore, the government has three choice variables, with the goal of maximizing welfare in the economy—that is, minimizing the aggregate collateral costs to both banks and the government. In turn, the banks choose the collateral ratio and the liquidity ratio to maximize the value of their shareholders, taking as given the actions of the other banks.

A natural question then is: What is the optimal thing for the government to do? The government would always want to minimize its balance sheet and simultaneously to relax both of the constraints for the banks. While these may seem to be conflicting goals, in principle, it is possible to achieve both by simultaneously issuing lots of reserves and saving a comparable amount in the form of private bonds. In other words, the government could create lots of liquidity and simultaneously save in other assets to reduce its leverage costs, by expanding its balance sheet. Hence, in order to make the problem interesting, the paper must impose an upper bound on how much the government can save in private assets—or, in other words, on the size of the balance sheet of the government, which is feasible without recurring to government leverage. Empirically, it is an interesting question why the governments shy away from large balance sheets and do not want to provide more of the liquidity services.

I will next turn to my comments on the modeling approach in the paper. There are two related trade-offs the paper must confront. The first is how detailed versus concise the model must be. The paper opts for a very detailed model of the banking system, with a lot of details that are often ignored in the macro literature. It is very impressive how far the authors can go with such a detailed model. The natural question, however, is which details are absolutely essential and which ones may be dispensed with in the future, when we incorporate these mechanisms into the workhorse macro framework. Does there exist a concise version of this model, which maintains the main mechanisms and trade-offs but which we can easily wrap into a full macroeconomic model with production and other features? Or, perhaps, there are circumstances when all these micro details do not matter and we can default to the baseline model (e.g., in "normal times"), and there are circumstances when these features become first-order for the macroeconomic outcomes and need to be modeled in full detail (e.g., in "crisis times").

Having "complained" that the model is perhaps too detailed, my second comment is that it is arguably not detailed enough. Luckily, the format of the discussion allows me to not be fully coherent, and just explore different directions. Indeed, the second trade-off the paper faces is between having some ad hoc constraints in the model and fully micro-founding them. It's not clear that is feasible at all given the state of the literature. The main ad hoc constraint the model relies on is the collateral constraint or, rather, the costs of leverage, on both the banks and the government. Literally speaking, when there is not enough collateral, the banks and the government need to burn resources. Of course, it is a parable for something. For example, in a partial equilibrium of the banking sector, it is perhaps not very consequential, and indeed intuitive. There are likely real costs for the banks of not being collateralized enough, and so one can just say that effectively the banks lose resources if that happens. But once we go to the general equilibrium, a specific model of such costs becomes consequential. Indeed, one needs to know whether the resources are burnt proportionally in every period or instead in certain infrequent states of the world, e.g., when there is a crisis. This, in turn, is likely consequential for the macroeconomic outcomes such as inflation and aggregate consumption. Do we have a sense of robustness concerning for which macro outcomes the stylized nature of the constraints is consequential and for which it is not?

Furthermore, and perhaps more important, once we go to a model with ad hoc constraints, studying optimal policy becomes very tricky. Indeed, the authors acknowledge this by carefully avoiding making strong policy prescriptions based on the model. Yet, of course, the questions of the optimal aggregate liquidity management are of the highest applied interest, and it is hard to avoid thinking about this issue in the context of this paper. Unfortunately, answering these questions without knowing more about the particular micro nature of the collateral costs is difficult. In particular, we do not know how specific policies may affect the collateral cost functions for the banks and the government, whether they would keep them unchanged or may alter them in some fundamental way. This is a version of the Lucas critique in the context of this model. And this is the main reason why the whole literature should think harder about the deeper micro foundations behind the liquidity and collateral constraints that are commonly adopted in the more positive work, which hence needs to avoid making strong normative recommendations.

It is also interesting to know the nature of the liquidity shock for the banking system. The banks need to have liquidity in certain states of the world. In partial equilibrium, this is very natural as a description of the environment for the banks. But once you start thinking about general equilibrium, you start wondering: With which aggregate shocks do the micro-level liquidity shocks interact, contributing to the cycle? Are these liquidity shocks something that could, in principle, be effectively diversified, so that the advances of technology would make these shocks less consequential for the macroeconomy? Or is it something about the aggregate state of the economy which does not allow it to effectively diversify the liquidity shocks, no matter what the market structure and technology used in the interbank market? Are these shocks rare, correlated events like the one that happened in 2007, and hence there is no effective way of avoiding them? If yes, how frequently do we expect to see such shocks in equilibrium?

A quick additional remark is about the welfare objective in the economy, which is exclusively to minimize the collateral costs, as it is an endowment economy. Of course, the natural next step is to extend the environment to a production economy, where sticky-price and/or financial constraints result in endogenous cyclical output fluctuations, which are then reinforced by the constraints in the banking system. The authors have a companion project where they do just that, and this is an important continuation to this research agenda.

I have three remaining comments, related to the empirical verification of the model's mechanism. First, the basic fact about the world is that deposit rates are low relative to other rates of return in the economy, even after controlling for the associated risk. One can go in at least two different ways about interpreting this fact. The way this paper interprets the fact is to say that liquidity constraints are binding, and hence return differentials. Thus, since we observe return differentials in the data, it must be that liquidity constraints are really binding and we must take this mechanism seriously. An alternative interpretation of the data is that of the market paper: perhaps the low deposit rates reflect the local monopoly power of the banks over retail customers. Is it possible to separate empirically the low rates on deposits due to market power versus those that are due to liquidity constraints? Perhaps the amount of market power changes slowly, at low frequencies (even though the recent crisis was followed by a wave of consolidation in the banking sector), and hence much of the cyclical fluctuation in the deposit spread is due to liquidity constraints. A further possibility is that the observed deposit spreads are due to some form of interaction between market power and financial frictions. Then it is interesting to know how the technological improvements in the high-tech financial sector may wipe out the market power of the conventional banks and what the implications are of such changes for the cyclical analysis.

My last two comments are about the more direct ways one can look at the data to get some empirical validation of the model's assumptions. I think there are two salient predictions of the model. The first salient implication is that the households don't want to hold the stock market other than the banking system, while the banking system will hold all of the non-banking equity. The banking equity offers high returns for the households, while the rest of the stock market is not particularly useful for the households, as it does not allow them to relax any of their liquidity needs. This is, of course, very stylized, and should not be taken literally. But one can ask a more nuanced question in the data. Specifically, in periods when liquidity constraints tighten, is it true that the expected equity returns for the banks are higher than equity returns on the rest of the stock market, and would an investor with deep pockets be able to take advantage of this?

The second salient implication of the model is about the cross section of countries with different institutions and, hence, arguably different reduced-form leverage cost functions. In some countries, leverage is very costly for the government, while in others governments run very large balance sheets with a lot of leverage. For some governments, it is very easy to borrow, and for other governments it is much costlier. Such variation in the leverage costs should translate into different choices of collateral and liquidity ratios in the private sector, through the endogenous mechanisms of the model. This, in turn, should translate into different macroeconomic outcomes. Can we look at the cross section of countries where governments have a differential ability to increase their balance sheets and see whether this indeed translates into different equilibrium outcomes in the banking system, as predicted by the model? Perhaps there exists anecdotal evidence of such effects.

This is a rich and insightful paper, and I look forward to the new developments in this exciting research agenda!

GENERAL DISCUSSION

MARTIN SCHNEIDER: I think we develop different types of models for different purposes. If we wanted to perform a full-on welfare analysis, more detail may be useful. The leverage cost in our model is basically a cost of breaking promises. It's effectively about expected bankruptcy cost—the probability of bankruptcy, how the legal system works during bankruptcy, and what investors typically recover. Adding more details about bankruptcy would make this aspect of our model more explicit.

We also have worked on a version of our model that has a more elaborate macro side. The key implication of our approach for macro modeling is that monetary policy targets the interest rate on an instrument that incorporates a convenience yield. This means that there is no direct transmission from the policy target to the marginal rate of substitution of households. Moreover, the wedge between the policy rate and the interest rate that matters for households depends on the current condition of the banking system. The map between this interest rate spread and variables that describe the banking system can be captured by a reduced form mapping. We can add details and other features to our model. The current version is the simplest way to derive the result that financial structure matters for the transmission of monetary policy.

And the other ideas you had I think were great. We'll follow up on that.

ARVIND KRISHNAMURTHY: In this model, you have interest on reserves, but yet there is a convenience yield on liquid assets and the quantity of liquidity matters. This world then appears different than the one that Bob Hall was telling us about where interest on reserves appeared sufficient to describe the monetary equilibrium. I was wondering if you could say more about that and clarify the difference between your model of the world and Bob's model of this morning.

MARTIN SCHNEIDER: I'll say two sentences about ours and then pass it on to Bob. So here the convenience of the reserves in our setting comes from two pieces. There is a liquidity benefit to the banks, and that is something that can shrink to zero. That is what happens in an abundant reserve regime in the liquidity trap. In this situation, T-bills and reserves become perfect substitutes for banks. However, because banks face a leverage cost, which is an additional financial friction, reserves have a convenience yield even when they are abundant because they are useful as collateral for the banks. The same is true for T-bills and other fixed-income instruments that banks hold. In other countries where banks can hold equity, equity values will also reflect a collateral benefit. In this sense, there is still convenience yield even in a liquidity trap. That's an important part of our theory.

ROBERT HALL: Reserves, as you point out, form the basis of the bottom of a transaction system. Ultimately, you need to transfer reserves to meet a financial obligation. On the other hand, the influential instrument that sets the interest rate is the RRP (reverse repurchase agreement).

[Note: Since the conference, the Fed has stopped using the RRP to set interest rates and reverted to using the interest rate on bank reserves.]

MARTIN SCHNEIDER: I consider the existence of the reverse repo program of the Fed, and the fact that currently the federal funds rate and the reserve rate are not exactly the same, but the fed funds rate is a bit lower, peculiarities of the payment system in the United States, where there are payment providers and other entities that use reserves but don't get interest on them. This goes back to US regulatory history. In other countries, it's not like that. In other countries, our model applies more cleanly in the sense that there are two regimes. There is an interbank market. There is the rate on interbank borrowing, and the central bank targets that rate. In the regime with abundant reserves, the interbank market essentially shuts down, and then one can think of equality between the reserve rate and the interbank rate.

In the United States, there are additional wiggles, which means that the fed funds market did not shut down completely, and then there was a reverse repo program introduced to make these other payment instrument providers more like banks, even though legally they're not.

From the perspective of our model, this is a feature that is left out. But I think for the main point of how policy transmission works across these two regimes, that is a detail. Adding more detail meant to put even finer tubes in the plumbing can be interesting, but I don't think it changes the overall spirit of the analysis.

JEFF LACKER: This idea of the RRP rate setting interest rates for the market has come up a couple times. It's important to clarify what Martin was saying. The Fed sets an interest rate on excess reserves. Any bank can borrow from anyone and put the resulting funds it obtains at the Federal Reserve at the interest rate on excess reserves. So the marginal cost of doing that will determine the spread between what they're willing to pay on, say, deposits or fed funds borrowed and the interest rate on excess reserves. When the Fed goes out and borrows money via RRPs, it auctions off that transaction. Where's the rate going to be? Well, it's going to be set in the market at a rate commensurate, risk-adjusted, with the rates banks are willing to pay and other intermediaries are willing to pay on those funds. Everything else is sort of just little wiggles and complications.

MARTIN SCHNEIDER: The way that we think about it in our model is that right now we're in a regime where all short paper is basically the same and moves in lockstep as the interest rate on reserves is changed. The last couple of years showed that when policy changes, as long as we stay in this regime, that's sort of how it works. There are small differences, but that's the main theme. The liquidity trap remains in the bank layer, not elsewhere in the economy, and everything moves together.

CHAPTER SEVEN

Liquidity Regulation and the Size of the Fed's Balance Sheet

Randal K. Quarles

Thank you very much to the Hoover Institution for hosting this important conference and to John Taylor and John Cochrane for inviting me to participate. In my capacity as both the vice chairman for supervision at the Board of Governors and a member of the Federal Open Market Committee (FOMC), part of my job is to consider the intersection of financial regulatory and monetary policy issues, the subject of my discussion today. This topic is both complex and dynamic, especially as both regulation and the implementation of monetary policy continue to evolve.

One important issue for us at the Fed, and the one that I will spend some time reflecting on today, is how post-crisis financial regulation, through its incentives for bank behavior, may influence the size and composition of the Federal Reserve's balance sheet in the long run. Obviously, the whole excessively kaleidoscopic body of financial regulation is difficult to address in the time we have today, so I will focus on a particular component: the liquidity coverage ratio (LCR) and its link to banks' demand for US central bank reserve balances. Besides illuminating this particular issue, I hope my discussion will help illustrate the complexities associated with

The views I express here are my own and not necessarily those of the Federal Reserve Board or the Federal Open Market Committee.

the interconnection of regulatory and monetary policy issues in general. Also, let me emphasize at the outset that I will be touching on some issues that the Board and the FOMC are in the process of observing and evaluating and, in some cases, on which we may be far from reaching any final decisions. As such, my thoughts on these issues are my own and are likely to evolve, benefiting from further discussion and our continued monitoring of bank behavior and financial markets over time.

MONETARY POLICY AND THE EFFICIENCY OF THE FINANCIAL SYSTEM

Before I delve into the more specific, complicated subject of how one type of bank regulation affects the Fed's balance sheet, let me say a few words about financial regulation more generally.

As I have said previously, I view promoting the safety, soundness, and *efficiency* of the financial system as one of the most important roles of the Board. Improving efficiency of the financial system is not an isolated goal. The task is to enhance efficiency while maintaining the system's resiliency. Take, for example, the Board's two most recent and material proposals, the stress capital buffer and the enhanced supplementary leverage ratio (eSLR). The proposal to modify the eSLR, in particular, initially raised questions in the minds of some as to whether it would reduce the ability of the banking system to weather shocks. A closer look at the proposal shows that the opposite is true. The proposed change simply restores the original intent of leverage requirements as a backstop measure to risk-based capital requirements. As we have seen, a leverage requirement that is too high favors high-risk activities and disincentivizes low-risk activities.

We had initially calibrated the leverage ratio at a level that caused it to be the binding constraint for a number of our largest banks. As a result, those banks had an incentive to add risk rather than reduce risk in their portfolios because the capital cost of each additional asset was the same whether it was risky or safe, and the riskier assets would produce the higher return. The proposed recalibration eliminates this incentive by returning this leverage ratio to a level that is a backstop rather than the driver of decisions at the margin. Yet, because of the complex way our capital regulations work together—with risk-based constraints and stress tests regulating capital at both the operating and holding company levels—this improvement in incentives is obtained with virtually no change in the overall capital requirements of the affected firms. Federal Reserve staff estimate the proposal would potentially reduce capital requirements across the eight large banks subject to the proposal by $400 million, or 0.04 percent of the $955 billion in capital these banks held as of September 2017.[1] So this recalibration is a win-win: a material realignment of incentives to reduce a regulatory encouragement to take on risk at a time when we want to encourage prudent behavior without any material capital reduction or cost to the system's resiliency. Taken together, I believe these new rules will maintain the resiliency of the financial system and make our regulation simpler and more risk-sensitive.

LIQUIDITY REGULATIONS

Let me now back up to the time just before the financial crisis and briefly describe the genesis of liquidity regulations for banks. Banking organizations play a vital role in the economy in serving the financial needs of US households and businesses. They perform this function in part through the mechanism of maturity

---

1. Required capital at the bank subsidiaries of these firms would be reduced by larger amounts—and would only allow the firm to move that capital to different subsidiaries within the firm—but, more important, the overall capital regime prevents this capital from being distributed out of the banking organization as a whole except in this de minimis amount. Thus, the overall organization retains the same capital levels without the structure of capital regulation creating an incentive to add risk to the system.

transformation—that is, taking in short-term deposits, thereby making a form of short-term, liquid investments available to households and businesses, while providing longer-term credit to these same entities. This role, however, makes banking firms vulnerable to the potential for rapid, broad-based outflows of their funding (a so-called run), and these institutions must therefore balance the extent of their profitable maturity transformation against the associated liquidity risks.[2] Leading up to the 2007–09 financial crisis, some large firms were overly reliant on certain types of short-term funding and overly confident in their ability to replenish their funding when it came due. Thus, during the crisis, some large banks did not have sufficient liquidity, and liquidity risk management at a broader set of institutions proved inadequate at anticipating and compensating for potential outflows, especially when those outflows occurred rapidly.[3]

In the wake of the crisis, central banks and regulators around the world implemented a combination of regulatory reforms and stronger supervision to promote increased resilience in the financial sector. With regard to liquidity, the prudential regulations and supervisory programs of the US banking agencies have resulted in significant increases in the liquidity positions and changes in the risk management of our largest institutions. And, working closely with other jurisdictions, we have also implemented global liquidity standards for the first time. These standards seek to limit the effect of short-term outflows and extended overall funding mismatches, thus improving banks' liquidity resilience.

---

2. While deposit insurance helps mitigate the incentive for many depositors to run, it cannot fully eliminate this risk. For a discussion of this vulnerability, see Douglas W. Diamond and Philip H. Dybvig, "Bank Runs, Deposit Insurance, and Liquidity," *Journal of Political Economy* 91, no. 3 (June 1983): 401–19.

3. "Risk Management Lessons from the Global Banking Crisis of 2008," Federal Reserve Bank of New York, October 21, 2009, accessed August 10, 2018, https://www.newyorkfed.org /medialibrary/media/newsevents/news/banking/2009/SSG_report.pdf.

One particular liquidity requirement for large banking organizations is the liquidity coverage ratio, or LCR, which the US federal banking agencies adopted in 2014.[4] The LCR rule requires covered firms to hold sufficient high-quality liquid assets (HQLA)—in terms of both quantity and quality—to cover potential outflows over a thirty-day period of liquidity stress. The LCR rule allows firms to meet this requirement with a range of cash and securities and does not apply a haircut to reserve balances or Treasury securities based on the estimated liquidity value of those instruments in times of stress. Further, firms are required to demonstrate that they can monetize HQLA in a stress event without adversely affecting the firm's reputation or franchise.

The rules have resulted in some changes in the behavior of large banks and in market dynamics. Large banks have adjusted their funding profiles by shifting to more stable funding sources. Indeed, taken together, the covered banks have reduced their reliance on short-term wholesale funding from about 50 percent of total assets in the years before the financial crisis to about 30 percent in recent years, and they have also reduced their reliance on contingent funding sources. Meanwhile, covered banks have also adjusted their asset profiles, materially increasing their holdings of cash and other highly liquid assets. In fact, these banks' holdings of HQLA have increased significantly, from fairly low levels at some firms in the lead-up to the crisis to an average of about 15 to 20 percent of total assets today.[5] A sizable portion of these assets currently

4. For a full description of the US LCR, including which banks are covered, see Regulation WW—Liquidity Risk Management Standards, 12 C.F.R. pt. 249 (2017), accessed August 10, 2018, https://www.gpo.gov/fdsys/granule/CFR-2017-title12-vol4/CFR-2017-title12-vol4 -part249.

5. See Jane Ihrig, Edward Kim, Ashish Kumbhat, Cindy M. Vojtech, and Gretchen C. Weinbach, "How Have Banks Been Managing the Composition of High-Quality Liquid Assets?" Finance and Economics Discussion Series 2017-092, revised February 2018, Board of Governors of the Federal Reserve System, accessed August 10, 2018, https://www .federalreserve.gov/econres/feds/files/2017092r1pap.pdf.

consists of US central bank reserve balances, in part because reserve balances, unlike other types of highly liquid assets, do not need to be monetized, but also, importantly, because of the conduct of the Fed's monetary policy, a topic to which I will next turn.

HOW DOES THE LCR INTERACT WITH THE SIZE OF THE FED'S BALANCE SHEET?

With this backdrop, a relevant question for monetary policy makers is: What quantity of central bank reserve balances will banks likely want to hold and, hence, how might the LCR affect banks' reserve demand and thereby the longer-run size of the Fed's balance sheet? Let me emphasize that policy makers have long been aware of the potential influence that regulations may have on reserve demand and thus the longer-run size of the Fed's balance sheet. And, of course, regulatory influence on banks' behavior, my focus today, is just one of many factors that could affect policy makers' decisions regarding the appropriate long-run size of the Fed's balance sheet.[6] In particular, in augmenting its Policy Normalization Principles and Plans, the FOMC stated in June 2017 that it "currently antic- ipates reducing the quantity of reserve balances, over time, to a level appreciably below that seen in recent years but larger than before the financial crisis" and went on to note that "the level will reflect the banking system's demand for reserve balances and the

---

6. For example, a separate factor that is relevant for policy makers in this regard is the FOMC's choice of a long-run framework for monetary policy implementation. For policy makers' discussions of this factor, see Board of Governors of the Federal Reserve System, "Minutes of the Federal Open Market Committee, July 26–27, 2016," news release, August 17, 2016, accessed August 10, 2018, https://www.federalreserve.gov/newsevents/pressreleases/monetary20160817a.htm; and Board of Governors of the Federal Reserve System, "Minutes of the Federal Open Market Committee, November 1–2, 2016," news release, November 23, 2016, accessed August 10, 2018, https://www.federalreserve.gov/newsevents/pressreleases/monetary20161123a.htm.

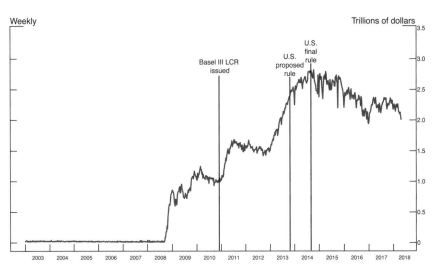

FIGURE 7.1.1. Reserve Balances

Source: Federal Reserve Board, Statistical Release H.4.1, "Factors Affecting Reserve Balances," https://www.federalreserve.gov/releases/h41.

Note: LCR is Liquidity Coverage Ratio.

Committee's decisions about how to implement monetary policy most efficiently and effectively in the future."[7]

With that said, it is useful to begin by examining banks' current reserve holdings. Figure 7.1.1 plots the aggregate level of reserve balances in the US banking system, starting well before the financial crisis. As you can see, the current level of reserves—at around $2 trillion—is many orders of magnitude higher than the level that prevailed before the financial crisis, a result of the Fed's large-scale asset purchase programs or "quantitative easing." The vertical lines in the figure show key dates in the implementation of the LCR, including the initial Basel III international introduction of the regulation followed by its two-step introduction in the United States. A key takeaway from this figure is that the Fed was in the process of adding substantial quantities of reserve balances to the banking system while the LCR was being implemented—and these two changes largely happened simultaneously. As a result, banks, in aggregate, are currently using reserve balances to meet a significant portion of their LCR requirements. In addition, because these changes happened together, it is reasonable to conclude that the current environment is likely not very informative about banks' *underlying* demand for reserve balances.

But now the situation is changing, albeit very slowly. Last October, the Fed began to gradually and predictably reduce the size of its balance sheet.[8] The Fed is doing so by reinvesting the principal payments it receives on its securities holdings only to the extent that they exceed gradually increasing caps—that is, the Fed is allowing securities to roll off its portfolio each month up to a specific maximum amount. This policy is also reducing reserve balances. So far, after the first seven months of the program, the Fed has shed about $120 billion of its securities holdings, which is a fairly modest amount when compared with the remaining size of its balance sheet. Consequently, the level of reserves in the banking system is still quite abundant.

So, how many more reserve balances can be drained and how small will the Fed's balance sheet get? Let me emphasize that this question is highly speculative—we have not decided *ex ante* the desired long-run size of the Fed's balance sheet, nor, as I noted earlier, do we have a definitive handle on banks' long-run demand for reserve balances. Indeed, the FOMC has said that it "expects to learn more about the underlying demand for reserves during the

---

8. The FOMC announced this change to its balance sheet policy in its September 2017 post-meeting statement; see Board of Governors of the Federal Reserve System, "Federal Reserve Issues FOMC Statement," news release, September 20, 2017, accessed August 10, 2018, https://www.federalreserve.gov/newsevents/pressreleases/monetary20170920a.htm.

process of balance sheet normalization."[9] Nonetheless, let me spend a little time reflecting on this challenging question.

How banks respond to the Fed's reduction in reserve balances could, in theory, take a few different forms. One could envision that as the Fed reduces its securities holdings, a large share of which consists of Treasury securities, banks would easily replace any reduction in reserve balances with Treasury holdings, thereby keeping their LCRs roughly unchanged. According to this line of thought, because central bank reserve balances and Treasury securities are treated identically by the LCR, banks should be largely indifferent to holding either asset to meet the regulation. In that case, the reduction in reserves and corresponding increase in Treasury holdings might occur with relatively little adjustment in their relative rates of return.

Alternatively, one could argue that banks may have particular preferences about the composition of their liquid assets. And since banks are profit-maximizing entities, they will likely compare rates of return across various HQLA-eligible assets in determining how many reserves to hold. If relative asset returns are a key driver of reserve demand, then interest rates across various types of HQLA will adjust on an ongoing basis until banks are satisfied holding the aggregate quantity of reserves that is available.

Recent research by the board staff shows that banks currently display a significant degree of heterogeneity in their approaches to meeting their LCR requirements, including in their chosen volumes of reserve balances.[10] Figure 7.1.2 shows a subset of this research to illustrate this point. The top and bottom panels represent estimates of how two large banks have been meeting their HQLA requirements over time. In each panel, the black portions of the bars denote the share of HQLA met by reserve balances, while the light, medium, and dark gray slices of the bars represent the

9. See Board of Governors, "FOMC Issues Addendum," paragraph 6, in note 7.

10. Ihrig et al., "Managing the Composition of High-Quality Liquid Assets."

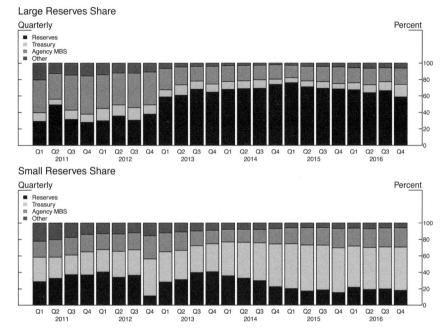

FIGURE 7.1.2. Reserve Balance Concentration in HQLA

Source: Jane Ihrig, Edward Kim, Ashish Kumbhat, Cindy M. Vojtech, and Gretchen C. Weinbach (2017), "How Have Banks Been Managing the Composition of High-Quality Liquid Assets?" Finance and Economics Discussion Series 2017-092 (Washington: Board of Governors of the Federal Reserve System, August; revised February 2018), https://www.federalreserve.gov/econres/feds/files/2017092r1pap.pdf.

Note: Key shows bar segments in order from bottom to top. HQLA is high-quality liquid assets; MBS is mortgage-backed securities; Other is other HQLA-eligible securities.

share met by Treasury securities, agency mortgage-backed securities, and other HQLA-eligible assets, respectively. Despite holding roughly similarly amounts of HQLA, the two banks exhibit very different HQLA compositions, with the bank depicted in the top panel consistently holding a much larger share of HQLA in the form of reserve balances than the bank shown in the bottom panel. This finding suggests that there likely is no single "representative bank" behavioral model that can capture all we might want to know about banks' demand for central bank reserve balances.

Some of the differences we see in bank behavior likely relate to banks' individual liquidity needs and preferences. Indeed, banks manage their balance sheets in part by taking into account their internal liquidity targets, which are determined by the interaction between the specific needs of their various business lines and bank management's preferences. In any case, this picture illustrates the complexities that are inherent in understanding banks' underlying demand for reserve balances, a topic for which more research would be quite valuable to policy makers.

So, what does this finding say about the longer-run level of reserve balances demanded by banks? The answer is that there is a large degree of uncertainty. In fact, the Federal Reserve Bank of New York surveyed primary dealers and market participants last December to solicit their views about the level of reserves they expect to prevail in 2025.[11] A few features of the survey responses stand out. All respondents thought that the longer-run level of reserve balances would be substantially *lower* than the current level of more than $2 trillion. In addition, there appeared to be a widely held view that the longer-run level of reserves will be significantly *above* the level that prevailed before the financial crisis. But even so, the respondents did not agree about what that longer-run level will be, with about half expecting a level ranging between $400 billion and $750 billion.

It is also important to point out that the Fed's balance sheet will remain larger than it was before the crisis even after abstracting from the issue of banks' longer-run demand for reserve balances. The reason is that the ultimate size of the Fed's balance sheet also depends on developments across a broader set of Fed liabilities. One such liability is the outstanding amount of Federal Reserve

11. The December 2017 Survey of Primary Dealers is available on the Federal Reserve Bank of New York's website at https://www.newyorkfed.org/medialibrary/media/markets /survey/2017/dec-2017-spd-results.pdf. The December 2017 Survey of Market Participants is available at https://www.newyorkfed.org/medialibrary/media/markets/survey/2017/dec -2017-smp-results.pdf. (Both accessed August 11, 2018.)

notes in circulation—that is, paper money—which has doubled over the past decade to a volume of more than $1.6 trillion, growing at a rate that generally reflects the pace of expansion of economic activity in nominal terms. When I left my position in the Bush Treasury in 2006, by contrast, the total amount of paper currency outstanding was not quite $800 billion. Other nonreserve liabilities have also grown since the crisis, including the Treasury Department's account at the Fed, known as the Treasury's General Account. Recent growth in such items means that the longer-run size of the Fed's balance sheet will be noticeably larger than before the crisis regardless of the volume of reserve balances that might ultimately prevail.

Putting the various pieces together, figure 7.1.3 illustrates how the overall size of the Fed's balance sheet may evolve. Given the uncertainties I have described, I have chosen to show three different scenarios, drawn from the most recent annual report released by the Federal Reserve Bank of New York, which was published last month.[12] These scenarios highlight the degree to which the longer-run size of the Fed's domestic securities portfolio—also known as the System Open Market Account, or SOMA, which accounts for the vast majority of the Fed's assets—will be affected by choices about the future level of reserve balances and the evolution of nonreserve liabilities. The assumptions underlying the scenarios are based on the distribution of responses from the surveys I described earlier, as those surveys also asked respondents to forecast the likely longer-run levels of several liabilities on the Fed's balance sheet other than reserves. The "median" scenario, represented by the solid (middle) line in the figure, is based on the fiftieth percentile of survey responses, while the "larger" and

12. See Federal Reserve Bank of New York, *Open Market Operations during 2017*, April 2018, accessed August 11, 2018, https://www.newyorkfed.org/markets/annual_reports.html. Among other things, the report reviews the conduct of open market operations and other developments that influenced the System Open Market Account of the Federal Reserve in 2017.

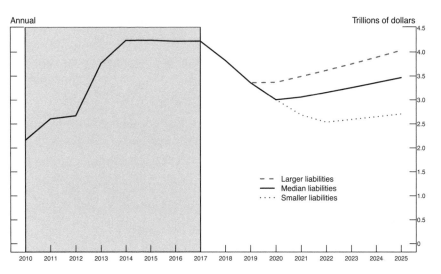

Annual   Trillions of dollars

FIGURE 7.1.3. Projected SOMA Domestic Securities Holdings: Alternative Liabilities Scenarios

Source: Federal Reserve Bank of New York (2018), *Open Market Operations during 2017* (New York: FRBNY), https://www.newyorkfed.org/medialibrary/media/markets/omo/omo 2017-pdf.

Note: Figures are as of year-end. Figures for 2010 to 2017 (shaded area) are historical settled holdings. Smaller and larger liabilities are based, respectively, on the 25th percentile and 75th percentile responses to a question about the size and composition of the Federal Reserve's long-run balance sheet in the Federal Reserve Bank of New York's December 2017 Survey of Primary Dealers and Survey of Market Participants. Projected figures are rounded. SOMA is System Open Market Account.

the "smaller" scenarios, denoted by the dashed (top) and dotted (bottom) lines, are based on the seventy-fifth and twenty-fifth percentiles, respectively.

The figure illustrates that the Fed's securities holdings are projected to decline about $400 billion this year and another $460 billion next year as Treasury and agency securities continue to roll off gradually from the Fed's portfolio. The kink in each curve captures what the FOMC has referred to as the point of "normalization" of the size of the Fed's balance sheet—that is, the point at which the balance sheet will begin to expand again to support the underlying growth in liabilities items such as Federal Reserve notes in circulation. All else being equal, greater longer-run demand for currency, reserve balances, or other liabilities implies an earlier timing of balance sheet normalization and a higher longer-run size of the balance sheet, as illustrated by the top line. And the converse—smaller demand for these liabilities and a later timing of normalization, illustrated by the bottom line—is also possible. In the three scenarios shown, the size of the Fed's securities portfolio normalizes sometime between 2020 and 2022. That is quite a range of time, so as the balance sheet normalization program continues, the Fed will be closely monitoring developments for clues about banks' underlying demand for reserves.

What will the Fed be monitoring as reserves are drained and the balance sheet shrinks? I would first like to emphasize that the Fed regularly monitors financial markets for a number of reasons, so I do not mean to imply that we will be doing anything that is very much different from our normal practice. As reserves continue to be drained, we will want to gauge how banks are managing their balance sheets in continuing to meet their LCRs, watching in particular how the distribution of reserve balances across the banking system evolves as well as monitoring any large-scale changes in banks' holdings of other HQLA-eligible assets, including Treasury securities and agency mortgage-backed securities.

And on the liabilities side of banks' books, we will be keeping our eye on both the volume and the composition of deposits, as there are reasons why banks may take steps, over time, to hold onto certain types of deposits more than others. In particular, retail deposits may be especially desired by banks going forward because they receive the most favorable treatment under the LCR and also tend to be relatively low cost.

Retail deposits have grown quite a bit since the crisis, especially in light of the prolonged period of broad-based low interest rates and accommodative monetary policy, limiting the need for banks to compete for this most stable form of deposits. However, the combination of rising interest rates and the Fed's shrinking balance sheet, together with banks' ongoing need to meet the LCR, may alter these competitive dynamics.

Of course, importantly, deposits will not necessarily decline one-for-one with reserve balances as the Fed's balance sheet shrinks. The overall effects of the decline in the Fed's balance sheet will depend both on who ultimately ends up holding the securities in place of the Fed and on the full range of portfolio adjustments that other economic agents ultimately make as a result.[13]

We will also be monitoring movements in interest rates. In part, we will be tracking how the yields and spreads on the various assets that banks use to meet their LCR requirements evolve. For example, to the extent that some banks will wish to keep meeting a significant portion of their LCR requirements with reserves, the reduction in the Fed's balance sheet and the associated drop in aggregate reserves could eventually result in some upward pressure on the effective federal funds rate and on yields of Treasury securities. This situation could occur if some banks eventually find that they are holding fewer reserves than desired at a given constellation of interest rates and, in response, begin to bid for more federal funds while selling Treasury securities or other assets. Interest rates will adjust up until banks are indifferent with regard to holding the relatively smaller volume of reserves available in the banking system.

Overall, we will be monitoring to make sure that the level of reserves the Fed supplies to the banking sector, which influences the composition of assets and liabilities on banks' balance sheets as well as market interest rates, provides the desired stance of monetary policy to achieve our dual mandate of maximum employment and stable prices. Of course, we will need to be very careful to

---

13. For a discussion of the overall effects of the decline in the Fed's balance sheet, see Jane Ihrig, Lawrence Mize, and Gretchen C. Weinbach, "How Does the Fed Adjust Its Securities Holdings and Who Is Affected?" Finance and Economics Discussion Series 2017-099, Board of Governors of the Federal Reserve System, September, 2017, accessed August 11, 2018, https://www.federalreserve.gov/econres/feds/files/2017099pap.pdf.

understand the precise factors that underlie any significant movements in these areas, because factors that are unrelated to the Fed's
balance sheet policies might also cause such adjustments.

CONCLUSION

To conclude, I would like to reemphasize that I have touched on
some highly uncertain issues today—issues that, I would like to
stress again, have not been decided by the FOMC. One such issue
that closely relates to my remarks today, and one I believe the
upcoming panel will likely address, is which policy implementation framework the Fed should use in the long run. That is, broadly
speaking, should the Fed continue to use an operational framework
that is characterized by having relatively abundant reserves and
operate in what is termed a "floor regime," or should it use one in
which the supply of reserves is managed so that it is much closer to
banks' underlying demand for reserves as in a "corridor regime"?

Of course, many complex issues underlie this decision, so
I would just like to emphasize two general points. First, a wide
range of quantities of reserve balances—and thus overall sizes of
the Fed's balance sheet—could be consistent with either type of
framework. Second, while US liquidity regulations likely influence
banks' demand for reserves, the Fed is not constrained by such regulations in deciding its operational framework, because US banks
will be readily able to meet their regulatory liquidity requirements
using the range of available high-quality liquid assets, of which
reserve balances is one type.

Importantly, additional experience with the Federal Reserve's
policy of gradually reducing its balance sheet will help inform
policymakers' future deliberations regarding issues related to the
long-run size of the Fed's balance sheet, issues that will not need to
be decided for some time.

The final and most general point is simply to underscore the premise with which I began these remarks: financial regulation and monetary policy are, in important respects, connected. Thus, it will always be important for the Federal Reserve to maintain its integral role in the regulation of the financial system not only for the visibility this provides into the economy but precisely in order to calibrate the sorts of relationships we have been talking about today.

DISCUSSANT REMARKS

Paul Tucker

Thank you very much to Johns Taylor and Cochrane for inviting me back to this conference. It is a great pleasure to be able to comment on Federal Reserve Vice Chair Randy Quarles's speech.

I liked the speech very much for a simple reason, which is that it sets out to discuss banking regulation, monetary policy, the implementation of monetary policy, and the Fed's balance sheet all in a joined-up way. That used to be rather more common when, a long time ago, I started out in central banking. The speech gives me hope that some lost years are being put behind us.

In that spirit, I am going to try to frame what Vice Chair Quarles has been saying in the broader context of what central banks are for (what social purpose they serve) and of how the imperative of monetary system stability should be part of what I call a Money-Credit Constitution.[1] I shall then use that framework to discuss the liquidity coverage ratio and the choice of monetary policy operating regime. When I reach the latter, I am going to make some observations about recent statements by the New York Fed which I believe to be deeply flawed, conceptually and factually, and so do not provide an adequate basis for the debate the Fed (and other central banks) need to have about how to manage the quantity of reserves and the overnight rate of interest in the unknown new normal the United States is now, happily, heading toward. Finally,

---

Adapted from *Unelected Power: The Quest for Legitimacy in Central Banking and the Regulatory State* (Princeton, NJ: Princeton University Press, 2018), accessed August 17, 2018, https://press.princeton.edu/titles/11240.html. Reprinted by permission.
    1. On the idea of a Money-Credit Constitution, see Ibid., Part IV.

I am going to air an option for addressing that challenge which I think merits consideration.[2]

WHAT CENTRAL BANKS ARE FOR

So, what are central banks for?

For an uncomfortable decade or so starting sometime in the 1990s, we lived in a world in which central bankers were seen as being for just one thing: price stability. Then early in the great financial crisis—in 2007, well before we reached meltdown in autumn 2008—the central banking community rediscovered that an awful lot of the monetary system is actually privatized, I might add for good reasons; and that, therefore, the stability of the issuers of private money, the banks, matters to the stability of the overall monetary system, including to the ability of the central bank to achieve price stability. For those central banks, such as the Fed, that had held onto their prudential supervision function over the decade leading up to the crisis, this amounted to recognizing that that work actually mattered and so deserved the attention of top management and the reassignment of some of the best staffers.

What is more, a new generation of top central bankers lived the reality that their monetary operations—as lender of last resort (LOLR) to the system as a whole and to individual intermediaries— were crucial to underpinning the stability of the private part of the monetary system. In other words, they discovered that they were actors in stability, not just more or less interested observers and commentators.

Reflecting that, there has been a growing realization that the public policy purpose of central banking is the preservation of

---

2. My thanks for comments from Roger Clews, my former colleague and co-architect of a decade-long series of reforms (from mid-1990s to late 2000s) to the United Kingdom's monetary operations and money markets.

monetary system stability.[3] While most certainly broader than the dominant pre-crisis view that all that mattered was low and stable inflation, this way of seeing central banking is still a lot narrower than a new habit of thinking that central banks are in the business of fixing or remedying all frictions and pathologies in financial economy–real economy interactions. That way lies nemesis.

Thought of in terms of monetary system stability, central banks have two related missions or objectives. One is to maintain stability in the value of their money in terms of goods and services. The other is to maintain an exchange rate of unity between money issued by the private sector monetary system *as a whole* and central bank money. The latter captures the objective of ensuring that the *aggregate* supply of monetary services to the real economy (payment transfers, liquidity insurance, credit) is maintained through distress. It does not imply that *individual* banking intermediaries should not be allowed to fail.

A Money-Credit Constitution

Now, if you accept that stability in the monetary system is a precondition for the operation of a market economy, then households and firms need to be highly confident that the monetary regime will not chop and change. That means that what central banks do and what private banks do need to be framed and constrained by a *Money-Credit Constitution*. This is somewhat broader than the late James Buchanan's proposal of a money constitution, for the simple but profound reason that we must face up to the existence of fractional-reserve banking (FRB).[4]

The broad concept of a monetary constitution will be familiar from the nineteenth century. This is what the gold standard

---

3. Again, see Part IV of *Unelected Power.*
4. For an example relatively late in his life, see James M. Buchanan, "The Constitutionalization of Money," *Cato Journal* 30, no. 2 (2010): 251–58.

became. It had three components. It imposed a particular kind of nominal anchor. It set a de facto, sometimes de jure, requirement that the core banks hold reserves with their central bank, which were an indirect claim on gold. And it was buttressed by the availability of emergency liquidity assistance to sound banks and other monetary-system intermediaries (Bagehot's lender of last resort).

I would suggest that a modern Money-Credit Constitution (MCC) needs not three but five components. One is a nominal target of some kind. That's what John Taylor was talking about at lunchtime. The second is a requirement for banks, and possibly what today are called "shadow banks," to hold reserves with the central bank or, alternatively, assets that can be readily converted into reserves. The third is a liquidity reinsurance regime, which normally goes by the name of lender of last resort but which I find helpful to think of in terms of liquidity reinsurance as it reminds us that the commercial banks are themselves, deep down, in the business of providing liquidity-insurance services via demand deposits and committed lines of credit. Fourth, a resolution regime, designed to ensure that fundamentally unsound intermediaries do not get bailed out by the monetary authority's loans but, also, that their distress and demise do not rupture the supply of core services. (That was missing in the nineteenth century for reasons that are worth discussing, but which I won't get into here.) And fifth—and this starts to build a bridge to the next session of this conference—constraints on the structure and uses of the central bank's balance sheet, given that the central bank's balance sheet is latently a fiscal instrument and so could in theory be used for almost anything, going well beyond the goal of monetary system stability.

In the light of Vice Chair Quarles's remarks, I will say something about the second, third, and especially fifth of those five MCC components.[5]

---

5. On how the second, third and fourth could become more joined up, via a second round of reforms, see Paul Tucker, "Is the Financial System Sufficiently Resilient?

THE PLACE OF THE LCR IN A
MONEY-CREDIT CONSTITUTION

In terms of the framework I have sketched, the liquidity coverage ratio (LCR) plainly performs a role in a money-credit constitution because, big picture, it specifies the level of reserves or other liquid assets that banks (and, at least conceptually, others) must hold relative to their short-term liabilities.

As I understand it, the matter at the heart of the vice chairman's speech is the relationship between the LCR and the Federal Reserve's monetary operations. From the regulatory end of the telescope, what proportion of the LCR should be met by banks holding reserves with the central bank? From the monetary policy and balance-sheet-management end, what quantity of reserves should be supplied to the system, and so end up being held by banks?

Big picture, there are two ways of ensuring that (sound) banks can meet a required degree of resilience against liquidity drains, enabling a unitary public/private-money exchange rate to be maintained. One is bottom-up, focused on individual intermediaries; the other top-down, starting from the system as a whole

The first is to require *each individual* bank to cover a specified minimum proportion (x%) of its short-term liabilities with assets that are eligible for discount at the central bank. The limiting case is what Mervyn King has called the "pawnbroker for all seasons," where *all* short-term liabilities must be covered (x = 100%).[6] The

---

A Research and Policy Agenda on Informationally Insensitive 'Safe' Assets within a Money-Credit Constitution," BIS Working Papers (forthcoming).

6. Mervyn King, *The End of Alchemy: Money, Banking and the Future of the Global Economy* (London: Little Brown, 2016). An idea of full "liquid-assets" cover for short-term liabilities was first floated in the Bank of England by David Rule when, before the great financial crisis, we were thinking about contingency plans for a 9/11-type disaster. Under such a scheme, ongoing industry lobbying (and associated political pressure) would be directed at the definition of "short term liabilities," the population of eligible instruments, and the level of haircuts.

LCR does not currently go nearly so far, but the sooner we have another crisis that looks like 2007 and early 2008, the more policy will move in that direction. It would give center stage to official policy on haircuts (or excess collateral), as among other things that would determine the proportion of assets that must be funded by equity (and longer-term debt liabilities).[7]

The second approach to effecting a desired liquidity standard is for the central bank to inject a quantity of reserves equal to or exceeding a specified proportion (x%) of the private banking sector's *aggregate* money-like liabilities. Conceptually, at the level of the system as a whole, that amounts to the central bank preinsuring against liquidity stress by buying or lending against eligible assets in advance rather than providing liquidity assistance only when needed to individual firms.

The two approaches are not mutually exclusive. Specifically, under the second, it would not be possible credibly to rule out *bilateral* liquidity assistance to sound banks, as reserves might not always be efficiently distributed via the market. But that could, in principle, be addressed by requiring each individual banking intermediary to hold the requisite level of reserves (x% of short-term liabilities) with the central bank. As will be clear, in that case the LCR is recast as a reserves requirement.

The higher the chosen rate of aggregate liquidity cover (x%), the larger would be the size of the central bank's balance sheet, *permanently* (rather than, as over recent years, temporarily in response to particular market and macroeconomic stresses and strains). As a thought experiment, then, this drives us to the vice chairman's question: Even with the current LCR, just how big should the central bank's balance sheet be?

---

7. Tucker, "Is the Financial System Sufficiently Resilient?"

THE MONETARY OPERATING FRAMEWORK
UNDER A MONEY-CREDIT CONSTITUTION

To find our way through these questions, we need to think about monetary-policy operating regimes and, in particular, to be alert to the transformation brought about by the move to paying interest on reserves (during the crisis in the United States, before the crisis in the euro area and United Kingdom).

Three Policy Instruments and a Principle of Parsimony

Paying the policy rate of interest on reserves gives a central bank more degrees of freedom. Most obviously, it can supply gigantic amounts of reserves (for example, via QE to stimulate aggregate demand as now, or to cover the banking system's liquid liabilities as described above) and so run a massive balance sheet while still keeping control of money market rates, since its policy rate provides a floor.

More generally, a central bank paying interest on reserves has not one but three policy instruments. The first and most familiar is the policy rate itself. The second is the size of the central bank's balance sheet. And the third is the composition of its asset portfolio (the instruments it has bought or the secured loans it has made in order to inject the desired level of reserves). The deep question—a political economy question, not just a matter for positive economics—is whether the Fed is going to adopt three objectives to go with those three instruments.

I want to argue that the answer should be: most of the time, definitely not. That is partly because I want to urge central banks to live by a *principle of parsimony* in order to aid public comprehensibility and accountability.[8] Central banks are very powerful bodies

---

8. Tucker, *Unelected Power*, chap. 21, 490–91, 501–02.

led by unelected technocrats who are insulated from day-to-day politics. In our democracies, the delegation of government power can be legitimate only if we can track what the legislature's agents are doing. Central banks should make that as straightforward as possible. And, in jurisdictions that have chosen to have a market economy, they should distort market mechanisms no more than required to achieve their objectives.

This precept entails that *central bank balance-sheet operations should at all times be as parsimonious as possible consistent with achieving their objectives.* Thus, if price stability can be achieved using only interest rate policy, it should be; and if banking system resilience can be maintained without a permanently enormous central bank balance sheet, it should be.

But if that general precept and its implications are reasonable, is it feasible here in the United States as the Fed eventually gets back to(ward) normality? I am going to argue that it is.

In doing so, I need to say something about the technicalities of monetary operating systems, as this will help to align the positive economics with my political economy precept of parsimony.

Monetary Operating Systems

In passing, Vice Chair Quarles noted that the New York Fed has framed the debate about the operating system in terms of whether the Fed should carry on with a kind of "floor system" or whether it should adopt what is described as a "corridor system."

Under a floor system, as touched on already, the central bank injects more reserves than are demanded so that the market rate falls to the rate the central bank pays on the marginal dollar of reserves. In consequence, if there are other options, a floor system violates the principle of parsimony as it involves the central bank choosing to have a larger balance sheet than is necessary for monetary policy.

The other option typically mentioned is a corridor system. Sadly, the New York Fed's discussion of corridor systems was highly misleading in three respects.[9] First of all, it is said that a corridor system relies on a scarcity of reserves. It need not do so at all. That is a defining requirement of a "ceiling system": a third type of system which, although unsuitable for prospective conditions in the United States, will help to explicate what is distinctive about a corridor system.

A ceiling system was used by the Bank of England in the early part of the twentieth century (with variants persisting until the early 1980s, when a mangled form of monetary-base control was introduced and conceptual confusion set in).[10] Under a ceiling system, the policy rate—Bank Rate, as it was called historically—is the rate charged on what the Fed calls (primary) discount window credit. When the market rate is not in line with what the central bank thinks is necessary to achieve its monetary objective, it undersupplies reserves via open market operations, creating scarcity and so pushing the banks into the window. Given reasonably efficient arbitrage, this asserts central bank control over the market rate, as banks will not pay a premium to square their books in the market when they could pay less at the window. The rate at which the open market operations are conducted does not matter very much, because that is a quantity exercise, designed to squeeze the banking system into the window.

A ceiling system would be quite inappropriate now and prospectively in the United States because, in common with other central banks, there is a structural surplus of reserves in the system (relative to demand) as a result of quantitative easing (QE). Expositionally,

---

9. William C Dudley, "Important Choices for the Federal Reserve in the Years Ahead," remarks at Lehman College, Bronx, New York, April 18, 2018.

10. I sometimes wonder whether similar confusions crept into US debates. For the UK saga, see Paul Tucker, "Managing The Central Bank's Balance Sheet: Where Monetary Policy Meets Financial Stability," *Bank of England Quarterly Bulletin*, Autumn 2004, especially Annex 3.

the concept is useful, however, because when thought about alongside a floor system it reminds us of the general economics of central banks' monetary operations.

What is a Corridor System?

To establish its policy rate in the money markets, the central bank needs to be either the marginal taker (floor system) or the marginal provider (ceiling system) of overnight money, or both. A corridor system simply combines the two: the central bank acts as *both* the marginal provider and marginal taker of funds, standing ready to borrow or lend in unlimited amounts at epsilon around its policy rate. Epsilon could be twenty-five basis points, the standard unit of change for monetary policy in most advanced economies, or less than that, or a bit more than that. The wider the corridor, the more an efficient money market is needed, which not all countries have.

This puts into relief the two other assertions made by the New York Fed about the characteristics of a corridor system. One was that such a system requires incredibly accurate forecasting of the demand for reserves and the other was that it requires the central bank to operate in the market frequently. Conceptually, neither proposition is true in general. Nor, for what it's worth, are they true in practice other than in rather particular circumstances.

Those circumstances are, broadly, where banks are set a reserves target; they have to meet it very precisely; the spread between the lending rate and deposit rate is large; and the maintenance period is effectively short (so that there is little or no intertemporal arbitrage across days). As it happens, nearly all those conditions held in the Fed's pre-crisis operating system, but they were *choices*.[11] Having

---

11. Technically, the Fed's maintenance period was not one day. But the low level of the reserves requirement and the system of penalties combined to make it operate somewhat like a one-day system so that large autonomous flows between the Fed and the banking system had to be offset via daily (or more frequent) OMOs.

to conduct frequent open market operations and to strive for precision in their forecasts of reserves-demand were consequences of those choices, nothing to do with corridor systems as such. When the governors debate the merits of floor versus corridor systems, they do not need to be constrained by the Fed's rather idiosyncratic pre-crisis system (which, as it happens, was not dissimilar to the equally idiosyncratic Bank of England system jettisoned in the 2000s).

So, specifying things more generally:

(a) Any system with two or more operating rates can be considered a "corridor," especially where the two rates are symmetric around the policy rate.

(b) There is a wide class of such systems, with none having an exclusive right to the label.

(c) Particular systems within the "corridor" family are distinguished by their other characteristics—daily or averaging and length of maintenance period, target range, etc., or not, and the distance between the two rates.

(d) These other characteristics powerfully influence the frequency and accuracy that are required or desirable in open market operations.

For example, the smaller epsilon relative to twenty-five basis points, say five basis points, the more the implementation of monetary policy—defined to mean establishing overnight money market rates broadly in line with the policy rate—does not require *any* open market operations at all or, indeed, any forecasting of the demand for reserves. The central bank just lets individual banks and the banking system as a whole come and borrow from it when the market rate is more than epsilon above the policy rate and, symmetrically, to place money with it when the market rate is more than epsilon below the policy rate. Instead, the size of the balance sheet fluctuates to the extent that banks square their books via the central bank's two facilities rather than meeting as counterparties in private markets.

Thus, it is possible for the central bank to set the overnight rate without having any kind of reserve system (or open market operations—OMOs) at all. That, broadly, is the setup in New Zealand.

This poses a big question: Why should a central bank want banks to hold a positive level of reserves? The arguments, I think, are twofold, perhaps threefold. First, the smaller the epsilon, the more banks will meet each other to balance their books across the central bank's balance sheet rather than in the money markets. The central bank might see positive value in the existence of a market. Second, a pure corridor system will not work effectively to implement monetary policy if stigma attaches to using the borrowing facilities of the central bank. Indeed, the greater the stigma of drawing on the borrowing facility in normal or exceptional circumstances, the more it is desirable in terms of the stability of the private part of the monetary system to ensure that the banks have *preinsured* themselves against liquidity shocks by holding reserves with the central bank.[12] And, possibly, third, the central bank might want to have some control, indirect or direct, over day-to-day fluctuations in the size of its balance sheet.

The prudent approach returns us, then, to the question: How to determine the level of reserves that the banking system should hold? Typically, that is debated in terms of: How should the central bank *set* the reserves requirement (direct control)? But, in fact, the central bank does not need to do that. The key is the design of the

---

12. In my view, stigma arises partly because a central bank can develop a reputation for being ready to lend to unsound banks. Fairly or unfairly, the Fed has that reputation with some members of Congress and some commentators. Shedding that perception is vitally important to giving the Fed space to choose its operating system and, of course, politically. The new resolution systems provide the basis for the Fed to bring about regime change in its LOLR function. For that and other reasons, together with other central banks it would rationally be a great advocate of resolution regimes and planning.

incentives to meet a target (and so how the target is specified), not who sets it: a form of *in*direct control.

Voluntary Reserves Averaging

This brings me to the option I want to air. A central bank can adopt what I am going to call "voluntary reserves averaging." Ahead of the start of a monetary maintenance period running from one Federal Open Market Committee (FOMC) meeting to the next, the central bank invites each reserve bank to specify the level of reserves it would like to target, on average, over the forthcoming period. They each set a target, t. The central bank then adds those up, to get an aggregate target, T. It must now provide something like that level of reserves over the maintenance period as a whole (technically, T times the number of days in the averaging period).

The system does not require daily (or more frequent) open market operations, because what matters is the final day of the maintenance period. So long as the policy rate is expected to prevail on that final day and provided the money markets are reasonably efficient, the policy rate will prevail on earlier days through the martingale properties of intra-maintenance-period arbitrage.

Nor does the central bank need to achieve pinpoint accuracy in the supply of reserves on the final day of the maintenance period, because it can create a very narrow de facto corridor by remunerating reserves at the policy rate so long as they fall, on average, within a range around each bank's target t. The wider the range, the less pinpoint forecasting is needed. More or less equivalently, the narrower the corridor between borrowing and deposit rates on the final day, the less super accurate reserves-demand forecasting is needed.

Further, because banks individually, and hence in aggregate, have an opportunity to reset their reserve targets at the beginning of each maintenance period, the system can accommodate swings in the demand for central bank money, and hence LOLR operations, without automatically having to conduct OMOs to drain "excess" reserves. Contrary to the New York Fed's statement, such draining operations are automatically needed only when reserves targets are static and so cannot accommodate shifts in demand.

The Bank of England employed this kind of system before the crisis, including a narrow corridor on the final day of the maintenance period, a wider corridor on earlier days, weekly OMOs plus a fine-tuning OMO on the final day, and reserves targets specified as a range. After the money-market liquidity crisis began in August 2007, banks progressively raised their reserves targets and we widened the permitted range around the targets. The system was, of course, suspended after the move to QE, when banks' own demand for reserves became irrelevant.

There are, of course, some practical constraints on utilizing this kind of system in normal conditions. First, and this might be relevant to the United States, it is important not to let nonbanks bank with the central bank unless they are subject to a system that replicates in some form the reserves system for banks. This might be relevant to the terms on which Fannie Mae and Freddie Mac are permitted to bank with the Fed.

Second, the integrity of collateral policy matters. If haircuts are too low or collateral valued richly, OMOs provide a cheap source of financing. In those circumstances, banks have incentives to choose high reserves targets simply in order to increase the aggregate size of OMOs. That would distort the allocation of resources in the economy and might help create debt bubbles. To be consistent with broad monetary system stability, banks need to choose their individual reserves targets guided only by their assessment of stochastic shocks to their payments flows and various other things that intrinsically matter (notably the system of penalties for missing reserves targets).

Provided those conditions are satisfied, the operating system I have been describing offers a solution to the problem outlined by Vice Chair Quarles.

That is because surely the answer to the vice chairman's question of what level of reserves the banking system will want to hold as conditions normalize is, absolutely: no one knows. But I am suggesting that the Fed does *not* need to know. It can find out through giving the banks the choice of selecting their own reserves targets.

I would not do that until the Fed's balance sheet has shrunk quite a bit. When introduced, the Fed would not know the extent to which the stock of reserves might still be massively greater than underlying demand. But a floor system could be synthesized, as a transitional measure, by remunerating reserves in a very wide range around the banks' targets.

The important thing, however, is that in steady state the Fed does not need to choose both the stock of reserves (the size of its balance sheet) and their price (the policy rate). Just as the public's holding of notes is demand-driven, so the banks' holding of reserve balances can be too. That fits with the principle of parsimony. Or put another way, do not try to control *both* the price and the quantity of reserves except where you really need to do so due to extraordinary circumstances.

There is, of course, a lot more to be said about the various options open to the Fed (and other central banks). But in evaluating them, the governors need not be worried that a corridor system entails creating a shortage of reserves, conducting OMOs very frequently, or forecasting the demand for reserves with pinpoint accuracy. The Fed is not condemned by those things to stick with a giant balance sheet and a "floor system" for rates forever.

SUMMING UP

It has been a great pleasure to respond to Vice Chair Quarles's remarks today. In doing so, I have offered some thoughts on how the LCR fits into an economy's Money-Credit Constitution and on the range of options available for operating monetary policy.

More important, however, are adopting a principle of parsimony in pursuing central banking's mission of monetary system stability and ensuring that the various arms of Fed policy are joined up and coherent.

By way of conclusion, I should perhaps stress that choosing the joined-up liquidity regime that complements the central bank's nominal target does not suffice to complete a money-credit constitution. Even a liquidity-reinsurance system providing 100 percent cover, in aggregate and individually, for the banking system's money-like liabilities would not cater for all seasons. That is because central banks cannot (legally or decently) lend to fundamentally insolvent firms (as to do so gives short-term creditors preference over similarly ranked longer-term creditors).[13] So while the LCR fits into the kind of MCC framework I have described, it needs to be supplemented with policies for the orderly resolution of intermediaries, which need to cover the permitted creditor hierarchy of operating banks and banking groups, and the availability of liquidity provision to recapitalized intermediaries. But that is another story.[14]

---

13. On the "no lending to fundamentally unsound firms" precept and the insufficiency of good collateral, see Tucker, *Unelected Power*, chapter 23; and Paul Tucker, "The Lender of Last Resort and Modern Central Banking: Principles and Reconstruction," BIS Papers No. 79, October 8, 2014. The important distinction between fundamentally sound and unsound borrowers arises because time-subordination exists while a firm is alive but not when in bankruptcy. Upon entry into bankruptcy, some debt claims are accelerated by their contractual terms and, more generally, liquidators are not permitted to pay out to short-term creditors if longer-term creditors of the same seniority would be left worse off as a result.

14. See Tucker, "Is the Financial System Sufficiently Resilient?"

GENERAL DISCUSSION

ANDREW LEVIN: The Federal Reserve regularly conducts stress tests for major banks. You ask them to consider how they would respond to key material risks. In my 2014 Hoover paper, I proposed that the Fed should also engage in stress tests for monetary policy, i.e., contingency planning for its policies and balance sheet. The Fed would refer to a benchmark scenario, like the ones that you've shown us, and then provide information about some salient risks over the medium run.

One obvious risk is the onset of a recession. The Fed will have some scope to cut interest rates or to launch a QE4 program. What would that look like in terms of the Fed's balance sheet? Another plausible risk is that paper cash could diminish much more quickly than in the benchmark scenario. As an analogy, when I visited Finland in 2007, everyone was confident that Nokia would continue to be the world's leading cellphone producer for many years to come, but then the iPhone was introduced and Nokia's business completely vanished within a couple of years. Don't we think that there's some nontrivial possibility that the same thing could happen to paper cash over the next five years or so? And if that happened, wouldn't it have major implications for the Fed's balance sheet? Again, you're asking the banks to do these sort of stress tests, so it seems sensible for monetary policy makers to start engaging in similar exercises regarding the central bank's balance sheet. What do you think?

RANDAL QUARLES: I guess there are two questions. One, is it worth considering those scenarios? And obviously, internally, we consider a lot of scenarios to be prepared for. And then the second question is, as we do with the stress tests on the financial sector, what's the public transparency around those considerations?

I think that there are pros and cons of that. Our current level of transparency, I think, sometimes results in an excessive level of Kremlinology around whose "dot" is whose [in the FOMC's periodic Summary of Economic Projections] and over parsing relatively arbitrary choices of words in statements. And so I shudder to think about the level of potentially misleading analysis that could come from transparency around how we were thinking about those other potential eventualities. But on the other hand, transparency, at least in the abstract, is a good, so I think it's something worth reflecting on.

CHARLIE SIGULER: I have a question for Vice Chair Quarles. I was thinking, in the world of post-QE2, we sort of had extraordinary monetary policy, and perhaps extraordinary moral hazard, and I'm wondering if the Fed put exists, and if the stock market were to fall by, let's say, 10 percent for no discernible reason, would the Fed be forced to take action?

RANDAL QUARLES: In general, I think it is not only our articulated stance, but I think it also actually reflects the fact that it's a complicated system of governance. But the Fed's decisions don't really reflect a targeting of asset levels. And certainly not equity market asset levels. You could come to some correlation, I suppose, to the extent that sudden changes in the value of equities are viewed as reflecting developments in the real economy that require a response. But I don't think that anyone should be expecting that a change in valuation, even a rapid change in equity valuations, that simply reflected sort of a reversion of asset prices to the mean as opposed to some signal about developments in the real economy, would result in action by the Fed.

DONNA BORAK: This question is for the vice chair. In the event that you don't take Paul's suggestion here at the end of his presentation, I'm curious, what do you think is a perfectly reasonable amount of time for the Fed to answer the two questions that you laid out in terms of what is the right size of the balance sheet and in terms of determining the deliberate demand that the banks have on these reserves? And second, are there external considerations that are weighing on your mind that might hasten how quickly you arrive at those answers?

RANDAL QUARLES: What I tried to walk through today was the mechanism through which we're essentially going to let the banks themselves reveal their demand for reserve balances as the balance sheet shrinks. It's one of the reasons for the gradual policy, precisely because we don't have a good handle on what that demand for reserve balance is going to be, and as the balance sheet shrinks, we will come to one of those inflexion points depending on where the underlying demand for reserves is, as well as some of these other factors, demand for paper currency and so forth. And when we hit that point, then the balance sheet will begin to grow and, essentially, we will see through the banks' actions what their demand for reserve balances is. We'll say, "Well, okay, it's not going down any lower." I view that as, essentially, we're going to allow the market to tell us through a gradual change in the environment when we have hit that inflexion point. We're changing it gradually so people sort of have a chance to change their practices and, indeed, discover their own preferences as the environment changes around them.

So, I don't know that it's really necessarily up to us to set the time frame on which that will happen. We're shrinking the balance sheet at a rate that's . . . with this batch, it could be faster, it could be slower. But it's one that's at least predictable, quite regular how that's going to happen. So, we've set kind of a very clear path for shrinking the balance sheet. And as that balance sheet shrinks, we will hit the point where we intersect the banks' underlying demand for reserves, which right now we think is unclear for a variety of reasons. And we will see it when we see it.

SEBASTIAN EDWARDS: This is a question for Paul. As you were talking about average voluntary reserves, it clicked in my mind that Mexico had such a system just before the last crisis. I quickly searched, and I found a paper by Moisés Schwartz. He used to be the head of the Independent Evaluation Office at the IMF and is a Mexican—a very good economist. And I find that there are a number of countries that have had zero reserve requirements, which in some way it is voluntary average reserve requirements. Because zero would be the lower bound. What is the evidence historically of these systems? I know that in Mexico, that story ended up badly, with a huge crisis. What is the story, the evidence in other countries—New Zealand and so on—and how would that affect your policy recommendation?

PAUL TUCKER: So, New Zealand is (or at least in the past has been), I believe, pretty close to operating a pure corridor system with no reserves requirement (voluntary or stipulated) at all, but instead just acting as the marginal provider and taker of funds. For normal times, I prefer the system of "voluntary reserves averaging" I described when responding to Vice Chair Quarles because it gives the banking system the option of *preinsuring* against liquidity runs. In terms of the voyage of discovery to gauging the demand for reserves that the vice chairman described, I think the difficulty that the Fed will intrinsically have is that (a) under a floor system, you cannot judge how far your (net) supply of reserves has exceeded demand; and (b) if, moving away from the floor system, you set a reserves target but the overnight unsecured rate (and perhaps also secured rate) falls below (or rises above) the policy rate, that is still not going to tell you very much about the elasticities. It's just going to tell you that you're in the zone when something's happening that you don't much like, and so those would be circumstances where open market operations *would* have to be actively used to discover the "right" quantities. Moving toward a system of voluntary reserve averaging would, by contrast, reveal to you the level of system-wide demand for reserves. (There are parameters that could be tweaked during the transition, including the permitted range around reserves targets, but that is getting rather techy for this discussion.)

The other thing about having that kind of system is that as conditions get more difficult but not terrible—I'll come back to that—the banking system will endogenously opt to have higher reserves targets (when each bank sets its target for a new monetary maintenance period). That is exactly what happened in the United Kingdom during the second half of 2007. The voluntarily chosen reserves targets doubled to tripled *before* we started QE. The point about QE, i.e., when you reach the zero lower bound, is that it's a game changer—because then the central bank is saying (precisely because it is at the zero lower bound), "We are not interested in demand for reserves anymore. We're actually trying to do something else in other markets through portfolio balance effects, etc." So, you have to think about a regime for normal times and one for non-normal times, and how you might design a system so as to be in receipt of signals that conditions are moving away from normal. And I want to underline, therefore, that the system I described gives you information through the choice that the banks make during normal times that non-normal times threaten.

WILLIAM NELSON: I have a question for Vice Chairman Quarles. So, as you noted, under the liquidity coverage ratio you can meet your liquidity requirements with reserves or with Treasury securities, other securities are, of course, limited, but you can use them to some extent. The most binding liquidity requirements right out there now are probably RLAP and RLEN and the liquidity requirements under living wills, resolution plans, we don't really know the details about, because those, of course, are secret. But one thing that I frequently heard back from banks or bank consultants is that, despite how the LCR is written, banks are told that they have to meet a material part of their high-quality liquid assets requirements with reserves. Now, of course, as you note, that does constrain the Fed, because if there's two trillion in HQLA out there, and say half of that has to be met with reserves, then you can't provide less than a trillion in reserves. I'd be curious to hear your thoughts on that and your reassurance that in fact it's Fed policy that banks can meet their liquidity requirements with alternatives and not just with the reserves.

RANDAL QUARLES: I do know that that message has been communicated at least in some supervisory circumstances in the past. I would say that that's in the process of being rethought.

PAUL TUCKER: Can I add something on this? Imagine that the QE had been so much bigger that the quantity of reserves had exceeded the aggregate LCR requirement. Well, then, assuming money markets are reasonably efficient, all of the LCR requirement would be met by every bank's holding of reserves. So, this isn't the LCR in normal monetary conditions, when reserves supply is lower than the aggregate LCR requirement.

WILLIAM NELSON: There are plenty of institutions that aren't banks that don't meet the LCR with reserves.

PAUL TUCKER: Well, there's a very deep, technical, but important question about the US monetary system in terms of who is allowed to have an account with Federal Reserve Banks and who is allowed to hold reserves. In terms of steering the overnight rate, that is a bigger question probably than anything we've discussed on this panel, but it is peculiar to the Fed's banking facilities.

MICHAEL BORDO: This is for Paul Tucker. It is an esoteric economic history question. When you were discussing the Bank of England in the 1930s, you should be aware of a new book by William Allen of the Bank of England which analyzes the history of the gilt market. It seems to me that what the Bank of England did in the 1930s is pretty close to what the Federal Reserve did in the 1920s: the Fed's main policy tool was the discount window, and it used open market operations to pressure the commercial banks to go to the window.

PAUL TUCKER: That's exactly right. I gave a speech in 2004 with, as I recall, more or less the same title as Randy's today. And, for me, the most interesting bit of the speech wasn't what I said but Annex 3, which is a series of extracts from notes written in the 1920s/30s and 1950s/60s, and so not my words at all. It operated exactly as you say: it was what, using today's metaphors, I called a ceiling system.

The Future of Central Bank Balance Sheets

Introduction

Kevin Warsh

Welcome.

If you are owing fealty to one side or the other in the curiously heated debate as to whether the Fed should add another "dot"—or twenty-five bps interest rate increase—to its forecasts this year, then our panel discussion will be of scant interest.

But if you are paying heed to the more consequential issues confronting the Fed and other large central banks, then my fellow panelists will not be strangers to you, nor will the issues we discuss.

The Fed's balance sheet is where the money is.

We will hear first from a leading Fed official who has day-to-day responsibility for the Fed's balance sheet. Then we will listen to the perspectives of a few of my fellow Fed retirees. The speakers will summarize their views, then I will encourage a discussion among my fellow panelists. Finally, we will open up the discussion to questions and comments from the assembled experts in the audience.

For those of us who were present at the creation of quantitative easing (QE), we cannot forget the ad hoc nature by which we initiated balance sheet expansion in the crisis. Nor should we lose sight of the frequent and consequential changes to the Fed's stated purpose of QE, its effects on real and financial assets, and the Fed's shifting exit plans in the decade that followed.

You will hear a range of views on benefits and risks of continued large central bank balance sheets in the post-crisis era. But one's ultimate judgment on the wisdom of the experiment—and the future of QE—may depend upon several things, which the panelists should explore:

- Whether the transmission mechanism and effects of QE are fundamentally different than standard interest rate policy
- Whether the implementation of QE injects liquidity neutrally
- Whether the Fed should possess a heightened, permanent role in the provision and allocation of credit in the financial system
- Whether a handful of large firms at the core of our financial system—they used to be called too-big-to-fail and now are deemed systemically significant—is necessary and desirable
- Whether market price signals are precious or should be readily supplanted by government-administered prices.

To put the moderator's cards on the table, I will offer a few words. The Fed appears lonely in its belief that post-crisis QE did not have significant effects on the prices of financial assets. And the Fed appears unmoved by the distributional consequences. Despite all-time highs in stocks and home prices, household net worth since 2007 is down for all income groups except for the top 10 percent since 2007. Net worth for the top decile is up an average of 27 percent; for the middle deciles, it's down 20 to 30 percent in real terms.

Central bankers, especially in non-crisis periods, ought not to be fiscal policy makers with tenure. Better, in my view, to yield fiscal policy to the other branch, no matter one's judgment on the wisdom of its policy choices . . . wiser for the Fed in peacetime to leave itself with a somewhat smaller, clearer responsibility in the conduct of monetary policy . . . and smarter for the Fed to possess a keen, concomitant focus on issues of financial resiliency in advance of the cycle turning.

Not long ago, General Jim Mattis roamed these halls at Hoover, reminding us that all war plans must have an end state. In our panel discussion, we will probe what is the end state for the Fed's balance sheet and question the prudence of unconventional policies' standing in the central bank's *conventional* toolkit in times of peace. In our discussion, we should be candid about our choices and humble about what we know of the Fed's incomplete experiment, even a decade later.

CHAPTER EIGHT

Normalizing the Federal Reserve's Balance Sheet and Policy Implementation

Lorie K. Logan

This chapter's topic—what we are normalizing to—is a key issue facing central banks as they normalize monetary policy after the crisis. I hope to bring to this discussion an operational perspective from my position on the Federal Reserve Bank of New York's Open Market Trading Desk. I will highlight three points. First, the Federal Reserve's balance sheet, once normalized, is likely to be smaller than it is today but considerably larger than it was before the crisis, regardless of the type of operating regime the Federal Open Market Committee (FOMC) adopts in the long run. Second, while the FOMC could maintain interest rate control through a corridor system for its longer-run monetary policy implementation framework, it would require a lot of learning by doing and would be unlikely to look like our pre-crisis corridor system. And third, based on what we've learned from operating a floor system thus far, it appears that this type of system can provide effective control of rates with operational simplicity. Before I continue, I should note that the views presented here are my own, and do not

I would like to thank Deborah Leonard for her assistance in preparing these remarks, as well as colleagues in the Federal Reserve System, including Antoine Martin, Simon Potter, Julie Remache, and Sam Schulhofer-Wohl, for comments and suggestions.

necessarily reflect those of the Federal Reserve Bank of New York or the Federal Reserve System.

Last October, the Federal Reserve began the process of reducing the size of its balance sheet—a significant milestone in the ongoing monetary policy normalization process. Using a program of progressively increasing caps, we are gradually reducing the Fed's securities holdings, which will reduce the supply of reserve balances in the banking system.[1] This process will continue until reserves fall to a level that reflects the banking system's demand for reserve balances and the FOMC's decisions about how to implement monetary policy "most efficiently and effectively," as noted in the FOMC's Policy Normalization Principles and Plans.

However, there remains much uncertainty over what the "normal" size of the Fed's longer-run balance sheet will be and how long it will take to get there. This uncertainty arises from numerous sources. We don't know how fast our MBS (mortgage-backed securities) holdings will pay down, how quickly currency outstanding will grow, how many bank reserves will be required for the efficient and effective execution of monetary policy, or how other liability items on the Fed's balance sheet will evolve. The economic outlook also poses an ever-present source of uncertainty.

Although the committee has not yet specified what a normalized balance sheet will look like, market participants' expectations may provide some helpful context. The New York Fed's most recent annual report on open market operations (released in April 2018) presents a set of projections for possible paths of the Fed's securities

---

1. Principal payments from the Federal Reserve's securities holdings each month are reinvested only to the extent that they exceed gradually rising caps, laid out in a schedule in the June 2017 addendum to the FOMC's Policy Normalization Principles and Plans. See Federal Open Market Committee, "FOMC Communications related to Policy Normalization," accessed August 16, 2018, https://www.federalreserve.gov/monetarypolicy /policy-normalization.htm. Around the time the caps reach their maximum levels in October 2018, Treasury reinvestments will typically occur only in mid-quarter months, while agency MBS reinvestments are projected to end altogether (assuming no downward shock in longer-term interest rates).

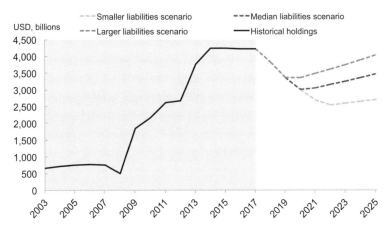

FIGURE 8.1.1 Historical and Projected SOMA Domestic Securities Holdings

Source: Federal Reserve Bank of New York Staff Projections (Report on Open Market Operations during 2017)

Note: Figures are as of year-end. Figures for 2018 onwards (dashed lines) are projected holdings and are rounded. Scenarios are based on the 25th, 50th, and 75th percentile responses to a question about expectations for the size and composition of the Federal Reserve's balance sheet, on average in 2025, conditional on not moving to the zero lower bound, in the Federal Reserve Bank of New York's December 2017 Survey of Primary Dealers and Survey of Market Participants.

portfolio.[2] As seen in figure 8.1.1, the report shows three scenarios constructed from distributions of market participants' surveyed expectations for the future size of the balance sheet.[3] Survey-based expectations for the path of interest rates and some staff modeling fill in additional details. While these scenarios by no

2. See the report and accompanying data file, *Open Market Operations during 2017*, Federal Reserve Bank of New York, accessed August 16, 2018, https://www.newyorkfed.org /markets/annual_reports.html.

3. The scenarios represent the twenty-fifth, fiftieth, and seventy-fifth percentiles of the combined responses to the New York Fed's December 2017 "Survey of Primary Dealers" and "Survey of Market Participants." See "Survey of Primary Dealers," Federal Reserve Bank of New York, accessed August 16, 2018, https://www.newyorkfed.org/markets/primarydealer _survey_questions.html; and "Survey of Market Participants," Federal Reserve Bank of New York, accessed August 16, 2018, https://www.newyorkfed.org/markets/survey_market _participants.html. The surveys asked respondents to provide their expectations for the composition of the Federal Reserve's balance sheet, on average in 2025, conditional on not moving to the zero lower bound at any point between now and the end of 2025.

means embody the full range of possible outcomes, they suggest the domestic securities portfolio's size could normalize at $2.5 trillion to $3.3 trillion, with the larger end of that range projected to be reached within two years. After its normalized size is reached, the portfolio is assumed to incrementally grow again as Treasury securities are purchased to keep pace with trend growth in liabilities, mainly currency.[4]

The projection exercise illustrates a key point: The Fed's future balance sheet will likely be considerably larger than its pre-crisis level. This outcome is likely regardless of the design of the operating regime that the committee ultimately uses to manage short-term interest rates. The normalized size will be determined by the liability side of the Fed's balance sheet, which will reflect two driving factors: growth in nonreserve liabilities and a potential shift in the structural demand for reserves.

First, there has been substantial growth in the Federal Reserve's nonreserve liabilities in recent years and some factors are expected to grow further, as seen in figure 8.1.2. US dollar currency in circulation tends to grow over time and has more than doubled since the start of the global financial crisis, to a current level of $1.6 trillion.[5] The median survey response implies an expectation for currency to grow to around $1.8 trillion at the time the size of the portfolio normalizes—in other words, the portfolio will need to be $1 trillion larger than before the crisis just to back currency in circulation. Meanwhile, various account holders—including the Treasury Department, foreign and international official institu-

---

4. Treasury securities would also be purchased to offset the ongoing runoff of the Fed's holdings of agency debt and mortgage-backed securities. Such rebalancing will support the continuing normalization of the composition of the Fed's securities portfolio, a process that is expected to take longer than normalization of the portfolio's size. The FOMC has stated that it intends to hold primarily Treasury securities in the longer run.

5. The December 2017 survey responses used in the three scenarios shown here imply average annual currency growth rates of 2.6 percent, 4.6 percent, and 5.8 percent through 2025—a deceleration from the actual average annual growth rate of roughly 7 percent over the past five years.

Billions of U.S. Dollars	Pre-Crisis Average (H1 2007*)	Current Level (4/25/18)	Expected Average Value in 2025**		
			Smaller Liabilities Scenario	Median Scenario	Larger Liabilities Scenario
Reserve balances	16	2,011	412	600	750
Non-reserve liabilities:					
Federal Reserve notes	772	1,596	1,900	2,200	2,400
Treasury General Account	6	403	200	300	365
Other deposits	0	80	50	75	100
Reverse repos (foreign official accounts)	34	235	120	200	250
Reverse repos (private counterparties)	n/a	4	58	100	150
All other liabilities and capital	40	45	50	50	57
Total	869	4,373	2,790	3,525	4,072

FIGURE 8.1.2 Federal Reserve Liabilities and Capital

Source: Federal Reserve Board; Federal Reserve Bank of New York

* Average of Wednesday levels.

** Expected average values in 2025 are based on the 25th, 50th, and 75th percentile responses to a question about expectations for the size and composition of the Federal Reserve's balance sheet, conditional on not moving to the zero lower bound, in the Federal Reserve Bank of New York's December 2017 Survey of Primary Dealers and Survey of Market Participants.

tions, government-sponsored enterprises (GSEs), and designated financial market utilities (DFMUs)—have increased their balances held in Federal Reserve accounts or investment services, which currently represent over $700 billion in additional liabilities.

Second, it is likely there has been a shift in the structural demand for reserves, driven largely by banks' response to changes in regulations and risk appetite that favor safe assets, particularly reserves. If the demand curve for reserves has indeed shifted out, the amount of reserves the Federal Reserve will need to supply to achieve a given interest rate target will be comparably larger than it once was.

The FOMC acknowledged in last June's addendum to its Policy Normalization Principles and Plans that it anticipates a future level of reserve balances that is "appreciably below that seen in recent years but larger than before the financial crisis."[6] In the three projection scenarios I've shown, reserve balances (as derived from market participants' expectations) are assumed to be around $400 billion, $600 billion, and $750 billion once a normalized balance sheet size is reached, well below the current level of $2 trillion and consistent with the committee's statement. However, we have insufficient information to identify what factors inform these views.

Taking reserves and nonreserve liabilities together, I see virtually no chance of going back to the pre-crisis balance sheet size of $800 billion. Thus, discussion of whether to have a large or small balance sheet in the long run partly misses the point. The conversation is really about the relative amount of reserves, which will be governed both by the banking system's demand for reserve balances—something we will learn more about during the process of balance sheet normalization—and by the committee's future decisions around how to implement monetary policy most efficiently and effectively.

Debates about monetary policy implementation regimes generally center on two frameworks, illustrated in stylized form in figure 8.1.3. The traditional framework—a version of which the Fed used before the crisis—is a corridor system, which is generally associated with a scarce supply of reserves. Policy is implemented through frequent adjustments to the supply of reserves, such that the supply intersects the steep portion of the reserve demand curve at the desired overnight interest rate. Fluctuations in reserves stemming from autonomous factors are borne by the private sector through the central bank's open market operations. In contrast, the framework used to implement policy today is a floor system, which is associated with an abundant supply of reserves and policy implementation that is achieved through periodic changes to

---

6. See the Federal Open Market Committee, "FOMC's Communications Related to Policy Normalization," accessed August 16, 2018, https://www.federalreserve.gov/monetarypolicy /policy-normalization.htm.

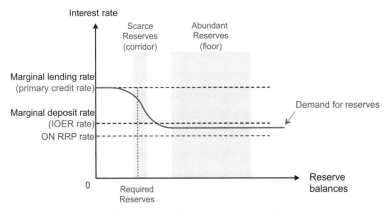

FIGURE 8.1.3. Stylized Monetary Policy Implementation Framework
Source: Federal Reserve Bank of New York

administered rates. A floor system is generally associated with a relatively larger balance sheet than a corridor system because the central bank needs to supply enough reserves to satisfy demand on the flat part of the reserve demand curve, perhaps with an additional buffer to accommodate reserve supply shocks. Such shocks typically stem from fluctuations in other liabilities.[7] However, we do not really know how large or small a difference in the amount of reserves would be needed to run an effective and efficient floor versus a corridor in the longer run. The answer will depend critically on the shape of the demand curve, which we will learn more about over time, as well as the specific design parameters of either framework.

I would emphasize that central banks have successfully implemented both types of frameworks, or variations of them, and that the Fed can achieve interest rate control with either one. Leaving aside some of the broader policy considerations, I'd like to make a few points about the technical operation of each framework in the longer run.

---

7. All else equal, changes in nonreserve liabilities have the opposite effect on the supply of reserves.

First, some observers see a return to the Fed's pre-crisis, reserve-scarce corridor system as the natural conclusion to the normalization process, highlighting that system's familiarity. But it is important to note that fundamental changes in the money market landscape over the past decade would likely make monetary policy implementation in a future corridor system look substantially different than before the crisis.

In the Fed's pre-crisis regime, hitting the target federal funds rate each day was a technically challenging exercise. Demand for reserves was driven largely by reserve requirements, in addition to intraday payment clearing needs. We started with a banking system that on most days was short of reserves. Then, using staff forecasts of various factors affecting the supply of and demand for reserves over multiple days ahead, we calibrated open market operations with the dealers in the repo market to bring the aggregate supply of reserves into balance at the target rate. With this aggregate balance achieved, individual banks distributed them. Banks facing a deficiency of reserves needed to find and trade with banks holding reserve surpluses, each balancing the costs associated with holding too many or too few reserves.[8] We were reliably proficient in hitting the FOMC's target rate in normal times, but interest rate control was more challenging at times when factors affecting reserves were harder to predict. This was particularly true in the early stages of

---

8. Reserve averaging over a two-week maintenance period provided a buffer around how precise the final distribution of reserves needed to be on any given day. Nonetheless, falling short of reserves could incur penalties or the need to borrow reserves at what might be relatively high rates. Since reserve balances were not remunerated, there was a steep opportunity cost to holding excess reserves. The degree to which such interbank trading, aimed at fulfilling a requirement imposed by the central bank, reflected fundamentals versus idiosyncratic factors is hard to assess. This ambiguity may obscure the value of its signal on market rates. Simon Potter explores this issue in "Discussion of 'Evaluating Monetary Policy Operational Frameworks' by Ulrich Bindseil," 2016 Economic Policy Symposium on Designing Resilient Monetary Policy Frameworks for the Future, Jackson Hole, WY, August 25–27, 2016, accessed August 16, 2018, https://www.newyorkfed.org/newsevents/speeches/2016/pot160826.

the crisis, when large changes in reserve demand caused significant intraday and interday swings in federal funds rates (figure 8.1.4).[9]

Today, with greater uncertainty and variability in factors affecting the day-to-day demand for and supply of reserves, it would be more difficult to anticipate fluctuations and achieve the necessary balance in reserve conditions even in normal times. In aggregate, reserve demand is likely to be guided by a more complex set of drivers, including post-crisis liquidity regulation, supervision, resolution planning, and intraday payments risk management. These needs have the potential to contribute to higher and more variable demand for reserves than banks had before the crisis.[10] Estimating reserve demand would need to take into account these factors, as well as banks' propensities to substitute between reserves and other relevant assets—something that may vary according to an individual institution's business strategy. Knowledge about the shape, position, and stability of banks' reserve demand curve will likely emerge only with experience.

---

9. Challenges operating in this environment are described by the SOMA manager in Federal Open Market Committee, FOMC meeting transcripts from September 18, 2007, and throughout the crisis, accessed August 16, 2018, https://www.federalreserve.gov /monetarypolicy/fomc_historical_year.htm. See also Spence Hilton, "Recent Developments in Federal Reserve System Liquidity and Reserve Operations," speech to the Reserve Bank of Australia Conference, July 14–15, 2008, accessed August 16, 2018, https://www.rba.gov.au /publications/confs/2008/hilton.html. A separate operational consequence of the corridor system, revealed during the crisis, is that it can constrain the Fed's ability to provide the types of lender-of-last-resort backstops that can help support financial stability. Accommodating broad-based, open-ended lending in a corridor system raises the need to drain any reserve additions to keep the federal funds rate close to the FOMC's target, thus posing a trade-off between the Fed's monetary policy and liquidity provision objectives. New York Fed President Bill Dudley recently highlighted this challenge in "Important Choices for the Federal Reserve in the Years Ahead," remarks at Lehman College, Bronx, New York, April 18, 2018, accessed August 16, 2018, https://www.newyorkfed.org/newsevents/speeches/2018 /dud180418a.

10. Morten L. Bech and Todd Keister explore the links between open market operations and short-term interest rate changes when banks face the possibility of a liquidity coverage ratio shortfall in "Liquidity Regulation and the Implementation of Monetary Policy," BIS Working Paper no. 432, October 2013, accessed August 16, 2018, https://www.bis.org/publ /work432.pdf.

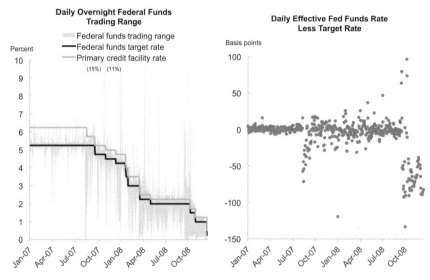

FIGURE 8.1.4. Intraday and Interday Volatility in Fed Funds Rates during the Crisis

Source: Federal Reserve Bank of New York

Note: Time series end on December 15, 2008, when the FOMC introduced a target range for the federal funds rate.

Additionally, we would need to consider shocks that affect the supply of reserves, such as those stemming from changes in the Fed's nonreserve liabilities. As seen in figure 8.1.5, net changes in nonreserve liabilities have become more variable in recent years.[11]

---

11. Increased variability arises from several changes over the past decade. Since 2008, the Treasury Department has managed its cash flows through the Treasury General Account (TGA) at the Fed. Balances in the TGA exhibit significant volatility, typically rising when auctions of Treasury securities settle and on tax receipt dates while shrinking when large payments are made. (Prior to 2008, the Treasury targeted a steady, low balance in the TGA. It also maintained private accounts, which absorbed the variability in cash flows.) DFMUs have gained access to Reserve Bank accounts since the crisis and GSEs now pre-position funds in their Fed accounts prior to making principal and interest payments. Overnight reverse repos have been introduced as a monetary policy implementation tool. Additionally, in response to foreign central banks' preferences to maintain robust dollar liquidity buffers and the reduced availability of alternative investments with private counterparties, the New York Fed has applied a less restrictive approach to the management of the foreign repo pool (a long-standing investment service through which foreign official and international account holders' balances are swept into overnight reverse repos).

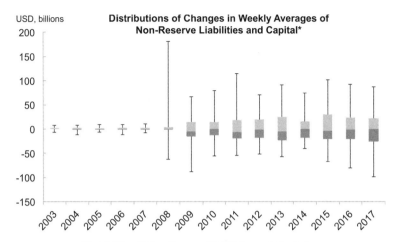

FIGURE 8.1.5. Variability of Non-Reserve Liabilities and Capital

Source: Federal Reserve Board; Federal Reserve Bank of New York Staff Calculations

* Boxes indicate interquartile ranges, and whiskers indicate minimum and maximum outcomes. Data show the distribution of changes in weekly averages of daily figures for liabilities outside the direct control of the Fed (currency, Treasury accounts, foreign repo pool, and other deposits) and capital. Liabilities associated with monetary policy instruments (overnight and term reverse repos conducted with private counterparties and term deposits held by depository institutions) are not included.

Even if fluctuations could be accurately forecast, in a corridor system, they would need to be offset through open market operations to maintain interest rate control. Larger fluctuations would likely require larger operations.[12] In the years before the crisis, the average size of daily overnight repo operations was around $5 billion—a relatively small amount given the size of the repo market and dealers' net securities financing needs. Roughly 95 percent of these operations were for less than $10 billion, and the maximum operation size in normal times was $20 billion. Looking just at recent variability in nonreserve liabilities and assuming overnight operations were used to offset their fluctuations, daily temporary

---

12. Changes in other features of the system could potentially help to smooth conditions. For example, certain alterations to the reserves averaging framework might allow the system to absorb more volatility.

operations in a corridor system might routinely need to be around
$25 billion, but could go as high as $100 billion.[13] We would need
to consider whether the Fed's repo and reverse repo operations
could be dependably scaled to that degree and whether their effects
would be transmitted to other rates.

One consideration in this regard is that there appear to be greater
frictions across funding markets today. Dealer balance sheets have
shrunk and become less elastic in the face of changes in regulation
and risk management.[14] While dealer caution contributes to the
overall safety and soundness of the banking sector, it could mean
we would need more or different types of counterparties for traditional repo operations, or perhaps different types of operations
altogether—particularly if federal funds trading became idiosyncratic or disconnected from other rates. In sum, a reinstated corridor might look less familiar than some expect.

For comparison, let me make a few observations about our experience with the floor system that the Fed is currently using. The
FOMC has successfully raised its target range for the overnight
federal funds rate six times since December 2015 and, as seen in
figure 8.1.6, the effective federal funds rate has reliably printed in
the prevailing target range over that time. The policy stance has
transmitted to a broad constellation of money market rates. The
system is simple and efficient to operate. The interest rate the Fed
pays on excess reserves serves as the primary policy implementation tool, with support from a standing facility that offers overnight

---

13. These estimates are based on variability of liabilities that are outside the direct control
of the Fed (such as currency, the Treasury General Account, the foreign repo pool, and other
deposits) and capital. They exclude reserves and liabilities associated with monetary policy
instruments (such as overnight and term reverse repos conducted with private counterparties and term deposits held by depository institutions).

14. Committee on the Global Financial System, "Structural Changes in Banking after
the Crisis," CGFS Papers, no. 60, January 2018, accessed August 16, 2018, https://www.bis
.org/publ/cgfs60.pdf.

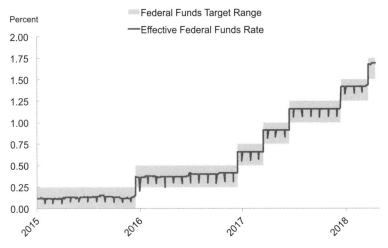

FIGURE 8.1.6. Effective Federal Funds Rate
Source: Federal Reserve Bank of New York

reverse repos (ON RRPs) at an administered rate.[15] There is no need to forecast specific factors affecting reserves or to conduct discretionary open market operations each day; overnight reverse repos are offered every day based on price, not quantity. Day-to-day fluctuations in factors affecting reserves are accommodated by the elastic reserve demand, given that reserve needs are widely met. Market forces keep the federal funds rate in the FOMC's target range by allowing a wide range of counterparties to price trades against the alternative option of investing with the Federal Reserve. And in the aggregate, use of the Fed's balance sheet is

15. The ON RRP facility helps to reinforce the floor under market interest rates by establishing an important investment option for a wide range of active lenders in short-term funding markets, including certain types of nonbank institutions that are not eligible to earn interest on reserves. Take-up in ON RRP operations is sensitive to the pricing of the Fed's reverse repos relative to the pricing and availability of comparable money market investments, including private repo, Treasury bills, and agency debt. Even with near-zero usage, as has been seen in recent months, the ON RRP facility supports market rates by ensuring that counterparties demand rates on other investments at least as attractive as the rate offered on the Federal Reserve's ON RRPs.

efficient by allowing private and official sector market participants to determine their preferred distribution across the range of Fed liabilities.[16]

This system could continue to work well with considerably lower levels of reserves, so long as the supply continued to intersect the flat part of the demand curve. If reserves fell too low, we could see high volumes of fed funds borrowing at interest rates well above the interest rate on excess reserves, which would indicate that we were no longer operating at the flat part of the demand curve.[17] As I noted earlier, maintaining a buffer of excess reserves to absorb reserve-draining shocks could prevent this outcome. An important trade-off arises between the size of that additional buffer and the frequency and size of open market operations.[18]

To sum up, the FOMC could choose to retain the floor system to implement policy in the longer run or it could choose to shift back to a corridor system. However, a reinstated corridor system may be less familiar than some expect. Such a framework would involve

---

16. In a preliminary discussion about the long-run monetary policy implementation framework, FOMC participants commented on the advantages of an approach to policy implementation similar to the one currently in use, in which the active management of reserves would not be required. Such an approach was seen as "likely to be relatively simple and efficient to administer, relatively straightforward to communicate, and effective in enabling interest rate control across a wide range of circumstances." However, policy makers made no decisions and acknowledged that they expected to learn from additional experience. See Federal Open Market Committee, "Minutes of the Federal Open Market Committee, November 1–2, 2016," accessed August 16, 2018, https://www.federalreserve.gov/monetarypolicy/fomcminutes20161102.htm.

17. We should also recognize that the fed funds rate might occasionally firm somewhat due to increases in interest rates in other money markets, which can affect the fed funds rate via arbitrage. Such developments are not necessarily a sign that reserves are becoming scarce. It is therefore important to understand dynamics not only in the fed funds market but also across a broader range of money market instruments and transmission across them. Simon Potter features some such analysis in "Money Markets at a Crossroads: Policy Implementation at a Time of Structural Change," remarks at the Master of Applied Economics' Distinguished Speaker Series, University of California, Los Angeles, April 5, 2017, accessed August 16, 2018, https://www.newyorkfed.org/newsevents/speeches/2017/pot170405.

18. I discuss these issues in more detail in "Implementing Monetary Policy: Perspective from the Open Market Trading Desk," remarks before the Money Marketeers of New York University, New York City, May 18, 2017, accessed August 16, 2018, https://www.newyorkfed.org/newsevents/speeches/2017/log170518.

uncertainties about reserve demand and greater variability in factors affecting reserve supply, and would likely require operations that are larger, more variable, or even very different from those used before the crisis. Meanwhile, those who favor a floor system may be encouraged by the performance of our current framework to date. We've learned that the floor system has proven to be highly effective at controlling the effective federal funds rate and other money market rates, is resilient to significant shifts in market structure, and is efficient to operate. Under either framework, the balance sheet will likely normalize at a level substantially larger than it was before the crisis to accommodate higher demand for reserves and nonreserve liabilities in the post-crisis landscape.

CHAPTER NINE

GET UP OFF THE FLOOR

William Nelson

My remarks today will focus on three things. First, I will make the positive case for a small balance sheet/corridor system for the Fed's monetary policy implementation framework in the longer run. Second, I will list shortcomings of a large balance sheet/floor system. And third, I will describe some pitfalls in the process that have left us where we are now.

But first, a little background. By "corridor system," I mean a monetary policy framework where the Fed supplies a sufficiently small quantity of reserves that the fed funds rate trades between the IOER rate (interest rate on excess reserves) and the discount rate. I will often refer to this as the pre-crisis framework even though the Fed couldn't pay interest before the crisis so the bottom of the corridor then was zero. What I currently have in mind is that the Fed would continue to pay interest on excess reserves, but that that rate would be well below market rates—perhaps fifty to a hundred basis points below.

The following figure, which I believe will be familiar to most of you, illustrates the situation. The dashed line is banks' demand for reserves at different levels of the fed funds rate. The black vertical line is the supply of reserves. As a result of large-scale asset purchases, the size of the Fed's balance sheet, and therefore the level of reserves, is enormous. The black line is currently far to the right, a bit over

These are my views, not those of The Clearing House or its member banks.

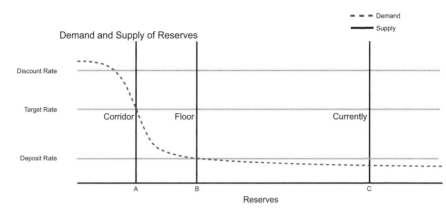

FIGURE 9.1.1. Demand and Supply of Reserves

$2 trillion. At that level, the fed funds rate has to be equal to or even a bit below the interest rate the Fed pays on reserves to leave banks content to hold the reserve balances supplied.

At present, the black line is creeping to the left as the Fed lets some assets mature without reinvesting the principal.

Eventually, supply will, or may, get to a point where it intersects the dashed line at the IOER rate, point B. That point is the minimum quantity of reserves at which the Fed can operate a floor monetary policy framework. Any smaller, and the federal funds rate would be above the floor. No one knows where that point is. I think it will be at a high level, perhaps not that far below where we are now, for reasons I will discuss in a minute. But really, we are all just waiting and observing. A number of the costs of a floor-based system go up with the minimum necessary size of the balance sheet, so knowing where that point is will help the Fed decide about its framework.

Even further to the left, point A is where the supply curve hits the demand curve right in between the discount rate and the IOER rate. That is the supply consistent with a corridor system. Prior to the crisis, that level was about $15 billion, with only $1 billion to

Federal Funds vs. Money Market Rates

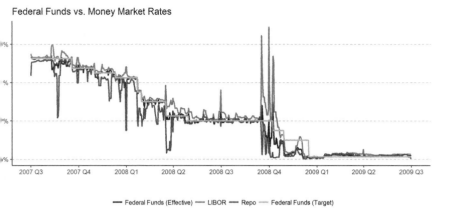

FIGURE 9.1.2. Federal Funds vs. Money Market Rates
Source: FRED and TCH Staff Calculations

$2 billion in excess reserves. No one knows where that point is now either, although I suspect it is quite low for reasons I will discuss.

We may, of course, never learn where point A is if the Fed decides to stick with a floor system. I think that would be a mistake, for a number of reasons.

Why is a corridor system preferable?

First, the Fed's pre-crisis framework worked well in normal times. The Fed conducted monetary policy by means of relatively small repos with broker dealers. Those transactions allowed the Fed to influence the fed funds market, a relatively small market where the Fed had tight control of both supply and demand. The Fed was usually not a counterparty in the fed funds market, except for the rare discount window loan. Changes in the fed funds rate were transmitted effectively to other money markets, including the repo market and term markets. Thus, without being an important counterparty to anyone, the Fed still had effective control of interest rates and thereby the economy.

Moreover, the pre-crisis framework also worked well in the crisis. From August 2007 through December 2008 the crisis was under way, but the FOMC's target range was not at zero. While spreads between money market rates became large and variable, as can be seen in the graph, reductions in the funds rate were still transmitted one-for-one into other money market rates.

For reasons I will come to, a small balance sheet is better than a large balance sheet, and a small balance sheet is only possible under a corridor system, not a floor system. Banks are currently holding over $2.5 trillion in liquid assets to meet the liquidity coverage ratio requirement. If the interest rate the Fed pays on reserves is equal to the fed funds rate and approximately equal to other money market rates, banks will choose to satisfy their liquidity requirement in large part with reserves. The Fed will, of course, then have to meet that demand by holding a large portfolio of securities.

By contrast, under the corridor system, the Fed would end up with a relatively small balance sheet. I spoke with a number of bank treasurers and CFOs about how they would adjust if the interest rate the Fed paid on excess reserves were fifty to one hundred basis points below the fed funds rate. Not surprisingly, they indicated they would find a way to minimize their excess reserves balances. They would reduce their LCR (liquidity coverage ratio) requirements by borrowing beyond thirty days or lending within thirty days. And they would hold Treasury or agency securities instead of reserves. There should be no shortage of securities: if the Fed is providing fewer reserves, it is holding correspondingly fewer government securities.

Finally, a smaller portfolio leaves the Fed better prepared if short-term rates again fall to zero. While theoretically it shouldn't matter, realistically, it would be easier for the Fed to conduct an asset purchase program starting with a small balance sheet.

What, then, is so bad about a floor system? In a nutshell, it will put the Fed at risk and increase its role in the financial system.

The first risk to the Fed is that it could lose completely the authority to pay interest on reserves. Currently, the Fed is paying

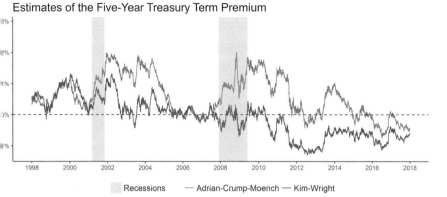

FIGURE 9.1.3. Estimates of the Five-year Treasury Term Premium
Source: Federal Reserve Board of Governors; Federal Reserve Bank of New York

interest at an annual rate of about $37 billion. If excess reserves decline and interest rates rise as projected by the FOMC, then interest payments will gradually fall. However, if the demand for excess reserves remains elevated, or if the Fed needs to increase the fed funds rate quickly to prevent an unwanted rise in inflation, interest payments would rise, possibly sharply. Congress might see such large payments to banks as unacceptable, and so take away or constrain the Fed's ability to pay interest on reserves.

The second risk is that a large balance sheet will reduce the Fed's income relative to a small balance sheet, which could have political implications. The Fed's expected net income is lower, not higher, for each Treasury security it holds in excess of currency outstanding. Treasury term premiums are negative, have been negative for years, and are likely to remain negative. If the five-year term premium remains about minus-fifty basis points, the Fed operates using a floor system, and excess reserves are about $2 trillion, then the Fed will earn and remit to Treasury $10 billion less each year than if the IOER rate were well below the fed funds rate and excess reserves were near zero.

More broadly, a large balance sheet/floor system framework for monetary policy may result in the Fed becoming a much more integral part of the financial system than under a corridor system. If the Fed decides that it intends to control money market rates broadly, rather than just the fed funds rate, and do so using deposit and lending facilities, not scarcity, it will inevitably find itself on one side or the other of a huge amount of transactions. It is particularly doubtful that the Fed can successfully control the repo market, a massive market for which the Fed controls neither demand nor supply, without massive interventions. While the corridor system offered good monetary control with a small footprint, a floor system may offer relatively poor control with the Fed counterparty to all.

PROBLEMS WITH THE PROCESS

Over the past decade, the FOMC made a series of decisions about its balance sheet to address immediate problems that ended up having implications for its longer-run framework. In some cases, the FOMC made time-inconsistent plans in order to forge an internal consensus to provide more accommodation, only to later conclude that those plans were unworkable. For example, when considering QE3, the committee based its decision on a staff balance sheet forecast in which the purchases would end in six months even though the staff economic forecast showed no decline in the unemployment rate over that period. The forecast for a limited purchase program was based in part on an implausible plan that, if necessary, the FOMC would simply announce that the program wasn't working. In the event, the program continued for twenty-one months.

Also noteworthy is the evolution of the committee's plans for reducing its balance sheet. In June 2011, the committee published "exit strategy principles" that included a plan to sell MBS (mortgage-backed securities) gradually once tightening had begun.

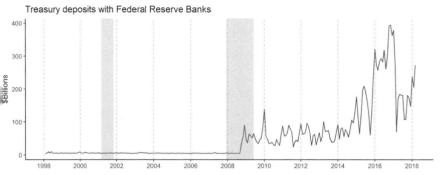

FIGURE 9.1.4. Treasury Deposits with Federal Reserve Banks
Source: Federal Reserve Board of Governors; Federal Reserve Bank of New York

But in June 2013, in order to continue the flow-based purchases without having to contemplate losses on future asset sales, the committee announced that it no longer intended to sell MBS, a decision enshrined in the new normalization principles it announced in 2014.

Lastly, the Fed has taken actions that have left it in a floor system for an extended period, and those actions make a floor system look attractive and a corridor system look implausible. With excess reserves topping $2.75 trillion, the fed funds market should have died entirely and today mostly consists of GSEs (government-sponsored enterprises) lending to FBOs (foreign banking organizations). Now floor system advocates ask, "How could the Fed target the interest rate in such an illiquid and odd market?"

With interest rates at zero, commercial banks were no longer able to provide the Treasury interest on its deposits, so the Treasury switched its deposits entirely to the Fed. The resulting increase in volatility of that account, shown in the graph, which causes corresponding volatility in the supply of reserves, hasn't troubled the Fed in a floor system but would make a corridor system unworkable.

With IOER above market rates, banks are satisfying liquidity requirements with excess reserves. Indeed, a number of bank consultants have told me that supervisors require that banks meet the requirements in large part with reserves, not with the alternatives. If that's true, then it is not just difficult, but impossible for the Fed to return to a small balance sheet.

Going forward, if the FOMC officially changes its monetary policy target from the fed funds rate to its new, broader overnight bank funding rate, or its new secured overnight financing rate, a large balance sheet/floor system becomes almost inevitable. On the other hand, I suspect that it will only take a few more grillings of Fed Chairman Jay Powell by Congress about the size of interest payments before a corridor system looks good again.

CHAPTER TEN

The Fed's Balance Sheet Strategy: What Now?

Mickey D. Levy

Since the Fed's unconventional emergency purchases of mortgage-backed securities and Treasuries at the height of the severe financial crisis in November 2008, the Fed's perception about a dramatically enlarged balance sheet has evolved toward believing that it is conventional and normal. The Fed's expanded scope of monetary policy has been supported by its overestimation of the benefits of its QE (quantitative easing) asset purchases and its underestimation of the economic and political risks of maintaining an outsized balance sheet. Of particular concern is the Fed's exposure to Congress's dysfunctional budget and fiscal policy making in the face of mounting government debt and debt service costs.

The Fed's emergency measures helped end the financial crisis and lift the economy from recession. After financial markets had normalized and economic growth had become self-sustaining, the Fed's QEs had a different purpose—to stimulate faster growth and improve labor markets.

While QE3, the Fed's low policy rates, forward guidance, and reinvestment policy clearly stimulated financial markets, and labor markets improved, there is scant evidence that economic growth was stimulated. Nevertheless, the Fed takes credit for the improved labor markets and now favors maintaining an oversized balance sheet.

So what began as an unprecedented response to the most severe financial crisis in generations has evolved into what is now perceived to be normal and conventional. But neither description is appropriate.

The Fed's current intention—to gradually reduce its Treasury and MBS (mortgage-backed securities) holdings but indefinitely maintain an enlarged balance sheet, including MBS, with sizable excess reserves—involves new procedures for conducting monetary policy that are simply more complex than are needed for the Fed to achieve its mandate. Also, they extend the Fed's footprint in financial markets more than is necessary.

The Fed should reset its strategy to rules-based guidelines for conducting monetary policy during extended normal times and move back toward its historic procedures that proved efficient in all but extreme circumstances. It should also establish a framework that would allow emergency monetary policies during abnormal economic or financial stress. The Fed should fully unwind its MBS holdings and reduce its balance sheet consistent with modest amounts of excess reserves. This would allow the Fed to gradually unwind its ON RRP (overnight reverse repurchase) program and reestablish the historic market-based "corridor system" of managing the federal funds rate.

QE AND THE BALANCE SHEET EXPANSION: PURPOSES, EFFECTS, AND PERSPECTIVES

In a speech on December 1, 2008, Fed Chairman Bernanke commented that the Fed's purchases of $600 billion of GSE (government-sponsored enterprises) debt and MBS initiated in November 2008 were extraordinary, unconventional steps. He stated, "To avoid inflation in the long run and to allow short-term interest rates ultimately to return to normal levels, the Fed balance sheet would eventually have to be brought back to a more sustainable level. The

FOMC will ensure that this is done in a timely way" (Bernanke 2008).

A month later, prior to the Fed's announced additional purchases of $750 billion agency debt and MBS plus $300 billion of Treasury securities in March 2009, Bernanke emphasized that the Fed's asset purchases involved emergency "credit easing" that "focuses on the mix of loans and securities that it holds and on how this composition of assets affects credit conditions for households and businesses" (Bernanke 2009). He set out an exit strategy: "A significant shrinking of the balance sheet can be accomplished relatively quickly" such that "the Federal Reserve will be able to return to its traditional means of making monetary policy— namely, by setting a target for the federal funds rate."

From crisis management to stimulating labor markets. The Fed and Bernanke ignored his crisis-related instructions. Following the QE2 purchases of $600 billion of Treasuries and maturity extensions through Operation Twist, at the Jackson Hole Symposium in August 2012 Bernanke outlined the rationale of the Fed's forthcoming QE3 and forward guidance, concluding that "the Federal Reserve will provide additional policy accommodation as needed to promote a stronger economic recovery and sustained improvement in labor market conditions" (Bernanke 2012).

Bernanke cited research suggesting that the Fed's QE1 and QE2 asset purchases lowered ten-year Treasury bond yields by an estimated eighty to 120 basis points and that "a study using the Board's FRB/US model of the economy found that, as of 2012, the first two rounds of LSAPs [large-scale asset purchases] may have raised the level of output by almost 3 percent and increased private payroll employment by more than 2 million jobs, relative to what otherwise would have occurred."

While the Fed's assessment of the benefits of QE1 in stabilizing financial markets and lifting employment from what would have occurred otherwise seems valid, it overestimated the effectiveness of QE2. QE1 was a successful response to a financial crisis and had a much larger interest rate impact than QE2. Estimates of the impacts of QE1 and QE2 should be unbundled. Importantly, the Fed board staff's estimates of the impacts of the QEs on GDP and employment that Bernanke cited were based on simulations of the FRB/US model that significantly overestimated actual growth over the period, which resulted in overestimates of job gains. It is noteworthy that the Fed's forecasting track record during 2010–16 was notably poorer than during pre-crisis periods (Levy 2018).

QE3 was an open-ended commitment by the Fed to purchase $40 billion per month of agency MBS until the labor markets improved "substantially." In December 2012, the Fed raised its total monthly purchases under QE3 to $85 billion with additional monthly purchases of $45 billion of longer-dated Treasuries that would be continued after Operation Twist concluded.

Financial markets thrived during QE3 but the economic responses were muted. Stock markets (and real estate values) rose sharply, bond yields stayed low, and risky assets appreciated. But nominal and real GDP did *not* accelerate during the four years after QE3 began as the Fed expanded its balance sheet to $4.5 trillion and reinvested maturing assets to maintain that level. Nominal and real GDP growth averaged 3.6 percent and 2.1 percent, respectively. Most striking, business investment did not respond as expected to the lower real costs of capital. The economic impacts of QE3 and subsequent reinvestment policy were significantly overstated and raise a lot of questions.

During this period, the Fed board's staff and the FOMC significantly overestimated real GDP growth (table 10.1.1 and figure 10.1.1). Actual real GDP growth in 2013 matched the Fed's forecasts but fell decidedly below the board staff's and FOMC's forecasts (summaries of economic projections, or SEPs) in 2014 and 2015. Actual growth also fell below the FOMC's forecast in 2016.

TABLE 10.1.1. Real GDP Growth (yr/yr % chg)—actual, and Fed Staff's and FOMC's forecasts

	2010	2011	2012	2013	2014	2015	2016	2017
Actual	**2.7**	**1.7**	**1.3**	**2.7**	**2.7**	**2.0**	**1.8**	**2.6**
Forecasts								
Q4-09								
Fed Staff	3.6	4.5	4.7	4.7	3.2			
FOMC midpoint	3.0	4.0	4.2					
Q4-10								
Fed Staff		3.7	4.4	4.7	4.7	3.5		
FOMC midpoint		3.3	4.1	4.1				
Q4-11								
Fed Staff			2.3	2.5	3.4	4.2	3.7	
FOMC midpoint			2.7	3.3	3.5			
Q4-12								
Fed Staff				2.5	3.2	3.6	3.2	2.5
FOMC midpoint				2.7	3.3	3.4		

Sources: The staff of the Federal Reserve Board's forecasts are from the Greenbook (2009) and the Tealbook (2010–12). The FOMC's forecasts are based on the Federal Reserve's quarterly Summary of Economic Projections. Real GDP growth forecasts are percent changes from Q4 to Q4.

The disconnect between the economy and the Fed's unprecedented monetary ease deserves closer scrutiny. More research on the factors that inhibited growth would clarify issues. Financial regulations and sustained low rates have been identified as sources that have constrained bank lending and harmed the monetary transmission channels (Calomiris 2016). Low business confidence, partially driven by the growing web of burdensome government regulations in an array of nonfinancial sectors, likely explains some constraint on growth, but more research is needed (Levy 2018).

The Fed's typical rationale for its QEs has relied on three themes: (1) if it had not taken the steps that it did, the financial crisis and economic contraction would have been magnitudes worse; (2) normalizing monetary policy any more quickly risked throwing the economy back into recession; and (3) with inflation generally below 2 percent, the Fed was appropriately pursuing its dual mandate.

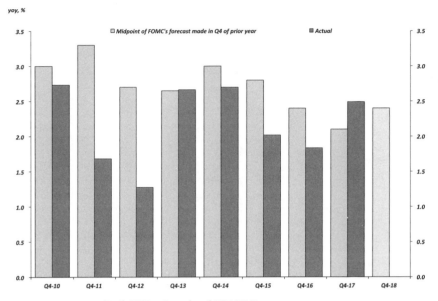

FIGURE 10.1.1. Real GDP—Actual and FOMC Forecasts
Sources: Federal Reserve Board, Bureau of Economic Analysis; Mickey Levy, "The Fed's Economic Forecasts, Uncertainties and Monetary Policy," paper presented to the Shadow Open Market Committee, New York, March 9, 2018.

The first rationale makes sense for QE1, but it is all-too-frequently used to inappropriately rationalize QE3 and the Fed's subsequent reinvestment policy. The Fed's excessive worries about rising rates ignore history that shows clearly that once economic expansions unfold following accommodative countercyclical monetary policy, normalizing interest rates and higher bond yields do not harm economic activity. Note that the recent sustained healthy economic growth as the Fed has raised rates is consistent with the historical pattern.

My assessment is that (1) if the Fed had not undertaken QE3, economic and labor market performance would have been very similar to what actually occurred; and (2) if QE3 had actually stimulated the economy as the Fed had forecast, inflation and interest rates would have risen significantly faster. Of course, the Fed's view of history is different. But it should be questioned in light of the persistent gap between the Fed's FRB/US model's forecasts and actual outcomes. A deeper and more reliable understanding of how unconventional monetary policy affects economic performance when the economy and financial markets are functioning normally would be very instructive.

The Fed's fears of jarring financial markets. The Fed's concerns about fragile financial markets and the economy were accentuated by the Taper Tantrum, a surprising 100 basis point rise in bond yields triggered when Bernanke suggested in May 2013 that the Fed would eventually need to reduce its asset purchases. This unanticipated sharp rise in bond yields had a negligible impact on GDP growth—temporarily weaker housing activity was offset by strength in other domestic purchases—and bond yields receded when the Fed actually tapered QE3 in 2014. Nevertheless, this episode jarred the Fed's confidence and led to its strategy of extending reinvestment of all maturing assets until well after it began increasing interest rates. As several Fed members noted in 2014, not reinvesting maturing assets would "send the wrong signal to markets."

These observations have several important implications: interest rates are not a reliable measure of monetary policy (which also calls into question the economic implications of "announcement effect" studies); the actual Fed balance sheet flows were less important to markets than earlier fears; and the Fed's concerns about market reactions to what it does and says are excessive.

The Fed's peak balance sheet grew to $4.5 trillion, comprising the world's largest holdings of US Treasury securities (various maturities) and MBS (mostly long-dated), financed largely by short-dated borrowings from commercial banks. This seemed to serve little economic purpose, other than satisfying the Fed's fears of jarring financial markets. The Fed's holdings contributed to low bond yields and mortgage rates and elevated the prices of stocks and real estate. The low interest rates encouraged reliance on debt and also encouraged risk-taking. But economic growth continued to disappoint through 2016.

Confidence jumped beginning in early 2017 and the economy gained momentum, even as the Fed gradually raised rates and announced and began its gradual balance sheet unwind. Bond yields have risen modestly since December 2017, but that likely reflects the strengthening economy rather than the Fed's policy of not reinvesting a minor portion of its asset holdings.

THE FED'S CURRENT UNWINDING STRATEGY AND POLITICAL ECONOMY RISKS

The Fed's official "Addendum to the Policy Normalization Principles and Plans," issued June 14, 2017 (Board of Governors 2017), established a schedule for passive runoffs of Treasury securities and MBS and stated that its intention is to maintain a balance sheet "larger than before the crisis." But the Fed has left unclear its ultimate balance sheet strategy. Projections of the Fed's holdings based on the schedule in the Fed's addendum are shown in figures 10.1.2–10.1.3. Note that the Fed's MBS holdings are projected to rise as a share of its total portfolio (figure 10.1.4).

Around the same time, Fed Governor Jerome Powell commented following a speech to the Economic Club of New York, "It's hard to see the balance sheet getting below a range of $2.5 to $3 trillion" (Powell 2017). With $1.5 trillion of currency, this would imply roughly $1 trillion of excess reserves. Powell's statements favoring the current "floor system" of managing the Fed's policy rate rather than the market-based "corridor" procedure used before the financial crisis reveal his preference to maintain ample excess reserves in the banking system and pay interest on excess reserves (IOER). Based on the Fed's schedule, the Fed's balance sheet would

$, trn

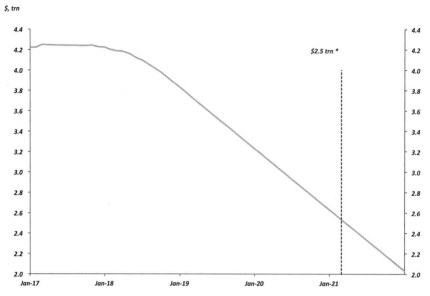

FIGURE 10.1.2. Projection of the Fed's Total Securities Holdings Based on the Fed's Addendum to the Policy Normalization Principles and Plans of June 14, 2017

Sources: Federal Reserve Board; Jerome Powell, "Thoughts on the Normalization of Monetary Policy," speech to the Economic Club of New York, New York City, June 1, 2017.

fall to $2.5 trillion in early 2021. At that time, the Fed would hold approximately $1 trillion of MBS.

My assessment is that the potential risks to the Fed's credibility and independence of maintaining an enlarged balance sheet overwhelm any possible benefits they provide as contingency planning for infrequent financial emergencies.

The Fed's MBS holdings should be fully unwound. There is no justification for the Fed's sustained holding of MBS and the Fed should adjust its strategy to move toward an all-Treasury portfolio. The Fed should not be involved in credit allocation that favors housing over other sectors years after the mortgage market has fully repaired. Policies affecting credit allocation should be left to fiscal policy and regulators and the Fed should stay away from the politics of housing policy and credit subsidies.

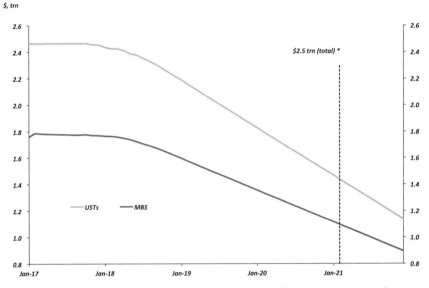

$, trn

FIGURE 10.1.3. Projection of the Fed's US Treasuries and MBS Holdings Based on the Fed's Addendum to the Policy Normalization Principles and Plans of June 14, 2017

Sources: Federal Reserve Board; Jerome Powell, "Thoughts on the Normalization of Monetary Policy," speech to the Economic Club of New York, New York City, June 1, 2017.

The Fed's reticence to unwind its MBS holdings is likely driven by concerns about mortgage rates. Estimates suggest that fully unwinding its MBS holdings may widen the MBS-Treasury yield spread by roughly 50 basis points. Although estimates involve uncertainties, such increases from current mortgage rates would not unhinge improvement in the housing market and would reduce the policy-induced distortions in credit allocation.

The costs and benefits of an enlarged balance sheet and changed operating procedures. An indefinitely enlarged balance sheet has been identified as a tool for enhancing financial stability and offering safe, liquid assets (Greenwood, Hanson, and Stein, 2016) and for facilitating the Fed's role as lender of last resort during financial crises. These arguments stem from the trauma of 2008–09 and are geared toward a discretionary monetary policy

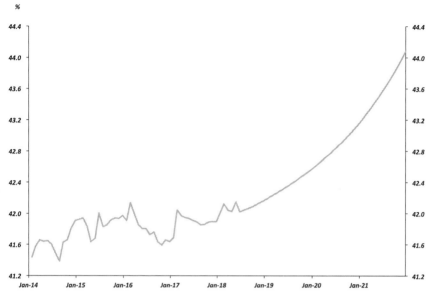

FIGURE 10.1.4. Projection of the Fed's MBS Holdings as a Share of Total Based on the Fed's Addendum to the Policy Normalization Principles and Plans of June 14, 2017

Source: Federal Reserve Board

framework that would provide flexibility to respond to rare bouts of financial instability.

Instead, it would be much more efficient to establish rules-based guidelines for the conduct of monetary policy consistent with the Fed's mandate that would be applicable during extended spans of normal economic and financial conditions and to also establish rules and triggers for infrequent emergencies, with sufficient flexibility for the Fed to provide liquidity and serve as lender of last resort. This would reduce the potential risks of maintaining an enlarged balance sheet during normal periods.

The Fed needs to better understand the interactions between maintaining an enlarged balance sheet and the Fed's interest rate policies, how they affect economic performance, and how the balance sheet fits into the Fed's task of achieving its mandate. The Fed has already expressed concern about establishing sufficient flexibility to ease monetary policy in response to the next inevitable downturn. A smaller balance sheet with fewer excess reserves would be a better basis for providing such flexibility and effectiveness under adverse conditions.

The Fed may be pressed on this issue if anticipated rate increases threaten to invert the yield curve which, based on history, would raise concerns about recession. In this situation, my assessment is that economic performance would be better served by more aggressive balance sheet reduction than by more aggressive rate increases, particularly through reductions in its MBS portfolio. Also, the Fed should consider reinvesting the portion of maturing assets above its designated caps into shorter-duration Treasuries, rather than maintaining the longer-duration objective of recent years. That would require a change in the FOMC's directive to the Federal Reserve Bank of New York's operating desk.

The blurred boundaries between monetary and fiscal policies. The Fed has been far from transparent about the sensitivity of budget outcomes to monetary policy, the economic and financial risks of its enlarged balance sheet, and how it encourages bad budget practices. The Fed's enlarged balance sheet and the sizable profits it remits to the Treasury are simply too tempting to Congress's fiscal policy makers who now perceive of the Fed as a source of risk-free money. The Fed should steer monetary policy clear of fiscal policy—and the most effective way of doing so is to shrink its balance sheet.

During fiscal years 2015–17, the Fed remitted an average of $98 billion per year to the Treasury. Along with low interest rates and bond yields, it significantly reduced the government's cash flow deficits. But these gains are likely temporary and can quickly turn to losses. In 2017, the Congressional Budget Office estimated that a 1 percentage point increase in interest rates would add $1.6 trillion to budget deficits during 2018–27 (CBO 2017). Year-to-date in 2018, both short-term interest rates and ten-year bond yields have averaged above the CBO's projections for all of 2018. The risks described by Marvin Goodfriend in "Monetary Policy as a Carry Trade" are becoming a reality (Goodfriend 2014). The CBO's latest budget projections of persistent government deficits, rising debt, and even faster increases in net interest outlays are striking (CBO 2018). The CBO's baseline projections of persistently high budget deficits increase publicly held debt from 78 percent of GDP in fiscal year 2017 to 96 percent in 2028 (up from 35 percent in 2007) and far higher in later years. (The Fed's holdings of Treasuries are counted as publicly held debt because the Federal Reserve District Banks, which hold the Fed's assets, are capitalized by commercial banks in their districts.) Over the next ten years, the government's net interest costs are projected to rise from $263 billion to $915 billion, nearly doubling as a percent of total federal outlays (from 6.6 percent in 2017 to 13 percent in 2028).

The potential risks facing the Fed were impressed upon me at a recent congressional hearing held by the House Financial Services Committee on the interaction between monetary and fiscal policies. Congressman Brad Sherman (D-CA) heaped praise on the Fed's outsized remittances to the Treasury and all of the additional spending they had financed. He then asked the expert witnesses, "What would the Fed have to do to double (to $200 billion) the amount it remits to the Treasury?" (US Congress House Financial Services Committee July 2017). This question may seem amusing to monetary economists, but the Fed should not take it lightly. The Congress has used the Fed's balance sheet twice to help finance spending legislation—the FAST Act in December 2015 and the Bipartisan Budget Act of 2018—and more intrusions seem likely. As Charles Plosser, former president of the Federal Reserve Bank of Philadelphia, has emphasized, the Fed has no defense against congressional misuse of its balance sheet (Plosser 2017).

The Fed's exposure to Congress's fiscal policy deliberations entangles it in Washington pressure politics in unpredictable ways. If things go wrong, the Fed may be blamed. And some of the Fed's operating procedures that it sees as important may draw heavy criticism from a Congress that puts its narrow perceptions above sound economics. The Fed's policy of paying IOER is a good example. While the Fed correctly argues that paying IOER is a long-run wash on the Treasury's balances, Congress's perception may be driven by other considerations.

In light of all the uncertainties about how an enlarged balance sheet affects economic performance and how it interacts with interest rate policy, and political risks posed by dysfunctional fiscal policy and the mounting debt and debt service costs, the Fed should be more circumspect about the potential risks and should move toward normalizing its balance sheet and operating procedures back to pre-crisis norms.

References

Bernanke, Ben. 2008. "Federal Reserve Policies in the Financial Crisis." Speech to the Greater Austin Chamber of Commerce, Austin, TX, December 1.

Bernanke, Ben. 2009. "The Crisis and the Policy Response." Speech to the London School of Economics, January 13.

Bernanke, Ben. 2012. "Monetary Policy Since the Onset of the Crisis." Speech at the Federal Reserve Bank of Kansas City Jackson Hole Symposium, Jackson Hole, WY, August 31.

Board of Governors of the Federal Reserve System. 2017. "FOMC Issues Addendum to the Policy Normalization Principles and Plans." News release, June 14.

Calomiris, Charles. 2016. "The Microeconomic Perils of Monetary Policy Experiments." Presentation to the Shadow Open Market Committee, New York, October 7.

CBO (Congressional Budget Office). 2017. "An Update to the Budget and Economic Outlook: 2017 to 2027." June.

CBO (Congressional Budget Office). 2018. "The Budget and Economic Outlook: 2018 to 2028." April.

Goodfriend, Marvin. 2014. "Monetary Policy as a Carry Trade." Presentation to the Shadow Open Market Committee, New York, November 3.

Greenwood, Robin, Samuel G. Hanson, and Jeremy C. Stein. 2016. "The Federal Reserve's Balance Sheet as a Financial-Stability Tool." Speech at the Federal Reserve Bank of Kansas City Jackson Hole Symposium, September.

Levy, Mickey. 2018. "The Fed's Economic Forecasts, Uncertainties and Monetary Policy." Presentation to the Shadow Open Market Committee, New York, March 9.

Plosser, Charles. 2017. "The Risks of a Fed Balance Sheet Unconstrained by Monetary Policy." Paper presented at the Hoover Institution Conference on The Structural Foundations of Monetary Policy, Stanford, CA, May 4.

Powell, Jerome. 2017. "Thoughts on the Normalization of Monetary Policy." Speech to the Economic Club of New York, New York City, June 1.

US Congress. 2017. "Monetary v. Fiscal Policy: Risks to Price Stability and the Economy." Hearing of the House Financial Services Committee Hearing, July 20.

CHAPTER ELEVEN

SHOULD THE FED 'STAY BIG' OR 'SLIM DOWN'?

Peter R. Fisher

Should the Federal Reserve plan to Stay Big and maintain a super-abundance of excess reserves? Or should it plan to Slim Down toward a significantly lower level of excess reserves?

Given the natural growth in currency as one of the Fed's liabilities, the size of its balance sheet in absolute terms (or relative to its pre-financial-crisis past) is not the relevant question. The policy choice the Fed confronts is whether to maintain a large portfolio of bonds on the asset side of its balance sheet and a correspondingly high level of excess reserves on the liability side, or to reduce significantly both the level of its excess reserve liabilities and its assets.

In my mind, Stay Big would imply maintaining a level of excess reserves that is *inconsistent* with a return to supply-demand dynamics allocating overnight reserve funds within the banking system via price signals. Slim Down, on the other hand, would imply reducing excess reserves to a level *consistent* with supply-demand dynamics eventually reasserting themselves in the allocation of funds among banks.

Compared to the current level of approximately $1.9 trillion of excess reserves, Stay Big might mean planning to maintain $500 billion or more, while Slim Down would mean planning on reaching a level of $100 billion or less.[1] Slim Down could, but need not, mean a return to the operating framework employed by the Fed prior to

---

1. Board of Governors of the Federal Reserve System, "Factors Affecting Reserve Balances— H.4.1 Release," June 21, 2018.

the financial crisis and the advent of the Fed's quantitative easing (QE) programs.

The expansion of the Fed's balance sheet under QE was explained as a means of reducing long-term interest rates and stimulating private credit creation.[2] Changes in the size and composition of the balance sheet were the means by which the Fed sought to stimulate aggregate demand through the "portfolio rebalance channel" to ease credit conditions and, thereby, encourage an expansion of private credit.[3] But the explanations offered, so far, in support of Stay Big are not made in the same terms. Rather, the focus has been on the mechanics of the Fed's operating procedures, the management of the very short end of the yield curve, and improving financial stability.

The influence of the Fed's balance sheet on the term structure of interest rates and in stimulating or retarding private credit creation should be central in the debate about whether the Fed should Stay Big or Slim Down. In these terms, the costs of Stay Big appear to be significant while the purported benefits of Stay Big are sketchy and raise more questions than they answer.

SPECIFYING MY PRIORS

My view is that QE1 (2008 to 2010) had a positive impact in liquefying the banking system during and immediately after the financial crisis and that it prevented more, and more rapid, deleveraging of the US financial system. But I am deeply skeptical about the

---

2. See Ben S. Bernanke, "The Economic Outlook and Monetary Policy," remarks at the Federal Reserve Bank of Kansas City Economic Symposium, Jackson Hole, WY, August 27, 2010 ("bringing down term premiums and lowering the costs of borrowing in a number of private credit markets"); see also Ben S. Bernanke, "Monetary Policy since the Onset of the Crisis," remarks at the Federal Reserve Bank of Kansas City Economic Symposium, Jackson Hole, WY, August 31, 2012 ("Declining yields and rising asset prices ease overall financial conditions and stimulate economic activity through channels similar to those for conventional monetary policy").

3. Bernanke, "Economic Outlook and Monetary Policy."

efficacy of QE2 and QE3 (2010 to 2016) in stimulating aggregate demand.

It is hard for us to know with any confidence what would have happened in the absence of QE. But we do have the imperfect counterfactual of history. Reinhart and Rogoff have provided us with a disciplined, 800-year review of the relevant economic history. They conclude that it has taken approximately eight to ten years for a country's economic activity to recover from a significant financial crisis.[4] The experience of the US economy over the last decade is entirely consistent with this history. As we did no better "this time," it is hard to conclude that the extraordinary monetary policies pursued by the Fed made much difference. Also, recent work by Greenlaw et al. suggests that the burden of proof for QE's effectiveness in stimulating aggregate demand has not been met.[5]

Thus, in my view, the use of QE "next time" should not be presumed, as former chair Janet Yellen appeared to do.[6] The effectiveness (in the past) and the appropriateness (in the future) of the use of quasi-fiscal powers by the Fed through QE should be addressed on the merits. The Fed should not simply rely on claiming that the burden of proof is on QE's side, nor rely upon the maintenance of a large balance sheet as implying the benefit of incumbency for QE.

Planning to fight the last war is likely to be a mistake. The political landscape is unlikely always to provide a vacuum in which usurping fiscal powers will be tolerated by either Congress or the executive branch.

---

4. Carmen M. Reinhart and Kenneth S. Rogoff, "Recovery from Financial Crises: Evidence from 100 Episodes," *American Economic Review* 104, no. 5 (May 2014): 50–55; see also Carmen M. Reinhart and Kenneth S. Rogoff, *This Time is Different: Eight Centuries of Financial Folly* (Princeton, NJ: Princeton University Press, 2009).

5. David Greenlaw, James D. Hamilton, Ethan Harris, and Kenneth D. West, "A Skeptical View of the Impact of the Fed's Balance Sheet," NBER Working Paper no. 24687, June 2018.

6. Janet L. Yellen, "The Federal Reserve's Monetary Policy Toolkit: Past, Present, and Future," remarks at Federal Reserve Bank of Kansas City Symposium, Jackson Hole, WY, August 26, 2016.

I also believe that much of the current debate about the size of the Fed's balance sheet is misdirected, particularly discussion about floors and corridors for the management of overnight interest rates on reserve balances.

The Fed, like any central bank, can use either administered rates or a targeted market rate as the reference point for the expected path of short-term interest rates. Too much is made of which one can more effectively "control" overnight interest rates. This is a minor issue. Prior to the advent of the euro, the Deutsche Bundesbank shifted back and forth between variable-rate and fixed-rate repurchase transactions and often chose to emphasize either its discount or Lombard rates in its communications.

The Fed has always used a combination of administered and market rates and this will likely always be the case. All that really matters for implementation of monetary policy is that there *be* a reference point for the expected path of short-term interest rates. For this purpose, the Fed can use administered rates, such as interest on excess reserves or the discount rate, or the Fed can use a "market rate" like the federal funds rate.

Even with the extremely high levels of excess reserves at present, the Fed continues to communicate its policy intentions expressed in terms of the federal funds rate.[7] This is at least suggestive of the idea that the technical framework for monetary operations need not constrain the Fed in how it communicates about the expected path of short-term interest rates.

Given the very high level of excess reserves at present, a decision to move toward Slim Down would, of course, require continued reliance on administered rates for some time, even if intending to put more emphasis on a targeted market rate in the future.

---

7. See Board of Governors of the Federal Reserve System, "Federal Reserve Issues FOMC Statement," news release, June 13, 2018.

THE COSTS OF STAY BIG ARE SIGNIFICANT

Maintaining a large Fed balance sheet and a correspondingly high level of excess reserves will be likely to impose significant costs on the effectiveness of monetary policy by constraining the Fed's ability to influence the level of long-term interest rates, by limiting the effectiveness of any future use of the Fed's balance sheet to stimulate the economy, and by impeding the efficient allocation of funds with the banking system via price signals.

Influence on Long-term Interest Rates

Maintaining high levels of excess reserves will be likely to diminish the Fed's ability to influence long-term interest rates and the shape of the yield curve. A perpetually available, super-abundant supply of excess reserves will tend to increase demand for long-term government securities from what it might have been without such a high level of excess reserves. This was precisely one of the key rationales for QE in the first place.[8]

By purchasing government securities (and agency securities) and expanding the supply of reserves, the Fed sought to reduce long-term interest rates both directly, by its own purchases, and indirectly, by encouraging market participants to replace the duration they had lost by purchasing longer-dated instruments themselves.[9] In this way, QE pushed demand out the yield curve. Stay Big leaves it there.

The market as a whole has a certain demand for duration. It is unlikely that the supply of zero-duration assets (in the form of excess reserves) can by itself change the market preference for

8. See Bernanke, "Economic Outlook and Monetary Policy," and Bernanke, "Monetary Policy since the Onset of the Crisis."
9. Ibid.

duration. So by maintaining a Stay Big level of excess reserves, the Fed continues to use its balance sheet to stimulate demand for longer-duration assets, dragging down the level of long-term rates.

Consider the reserve. At some point the Fed might want to see higher long-term interest rates or a steeper yield curve. How would Stay Big enhance the Fed's ability to influence long-term rates *regardless of sign*? How would a high level of excess reserves help the Fed *increase* long-term interest rates?

You can also think of this by analogy to Gresham's Law that "bad money drives out good money." In this case, the super-abundance of the "bad money" of zero-duration central bank liabilities leads to the hoarding of positive-duration "good money" of central government liabilities, pulling down the level of long-term interest rates.[10]

Thus, maintaining a large balance sheet is likely to cause the yield curve to be flatter than it otherwise would be.

Perhaps the Fed is happy with the current, almost flat yield curve.[11] In that case, perhaps it intends to hold down the level of long-term rates. If so, the Fed should explain that maintaining a high level of excess reserves is an ongoing policy choice aimed at compressing the term premium from what it would otherwise be.

The Effectiveness of QE "Next Time"

A Stay Big level of excess reserves will be likely to reduce the effectiveness of any future use of QE.

As noted, I am skeptical that QE2 and QE3 stimulated aggregate demand in the economy. I may be wrong. More importantly, former chair Yellen took the position that any and all of the extraordinary actions the Fed took, including specifically QE, should be and will

---

10. For an extended discussion of the analogy to Gresham's Law, see Peter R. Fisher, "What is Money and Who Says So?" remarks at SUERF/Bank of Finland Conference, Helsinki, July 3, 2015, *SUERF Policy Note*, no. 1 (September 2015).

11. "10-Year Treasury Constant Maturity Minus 2-Year Treasury Constant Maturity," FRED Economic Data, Federal Reserve Bank of St. Louis, June 26, 2018.

be available to the Fed to use in the next downturn—particularly if the Fed is again constrained by the effective lower boundary of interest rates.[12]

But if the Fed does choose to Stay Big, then "next time" it will be starting with an enlarged balance sheet and already high levels of excess reserves.

Having already provided the banking system with a super-abundance of excess reserves, it seems unlikely that adding to that super-abundance will have the same impact of encouraging market participants to shift into longer-duration and riskier credit assets.

There is a debate about whether—in monetary policy and in markets—it is the stocks or the flows that matter. For both purposes, it seems to me that what matters most are changes in expectations. So it is the changes in expected stocks or the changes in expected flows—whatever moves you—that will influence market participants to change the prices of financial assets.

In order to create a comparable sense of "shock and awe" in its impact on market expectations and the level of long-term interest rates, it seems likely that the Fed would feel the need to act bigger, to try to expand its balance sheet even more rapidly.

Already holding a large share of US Treasury securities will likely complicate the execution of further substantial purchases. At its peak, implementation of QE2 and QE3 involved the purchase of $85 billion worth of government and agency securities per month, a number that was targeted on the theory that more rapid purchases would be likely to impair the functioning of the government securities market.[13] By maintaining large holdings of Treasury securities, by starting with a bigger balance sheet, the Fed would be likely to hit these "speed limits" more rapidly, reducing

---

12. Yellen, "The Federal Reserve's Monetary Policy Toolkit." Current Fed Chairman Jerome Powell does not appear to have addressed the question of QE next time as explicitly as former chair Yellen.

13. See transcript of Federal Open Market Committee, July 31–August 1, 2012, remarks of Simon Potter, manager, System Open Market Account, p. 43.

the potential efficacy of QE next time compared to whatever it might have been the first time or would be in the event that the Fed started with a smaller balance sheet and a smaller share of Treasury securities already on its balance sheet.[14]

The Fed should explain whether, in its view, a Stay Big level of excess reserves and bond portfolio will enhance the effectiveness of any use of QE in the future and, if so, how.

Impact on Short-term Funding Market.

Stay Big will also be likely to impede the efficient allocation of reserve balances within the banking system via price signals. In the current environment, banks have much less incentive to manage their own funding positions and to trade fed funds with one another. While this may not impede the ability of the Fed to communicate about the expected path of short-term interest rates, it will make short-term funding markets less efficient.

By impeding a market allocation of funds in normal times, Stay Big will make it less likely that price signals can serve as a warning sign of financial stress at individual firms. In the past, the relative scarcity of reserve balances and the need for banks to actively manage their balances with the Fed have provided both market participants and the Fed with a source of information about the willingness of banks to lend reserve balances to one another, as reflected in the premium that individual banks may have to pay.

The market for repurchase agreements in government securities does not provide the same information because of the secured nature of these transactions. The market for single-name credit

---

14. Perhaps the advent of the Trump deficits, caused by the tax cuts enacted by Congress in 2017, will expand the supply of Treasury securities sufficiently to make this less of a worry.

default swaps might provide this information but might also be considered untrustworthy.[15]

Given uncertainty about the transition from normal times to times of financial stress, I think it is likely that "next time" market-based price signals about the credit standing of individual firms will be missed.

Possibility of Losses on Bond Holdings

With an enlarged portfolio of bonds, the Fed faces the increased probability of potentially large losses in the event of an appreciable increase in interest rates.[16] Just as the Fed routinely passes on its income from its large asset holdings to the US Treasury, any decline in this income would contribute to wider fiscal deficits. If losses were significant, in extremis, the Treasury would confront whether and how to address any impairment of the Fed's balance sheet. This is really a matter of fiscal policy, not monetary policy, but one that might generate a legislative response that could threaten the Fed's independence.

Having implemented QE, the Fed has indeed moved into the "fiscal space" and, as already noted, is now dependent on both Congress and the executive branch to tolerate the Fed's use of quasi-fiscal powers. This issue is much broader and more significant than the potential for losses to impair the flow of income to the US Treasury. This is only one way that Congress might become interested in the use of the Fed's balance sheet for fiscal purposes.[17]

---

15. See "Statement on Manufactured Credit Events by CFTC Divisions of Clearing and Risk, Market Oversight, and Swap Dealer and Intermediary Oversight," US Commodity Futures Trading Commission, April 24, 2018.

16. See Christopher A. Sims, "Fiscal Policy, Monetary Policy, and Central Bank Independence," remarks at Federal Reserve Bank of Kansas City Economic Symposium, Jackson Hole, WY, August 26, 2016.

17. See Charles I. Plosser, "The Risks of a Fed Balance Sheet Unconstrained by Monetary Policy," paper prepared for the Hoover Institution Conference on the Structural Foundations

THE BENEFITS OF STAY BIG ARE SKETCHY

Enhanced Financial Stability

It has been argued that maintaining a high level of excess reserves will help prevent excessive maturity transformation and unnecessary private money creation which, in turn, will make the financial system more stable and less prone to crisis.[18] By satisfying more of the market's demand for money with Federal Reserve liabilities, it is reasoned, there will be less demand for private money creation.

Assuming that this is so, how would it work? How would maintaining a high level of excess reserves prevent banks from engaging in maturity transformation and private money creation?

To accomplish this, banks would need to hold such a high level of zero-duration, excess reserve assets that they would be unable to create other, longer-duration credit assets of their own in the form of loans that they would write. To constrain their ability to engage in maturity transformation, between their deposit liabilities and their assets, the level of Fed liabilities would need to be so high as to be an effective constraint on the mismatch that the banking system as a whole incurs between the average duration of bank assets and the average duration of bank liabilities.

If the Stay Big super-abundance of excess reserves were to be so large as to constrain maturity transformation and the creation of private money, so large as to crowd out the ability of banks to create loans and money-like substitutes, then it would be a restrictive

---

of Monetary Policy, Economics Working Paper no. 17102, Stanford University, Palo Alto, CA, May 4, 2017.

18. See Robin Greenwood, Samuel G. Hanson, and Jeremy C. Stein, "The Federal Reserve Balance Sheet as a Financial Stability Tool," paper prepared for the Federal Reserve Bank of Kansas City Symposium, Jackson Hole, WY, September 2016, cited approvingly by Ben S. Bernanke, "Should the Fed Keep Its Balance Sheet Large?" blog, Brookings Institution, September 2, 2016; also see Bernanke, "Shrinking the Fed's Balance Sheet," blog, Brookings Institution, January 26, 2017.

monetary policy. It would prevent the normal operations of the credit channel and suppress credit creation.

If a large balance sheet is how the Fed intends to stimulate the economy—the E in QE stands for "easing," after all—the apparent benefit of using high levels of excess reserves to prevent maturity transformation would have the opposite effect. Which is it: Is a large balance sheet an easy monetary policy or a tight one?

An enlarged central bank balance sheet might be neither an effective way to stimulate nor an effective way to restrict maturity transformation and the creation of credit and private money. But it seems unlikely that it could simultaneously be both. This "benefit" of Stay Big appears to be especially sketchy.

Reduced Financial Stress and Stigma

A Stay Big super-abundance of excess reserves could reduce the likelihood of financial stress and the potential stigma, or reluctance, of banks to borrow reserves from the Fed when needed.[19]

If the Fed permanently smothers the short end of the yield curve with a quantity of reserves well in excess of the plausible, normal operating needs of the banking system, banks would, indeed, be less likely to find themselves "short" of reserve balances. In effect, Stay Big would "pre-fund" liquidity to those institutions that hold accounts at the Fed. However, we have normally thought of liquidity provision by the central bank, particularly in the lender-of-last-resort context, as a way to *alleviate* financial stress. How would Stay Big prevent financial stress in the first instance?

A super-abundance of reserves might make it difficult for the banking system to be both illiquid and highly leveraged at the same time. Banks might still operate principally on the borrowed liabilities of their deposits and other short-term funding. But by forcing

---

19. Bernanke, "Should the Fed Keep Its Balance Sheet Large?"

banks to hold high levels of reserve balances on the asset sides of
their balance sheets, banks could more readily meet withdrawals of
their deposits and reduce the risk of bank runs and panics. In this
sense, a high level of excess reserves might operate as a minimum
liquidity requirement for the banking system as a whole.

But this seems unlikely to act as a binding constraint on individual banks. It would also not have an impact on nonbank financial
firms that lack accounts with the Fed.

An individual bank might still sell its fed funds to other banks.
While a given bank's own regulatory liquidity requirements would
be a binding constraint, the total supply of reserves would not.
So individual banks would still be able to be both illiquid—up to
the point of their liquidity requirements—and highly leveraged.
Moreover, the absence of a deep and robust funds market, operating on price signals, would likely make it more difficult for an
individual bank in need to purchase fed funds when desired.

Also, to the extent that Stay Big helps make the banking system
more liquid and, thereby, less likely to be both highly leveraged and
illiquid at the same time, this would only apply to banks that hold
accounts at the Federal Reserve. This would do nothing to prevent firms in the nonbank financial sector—the notorious shadow
banks—or firms in the corporate sector from being both highly
leveraged and illiquid.

This would suggest that "next time" it is more likely that financial stress will emerge outside the banking system than within it.
This would make it (even) more likely that, in the event of financial
stress next time, the Federal Reserve will be called upon to consider
using its powers to lend to nonbanks under Section 13(3) of the
Federal Reserve Act.

Overwhelming the fed funds market and impairing the efficient
allocation of reserves via price signals within the banking system
have the "benefit" of reducing, somewhat, the likelihood that individual banks end up "short" of funds. But whether and how this

might actually reduce the likelihood of stress in the financial system remains to be explained.

IMPROVED "TRANSMISSION MECHANISM"

It has also been suggested that a larger balance sheet that incorporates the Fed's reverse repurchase program (RRP) could improve the transmission of the Fed's intended level of short-term interest rates to other markets more effectively.[20]

While this may be so, it conflates the size of the Fed's balance sheet with the number and type of the counterparties with whom the Fed acts. The Fed could have an expanded set of counterparties, beyond the banks and primary dealers with whom it dealt in the past, but still seek to influence overnight rates "at the margin" rather than by re-pricing most or all of the enlarged stock of reserves.

The RRP program was designed to help the Fed mop up the super-abundance of excess reserves.[21] Given that the Fed has a super-abundance of excess reserves, the RRP tool is certainly a useful means of coping. But this is an unpersuasive rationale for maintaining any particular level of excess reserves.

It is important to note that this claim is only about the "transmission mechanism" of monetary policy to other short-term interest rates. I was unaware that anyone thought that this was an especially important constraint on the Fed's effectiveness—other than in the conditions of extraordinarily high levels of excess reserves. The argument that the Fed can better cope with an enlarged balance sheet is not a compelling rationale for maintaining a large balance sheet.

---

20. Darrell Duffie and Arvind Krishnamurthy, "Passthrough Efficiency in the Fed's New Monetary Policy Setting," paper presented at the Federal Reserve Bank of Kansas City Symposium, Jackson Hole, WY, September 2016, cited approvingly by Bernanke, "Should the Fed Keep Its Balance Sheet Large?"

21. Ben S. Bernanke, statement prepared for the Committee on Financial Services, US House of Representatives, February 10, 2010, p. 7.

But even if one does consider the transmission of the Fed's policy impulse among short-term rates to be important (other than specifically to address the problem of high levels of excess reserves), one would still want to consider the trade-off between maintaining a Stay Big level of excess reserves for purposes of more effectively transmitting the Fed's signals to other short-term rates against the cost of diminished influence over the level of long-term rates and the shape of the yield curve.

WHAT'S GOING ON?

There are only three tools of monetary policy that matter: (a) the size and composition of the central bank's balance sheet; (b) the price of the central bank's liabilities; and (c) expectations about (a) and (b).

Quantitative easing was justified by the theory that, even at the effective lower boundary of the price of the Fed's liabilities, expectations about the size and composition of the Fed's balance sheet would lower long-term interest rates and stimulate private credit growth and aggregate demand. But keeping the Fed's balance sheet large is now being justified by the theory that doing so will help the Fed reduce volatility in the price of its liabilities, prevent banks from creating too much credit, and reduce the need for banks to manage the liquidity of their asset portfolios.

Maybe these are all "good" things, but they seem more like a sideshow than the main event.

It is possible to imagine that monetary policy can work without the credit channel. We can imagine that somehow expectations about interest rates will operate directly upon our propensities to consume, to invest, and to save without involving the business of dis-saving and private credit and money creation. But even if we can imagine this, it is unlikely that private credit creation will cease to exist. The credit channel will still be out there.

Accepting the economic benefits of the credit channel when it is convenient but ignoring the credit channel when it is inconvenient is a mistake that the Fed could usefully avoid.[22]

You may not agree with my assessment of the costs and benefits of Stay Big. But I hope you will ponder whether maintaining a large balance sheet and a super abundance of excess reserves enhances or impedes the transmission mechanism to aggregate demand that we actually have today rather than some other transmission mechanism of your imagination.

If it is nostalgic to expect that the Fed should be able to explain the benefits of keeping its balance sheet large in terms consistent with how it has explained the transmission mechanism of monetary policy for the last ten years, then call me nostalgic. It seems more than a mere oversight for the Fed *not* to address how Stay Big might affect long-term interest rates, the credit channel, and aggregate demand in the same terms that were used to justify QE in the first place.

---

22. See Peter R. Fisher, "Financial Stability and the Hemianopsia of Monetary Policy," *Business Economics* 51, no. 2 (2016): 68ff.

GENERAL DISCUSSION

KEVIN WARSH: Lorie, you must be saying, "Why did I sign up for this? Why did I come to Hoover?" [Laughter] Our fellow panelists did not come to bury the Fed, but to praise it. So, let's give you an opportunity to respond to a set of issues that were raised.

Allow me to frame the question. Randy Quarles rightly said that the Fed has an unenviable task of trying to make monetary policy and regulatory policy at the same time with an existing mix of tools. So, first, is the asset side of the balance sheet going to determine the new equilibrium for the size of the Fed balance sheet? Or will the liability side? That is, will it be driven by the Fed's decision on optimal monetary policy? Or will the ultimate size of the Fed's balance sheet be dictated by the optimal amount of reserves demanded by the banks to satisfy regulatory standards?

And second, if the Fed decided to keep larger levels of excess reserves, need they be of the same average duration as the assets currently held on the Fed's balance sheet?

LORIE LOGAN: Well, let me touch on a couple of things. I'm just first going to go back to Mickey's presentation. I think in the $2.2 trillion that you had, and why you came up with such a high number of excess reserves, is because you were taking out the other noncurrency, nonreserve liabilities. So, one of the points I wanted to make here is that people often forget about the other, nonreserve liabilities on the balance sheet that are there. And as I said, if you look at them currently, they make up about $700 billion. So, I don't think when you cited those numbers that it was that high for excess reserves.

And then the other point I would make is on the mortgage-backed securities caps. If interest rates were to follow the current market path, even if the FOMC were to raise the caps, it wouldn't change the pace of the runoff, because toward the end of the year the prepays are going to come in well below the cap that we have at the maximum level. So, at that point, the only reason that we would end up reinvesting is if the prepayments come in above the cap, which would likely happen if there was a big shock and interest rates were really to fall. So, I don't think a change in the caps to a higher level would necessarily change the pace of that runoff.

I think there's this larger question about mixing the asset side with the monetary policy framework in the conversation on the panel. As I said, we're going to be moving into a liability-driven size of the portfolio. The size of the portfolio will be driven by the liability side, not the asset side. And you can really think about the asset side in a variety of ways. And some of the concerns about being in a floor system with having some abundant reserves was, well, you'll be starting from a higher level. I think you could structure that asset side with a large proportion of Treasury bills, for example. It doesn't need to be in a portfolio that looks so long-term. So, you would still have the same sort of interest rate risk that you could take if you restructured the asset side of the portfolio. I don't think that that's a limiting factor, and it would also, of course, change your influence that you're having in financial markets.

One of the things I guess I struggled with in the conversation was the price signal. Maybe I just need to talk through that a little bit more. But when I think about the price signal in the old regime that we had pre-crisis, individual bank rates, they could move. It could be because of credit, but it could also mean they just got a payment shock late in the day. And so I think actually, in the other system, the price signal was really confused, because you couldn't tell the difference, necessarily, between those two. And I think during the crisis, we discovered that that price signal didn't turn out to be very useful. The system that we are in now, if that were to happen, it clearly wouldn't be because of the late-day payment shock, it would be because there was a credit issue with a particular bank. So, maybe I wasn't following the full price signal argument Peter made. But I think the current framework is better in that sense.

And another point that I would make is this large role in the financial markets with the floor system. I guess I'd want to talk more about that too. I agree that we have an abundant supply of reserves, and I don't think to run the floor system we need anywhere near the level of excess reserves that we have now. I think that number can come down quite a bit. And I think that we're doing that with an open market operation, the overnight RRP facility that's enhancing competition in money markets with very little usage. I think last month we might have had a day where it was one and a half billion dollars only. So, I think that that facility being there is not necessarily having a big impact. It's just enhancing competition in money markets, which is a good thing.

I would just go back to the main point I wanted to draw out today, which is I think that we can implement in either a floor or a corridor system. And I think there is a whole variety of corridor-type systems. It's simplified by just talking about the version that we used pre-crisis, and I don't think this should be surprising, because the committee had undergone a fairly extensive set of work before the crisis to relook at the system and explored a variety of corridor-type regimes. One was the voluntary reserve requirements. But there are a whole host of others that could be considered.

One might improve some of the concerns we had with the pre-crisis system. You know, it had this liquidity tax on reserves, it was not very transparent, it was fairly complex, and there were a lot of times when there were fairly discretionary open market operations that were required. So, I agree we could return to a corridor system. My main point was that if we were going to return to a corridor system, doing so would probably look different than the one we used, but there are some other ones that we certainly could turn to.

KEVIN WARSH: Thank you, Lorie. Let's turn next to you, Bill. Our audience should know that Bill was in the heart of the beast in the darkest days of the crisis. He overlapped with a couple of us on this panel and was among the designers of the Fed's extraordinary crisis-response facilities. Bill, you've done an exceptional job on this panel atoning for your past sins. [Laughter]

A couple of questions. First, you indicated, in some sense, you were concerned that short-term securities that were issued by the Treasury market might be quasi-substitutes for the Fed's excess reserves. I query whether there could be crowding out or competition among similar situated risk-free securities. Perhaps you could speak to that in addition to responding to other issues raised by our fellow panelists.

WILLIAM NELSON: Happy to. And I don't want to take any incorrect credit for the QE programs. [Laughter] I was the 13(3) facilities all the way. Lorie would be on me in a minute if I tried to take credit for QE.

The point that I was making and discussing with Vice Chairman Quarles was that liquidity regulations are designed so that institutions can hold reserves or can hold Treasuries. And if you want to return to a small Federal Reserve with a smaller balance sheet, with a low quantity of excess reserves, that option needs to be there if you want to have liquidity requirements. So that substitutability within the requirements is very important.

And I was trying to make the case—and I may be alone here—in thinking that if the interest rate on excess reserves was actually 50 to 100 basis points below the fed funds rate, so something back towards a classic, pre-crisis kind of configuration, that banks would actually go a long way to getting their excess reserve holdings down, much more than the forecast in the New

York Fed's survey, or what's being used in their models, because they would have a number of levers that they can turn to do so.

It could, as Lorie and I have discussed, be quite stressful in markets to get there. Like everything in policy design, gradualism, I think, would be very important. This would be something which would have to take place slowly. And as reserves got scarcer and scarcer, you could get banks to substitute, I believe. But not all at once. However, if it's required that banks have to hold a material part of their HQLA as reserves, then you're going to have a big balance sheet. There's no way around it. Only the Fed can provide those reserves. It can only provide those reserves by holding a large portfolio of securities.

KEVIN WARSH: Mickey, the Fed appears somewhat lonely in its belief that quantitative easing has had no material effect on asset prices, which I always found to be a striking judgment at odds with most market participants. I also heard you say that the Fed is overstating the effects of its large balance sheet on the real side of the economy. Please expand on these points, if you would.

MICKEY LEVY: Well, sure. First, I was thinking about Lorie's responses. Look, I have absolutely all the confidence in the New York Fed. The work it did on the overnight reverse repo market and the research you did in rolling it out just show how good and efficient it is. But the broader macroeconomic question is: What's the most efficient way for the Fed to achieve and pursue and maintain its dual mandate? And do you need that broader financial market footprint? Do you need the size of the balance sheet?

Kevin, regarding your question, it just seems clear to me QE3 did not work to stimulate the economy as planned. Going back to when Chairman Bernanke rolled out QE3 and forward guidance, he described the portfolio balance effect in which the Fed would pump a ton of money into the financial system, convince markets that interest rates would stay low, encourage risk taking, and push up asset prices, and all that would stimulate aggregate demand. Everything worked to stimulate financial markets—bond yields stayed low, the stock market and home prices rose—but if you look at what actually happened in the next four years, nominal GDP growth, the broadest measure of current dollar spending, did not accelerate. Certainly, the unemployment rate fell. But if you went back to mid-2012 and ran simulations of the Fed's macro model based on the actual QE3, lower interest rates, and the actual lower real cost of capital, and the modest increase in the real cost of labor, the results would have been a significant acceleration in economic growth with booming capital spending and relatively weak employment growth. The opposite happened. Once again, the Fed affects the unemployment rate through real economic activity, which didn't respond. I completely agree with Peter. QE1 really helped. But I think we need to do more research on why QE3 really didn't work.

Let me just add one other point on empirical studies of the effects of Fed policy announcements. I think we have to take the economic impacts of the empirical findings with a grain of salt because they tend to be short-run effects with questionable impacts on the economy. The best example is the "taper tantrum": ten-year bond yields rose surprisingly 100 basis points, which definitely affected the Fed's subsequent conduct of monetary policy but didn't have any impact on GDP growth.

KEVIN WARSH: Peter, let's turn to you for the final word in this segment of our discussion before we take a couple questions from the audience. Peter, the most intriguing part of your remarks centered on the role and responsibility of the Federal Reserve. And to paraphrase you with some license: we central bankers are not fiscal policy makers with tenure. We have a fundamentally different role. I'll give you the last word before we turn to the audience.

PETER FISHER: Well, I certainly agree with that, and I think we've had that theme all day, from the get-go this morning of Raghu

Rajan trying to get us to think about how we're going to contain monetary policy in a somewhat smaller box.

But I also want to note that the Fed's mandate is not just to manage aggregate demand. Section 2A of the Federal Reserve Act is not a Phillips curve-only mandate, whatever the FOMC says; go read Section 2A for yourselves. Providing an elastic currency is a necessary means of ensuring that the monetary and credit aggregates don't contract too quickly. We do need to figure out how to manage the discount window, how to do the elastic currency thing without stigma, but I don't think flooding the system with excess reserves is the best means of doing that.

KEVIN WARSH: So, we're going to take a couple questions from the audience. I see John Cochrane, our fearless leader. His name was invoked, so he gets the first question.

JOHN COCHRANE: Thanks. In 1970, Milton Friedman propounded the optimal quantity of money, which in our current circumstance would be that the Fed pays interest on reserves and floods the market with reserves. Why is that optimal? Well, money is to the economy like oil in a car. It's better to drive a car with the oil full, not to starve it of oil in order to slow it down. Now, Friedman didn't take that prediction seriously, because the Fed would lose control of the price level at zero interest or if it allowed money to pay interest so money becomes a perfect substitute for bonds. We need MV=PY. Friedman didn't know about John Taylor, who taught us that by changing interest rates, the Fed can maintain price-level control and give us the optimal quantity of money. In 2008, the Fed tried the experiment, flooding the economy with interest-paying reserves, and lo and behold, it works! You *can* flood the economy with interest-bearing reserves and retain price-level control. We learned something over these years.

That seems to me like a strong argument for maintaining a large balance sheet. Why not? Yes, we may not like the kinds of assets the Fed buys in order to issue reserves. Fine, let them buy short-term Treasuries. Better yet, let the Treasury issue more short-term debt—ideally, fixed-value floating rate debt.

Other than that, all I've heard is nostalgia. The good old days were kind of nice, but we've learned something. Monetary policy advances. So, I think, the lesson of theory and experience is now pretty clear: keep the large quantity of interest-paying reserves. The asset side can be an all-Treasury short-dated balance sheet. Let's live the optimal quantity of money!

PETER FISHER: I want you to go visit Japan, where the central bank is flooding the system with reserves and hoarding duration and other assets. You can crush the credit channel. You may like what it does to your model of the economy, that we can have fewer Greek letters and not have to worry about modeling a financial system, but I just don't think it actually will help us manage the economy going forward. We can imagine that we want to go to a place where the only financial intermediation is done by the central bank, and that central bank money is the only money we use, but I don't think that is either necessary or desirable.

ANDREW LEVIN: This question is for Lorie Logan, although maybe Bill Nelson can also weigh in. You showed a chart of balance sheet projections with alternative trajectories—the same chart that Vice Chair Quarles showed earlier. The first decision point or "kink" is only six months away, the second kink is about eighteen months away, and the third kink is a bit further off. So, it seems like there should be some sense of urgency in addressing the questions that have been raised this afternoon. Market participants need to be able to anticipate what's coming so that the process isn't disruptive. That means that there isn't necessarily much more time to clarify the Fed's "new normal" for the balance sheet, especially given Bill's concern that moving soon would foreclose some other options.

LORIE LOGAN: I think with the chart, we do have more than six months, if that larger projection were to hold. So, I think there is time. We're monitoring a whole variety of factors in money markets to understand whether we're getting anywhere close to showing some signs of scarcity, and I don't think we're seeing anything in those.

I think the point is that we don't know, and I think those projections were just dealer estimates. So, the broader point is we have to be watching for signs of scarcity, and I think we have a variety of measures, and we aren't seeing any signs of that. So, I think there's still time for the committee to continue to learn by monitoring what's happening in money markets today.

KEVIN WARSH: I want to just thank my fellow panelists. The robustness of the discussion inside the Fed system is, we should hope, no less robust than the discussion we just completed. We especially appreciate Lorie's attendance, because she is compelled to implement the decisions of the board and the FOMC.

··

PART III

CHAPTER TWELVE

ANCHORING INFLATION EXPECTATIONS IN A LOW R-STAR WORLD

John C. Williams

First I want to thank both John Taylor and John Cochrane for inviting me to this event. I did make a bit of a trade. I said that I'd like to have invitations every year for the next ten years while I'm in New York. That gives me a good excuse to come back to Stanford and enjoy not only what is always a great conference but, of course, the amazing Stanford campus. I'm going to miss it and California very much when I'm in New York.

In his introduction, John Taylor mentioned that when I was a graduate student at Stanford, I worked on his multicountry model, which required solving a seven-country, 115-equation rational expectations model. It was very cutting-edge at the time, and it gives me some street cred with the young economists today. When we're interviewing a freshly minted PhD who says, "Oh, I'm working on a very elaborate way of solving a nonlinear model," or something like that, I say, "We were working on nonlinear models with rational expectations nearly thirty years ago." But then I mention we did it in Fortran, and some of that newfound credibility slips away.

One of the reasons the annual Hoover conference is so good is because it brings together policy makers, academics, and people in the private sector to think about the most important long-term issues. Secretary Shultz highlighted this aspect in his comments, as did John in his comments: that this is a way to get away from the day-to-day debates about the ups and downs of the economy or the markets and really think about the fundamental issues regarding monetary and other policies. We've seen a lot of active discussion already this morning.

Before I go any further, I need to give the standard Fed disclaimer. Given my upcoming transition between jobs, this seems a particularly important time to say this: everything I say reflects my own views, not necessarily the views of the New York Fed, the San Francisco Fed, or any other Fed at all!

I will focus on a narrow question regarding monetary policy strategy. We talked about a lot of really big questions this morning and we're going to talk this afternoon about another important monetary policy question: namely, the operational framework of monetary policy. But I'm going to look at monetary policy framework in terms of its overarching strategy. And I'm going to focus even more narrowly on these questions: How do we best achieve price stability and anchor expectations in the future? What are the implications of some changes in the global economic environment that are going to make achieving those goals more challenging? And finally, what are some of the options that policy makers need to be considering in order to achieve price stability and strong anchored inflation expectations in the future?

Throughout my comments, I will be thinking of this issue in terms of a long-run monetary policy strategy or framework, not about what needs to be done at the next meeting or next year or next two years.

If you go back in time to the 1980s, when the current inflation-targeting framework and similar approaches were developed and put into place, it was in the context of very high and variable inflation across the world. The focus of those strategies was to bring inflation down and create stable, well-anchored inflation and inflation expectations. This focus was completely understandable given the context of the times.

Today, we face a very different set of issues stemming from very low levels of interest rates not only in the United States but around the globe. Crucially, these low rates are not merely a reflection of cyclical monetary policy actions but also reflect longer-term factors that affect interest rates globally.

The outline of my talk is to discuss why interest rates are so low, how I see them moving ahead in the future, what kind of challenges that brings to price stability and anchoring expectations, and, finally, what sort of policy options exist for a persistently low-rate environment.

I'll cover the past, present, and future of the neutral interest rate, often referred to as r-star. This is the neutral real interest rate, that is, the short-term real interest rate that's consistent with an economy growing at its trend rate, consistent with price stability and constant low inflation. If you asked me what the equilibrium neutral real interest rate in the United States was twenty-five years ago, I would have said something like 2 or 2½ percent. In fact, in John Taylor's famous policy rule, 2 percent is the assumed level of the neutral real interest rate.

Such estimates of the neutral rate were reasonable given historical averages over the post-World War II period through the 1990s. However, in the past twenty years or so there has been a clear downward trend in real interest rates, not only in the United States but in many advanced economies.

In thinking about the neutral interest rate, one needs to distinguish cyclical and transitory factors from structural, longer-term factors. After all, we experienced the worst recession and global financial crisis of our lifetimes, and that has been an important cause of low interest rates. But there's been a great deal of research that finds longer-term factors also play a significant role in explaining why rates have been so low.

Admittedly, there's a lot of uncertainty around estimates of the neutral rate. But if you compare today to twenty years ago, a typical estimate of a neutral real interest rate in the United States is between 0 and 1 percent, instead of 2 to 2½ percent twenty years ago. We've seen similarly large declines in estimates of the neutral interest rate in other advanced economies as well.

Research has identified three big drivers of why real interest rates have been declining for decades. One is demographics. In general, people are living longer around the globe, which typically generates an increase in savings. Another is productivity growth, which has slowed not only in the United States but also around the world. This productivity slowdown reduces the demand for investment. Now, I'm sure there will be questions about measurement issues, but I would point to the research by my colleague John Fernald, who finds that these issues cannot explain the productivity slowdown. The third factor is the heightened demand for safe assets, a topic that was discussed this morning. This has created a wedge between yields on safe government securities or central bank reserves and yields on riskier assets like corporate bonds or equities. This pushes down yields on safe assets like the federal funds rate. These three trends have been occurring for the past couple of decades and together account for the significant decline in the neutral rate we've seen.

In summary, we have seen the neutral interest rate decline from between 2 and 2½ percent to somewhere between 0 and 1 percent. The big question is: Will we see the neutral rate rise back to levels of the past? Or is the downward trend of the past two decades going to continue because of ongoing changes related to demographics? Or is the future likely to look similar to today?

I usually quote Yogi Berra about not wanting to make forecasts, especially about the future. But in this case, although it is very difficult to see into the future, I do want to highlight a few issues that shape my thinking about the likely future course of r-star.

The first driver is demographics. Those are baked in the cake in the sense that we do have a pretty good ability to forecast demographics in terms of living longer and the slower population growth we've been seeing around the world. So, I don't see hope of a reversal in r-star coming from demographics.

In terms of productivity, that's a harder one. Experts are actively debating whether productivity growth in the last decade or fifteen years of about 1 to 1¼ percent represents a "new normal." That is, periods of 2 to 3 percent productivity growth like we saw in the late 1990s and early 2000s are the outliers. Of course, I live in a region where everyone feels the world is being reinvented every week. And that has led some commentators to predict that we're going to see this huge surge of productivity down the road. Obviously, that could be true. But so far, we haven't seen that, not at all. So far, at least, productivity trends in the United States and around the world are consistent with steady, incremental increases in productivity, not the big surge that some people are hoping for.

The third factor is the demand for safe assets. And this is the one where there is greater uncertainty about how it will go in the future. There's some evidence that the demand for safe assets may be receding a bit, but it has not gone back to historical levels.

Two other considerations also come into play in thinking about the likely future of r-star. The first is fiscal policy. A common question today is whether the recent tax cuts and the spending increases in the United States will push up the neutral rate of interest. The analysis I've seen argues that they may well boost the neutral interest rate, but by no more than a quarter percentage point or so. One reason for this relatively modest effect on r-star is that a lot of the effects of the tax cuts and the spending bill are front-loaded. If you look ahead to five to ten years from now, some key provisions expire and, as a result, the longer-term effect on r-star is muted.

The second is the effects of the changing size of central bank balance sheets. Currently, the Fed owns over $4 trillion of assets. We're in the process of normalizing, that is, reducing our balance sheet. It's going to take a few years to get to the new normal. Arguably, purchases of assets by the Fed and other central banks boosted economic growth, raising r-star for the time being. As this stimulus is removed, this positive effect on the neutral rate will diminish and r-star may decline.

I don't pretend to have a crystal ball. R-star could move back closer to more historical levels or it could continue to trend down. My best guess is that what we're seeing today—longer-term neutral interest rate or r-star of between 0 and 1 percent—is likely to be with us for the foreseeable future.

I will now turn to some uncomfortable implications of a very low neutral interest rate. The standard argument is that, with a low neutral rate, when the next recession hits we can't lower interest rates, we can't stimulate the economy as much as we would like. And that's absolutely true. But I want to stress another aspect of a low neutral rate—the challenge it creates to anchoring inflation expectations and consistently achieving a desired inflation rate.

When the next recession happens, which will happen someday, if we start with an interest rate of, say, 3 percent, we don't have as much room to cut interest rates to stimulate the economy and get inflation back to its target level. This would be true in most advanced economies, because they are all experiencing this low neutral interest rate.

What does this mean in terms of inflation expectations and price stability? In a recent paper coauthored with my colleague, Thomas Mertens, we examined this issue. Let me give a concrete example. Say that 80 percent of the time, the Fed can hit its 2 percent goal on average, everything is good, no zero lower bound, no constraints on policy, we're okay. But then, say, 20 percent of the time, the economy falls into a recession that's severe enough that the central bank cannot achieve its goals as effectively owing to the lower bound on interest rates. As a result, there is a period of inflation below the 2 percent target. This, of course, is exactly the situation the Fed and other central banks have faced the past seven or eight years.

If you think about that, 80 percent of the time you're at 2 percent and 20 percent of the time, you're at, say, 1 percent inflation. Averaging over the two periods, inflation will be 1.8 percent over the long run. You're 2 percent when things are good, but you're at 1 percent when things are bad. There's an explicit asymmetry as a result of the lower bound. As a result, inflation expectations could become anchored at 1.8 percent, below the desired 2 percent target.

There's a secondary effect of this downward bias to inflation expectations and that is the spillover from expectations back to the present. Even in good times when the current inflation rate is 2 percent, people will still expect that future inflation will average 1.8 percent, and that will affect their decisions today, exacerbating the downward bias to inflation. In other words, you're always swimming upstream, fighting a current of too-low inflation expectations.

In fact, in our model, if the neutral interest rate is low enough, there is no equilibrium inflation rate in the model. The point is that the expectation of possible future constraints on monetary policy affects the ability to achieve the inflation target, even at times when policy is not constrained by the lower bound.

The debate about monetary policy frameworks aims to tackle these problems associated with the lower bound on interest rates. There are three main policy options in terms of thinking about long-run strategy. One is the status quo of inflation targeting, relying mostly on conventional monetary policy and accepting any resulting deterioration in macroeconomic outcomes resulting from the lower bound.

The second is to aggressively follow the same playbook that the Fed and other central banks wrote over the past decade—a combination of rapid rate cuts, large-scale QE (quantitative easing), and strong forward guidance. Some people would argue we've gotten through the last ten years reasonably well, especially given how bad the crises and recession were. In less severe recessions, this recipe may be sufficient to counter the effects of the lower bound.

The third is to think hard about how we can best achieve price stability and maximum employment even in the presence of severe downturns. And that means contemplating a somewhat different regime than inflation targeting. You can call it price-level targeting, or temporary price-level targeting in Ben Bernanke's proposal, nominal GDP-level targeting, or average inflation targeting that basically says our goal is to have inflation average 2 percent over a ten-year span.

It is easy to get caught up in the details of these various proposals—and they're important. But the critical common element of these proposals is that they are designed to attain well-anchored inflation expectations, with the anchor set at the target rate.

What is my view? Well, I gave a talk at the Shadow Open Market Committee some time ago, so I will repeat what I said there. Price-level targeting and its variants have some significant benefits over inflation targeting, especially in the context of the lower bound. For example, if you put a price-level target into a standard Taylor rule, you can potentially achieve better anchoring of inflation expectations and price stability. And this is in no way a radical departure from inflation targeting or the original Taylor rule.

I want to come back to the themes of these conferences the past several years that I've attended. These meetings have emphasized the importance of thinking about policy issues in terms of a long-run, coherent, systematic strategy. One should not think about whether price-level targeting or nominal GDP targeting or any of these alternative approaches is a way to fix a problem that we're in today or deal with a short-run situation. Instead, these are best analyzed and debated with a long-run perspective focused on how we can best achieve our policy goals.

Academics, policy makers, and others from here and around the world all have an important part to play in that discussion, sharing ideas, debating them, and comparing experiences to help think through these issues. It's also essential to think that we're really trying to solve the same problem that the academics and the policy makers of the 1970s and '80s were addressing, which was how to anchor inflation expectations and attain price stability, both of which are essential to successful monetary policy. What is unique this time is that the problem is inflation that is too low, not too high as in the past.

The last thing that I would say is that, even if you're not convinced that the neutral interest rate is going to stay low, the question of the best policy framework is nonetheless a healthy discussion for all of us to have. We need to make sure that whatever decision we make around frameworks, whether it's at the Federal Reserve or other central banks, we've gone through this process of challenging our assumptions, looking at alternatives, thinking seriously and carefully about them, and coming to good decisions. That's one of the reasons I've advocated for the Fed and other central banks to make this a regular part of how we approach monetary policy strategy. In particular, every five years or so, we should reassess our policy framework along the lines that the Bank of Canada does. They make a very serious and productive effort to think through these issues on a regular basis and, even if the decision at the end of the day is to stay with the status quo, it's better to have gone through that very open, transparent, and accountable way to think about these issues.

GENERAL DISCUSSION

ROBERT HELLER: You talked a lot about achieving the goal of price stability, as mandated by Congress. Well, 2 percent inflation means doubling the price level every thirty-five years. How can you possibly argue that that's price stability? If you look at the beginning of the republic from 1776 until the Federal Reserve was founded, there was no overall change in the price level. And then comes 1913, the Federal Reserve starts doing its thing, and since then, there's been an explosion of prices. And you want more of an explosion of prices. That's not price stability.

JOHN WILLIAMS: I'll take that last part as a question. We obviously have thought hard about the questions, "What is price stability?" and "What is the inflation rate that's consistent with our dual mandate goals of price stability and maximum employment?" I will say, among friends, that the track record before 1913 on economic performance wasn't that great.

But I think you're absolutely right. We don't want high inflation and we don't want variable inflation. Over the last twenty years, we've had relatively low inflation, but the question is, why not lower? The discussions we've had at the FOMC led to the January 2012 statement of long-run goals and strategy, and I think it was framed exactly right. We're trying to achieve both maximum employment and price stability. We can't think of maximum employment as zero unemployment or just the economy having as many jobs as possible, because that's inconsistent with price stability. At the same time, we know that if we shoot for too low of an inflation rate, say zero or one, the concerns about the zero lower bound, deflation risks, or asymmetry of behaviors of wages and prices at very low inflation suggests that that might interfere with achieving our maximum employment mandate over the long term.

It's also a question we debated, by the way. You know, going back to the nineties, the Fed has debated: What should the inflation goal be?

The 2 percent is a compromise between these goals. I personally think it's served us well. A lower inflation rate would make the zero lower bound issues bigger. But it should be among the topics of conversation if we start to have regular reviews of monetary policy strategy.

[UNIDENTIFIED SPEAKER]: When you mentioned the primary reasons for the lower real rates, you mentioned demographics, productivity growth, and safe asset demand. One thing you didn't mention was regulation, and there's obviously a school of thought that more regulation leads to slower growth and so forth. What framework do you use to look at the regulatory impact on the natural rate?

JOHN WILLIAMS: Obviously, productivity growth is influenced by regulation, alongside other issues. Whether you have free trade, free flows of capital markets, and things like that, they all feed into the level of productivity in our economy and the growth rate of that productivity. Changes, whether in regulation or increased investment in infrastructure or education, would affect the potential growth rate of the economy and therefore boost the natural rate of interest. The best solution for this low r-star issue is not a monetary policy solution. It's about increasing the potential of our economy, it's about increasing investments across the board, whether it's in education or infrastructure. I haven't seen that happen as much as is needed to move the dial and boost the natural rate.

[UNIDENTIFIED SPEAKER]: I would love to hear your thoughts on whether you think inflation is driven more by demand factors, as one has thought about it for a long time, or is it being driven more by supply factors and areas like regulation and changes in health care or technology and so on.

JOHN WILLIAMS: I'm an economist. It's both demand and supply! That's the answer to every question in life, right? It depends on what time period you are talking about. If you asked me this question in 2009–10, when inflation was, depending on the measure, 0 to 1 percent, I would attribute that to weak demand. Unemployment was 10 percent, and it stayed very high for a long time. We also saw wage growth stall. So, for that period I would be talking about demand. And in fact, if you look at my speeches from that period, I talked about employment, employment, employment.

Today, we're in a very different situation. Unemployment's below 4 percent. As we now know, wage growth is picking up. I do think supply plays a role. Inflation's really near 2 percent, so what are we talking about all the time? We're talking about tenths and half-tenths and .03 percentage point things. But I think some of these changes, the Affordable Care Act and other government program changes from Congress over the past few years, have actually reduced prices of Medicare services, and those tend to spill over into private-sector prices. My colleagues at the San Francisco Fed, Adam Shapiro in particular, have studied this, and their research shows these changes took a couple tenths off inflation in 2016 and maybe 2017. With inflation around 2 percent and the economy around full employment, it's actually some of these special supply factors that are pushing it around more. Right now, the demand seems to be kind of keeping inflation close to 2 percent, but supply is causing some ups and downs.

SEBASTIAN EDWARDS: So—since we think about the long run—what about Ken Rogoff's view that we have to get rid of cash, and once we do that, dealing with the lower zero bound is easier? So, (a) do you think we're going in that direction? There are some countries where basically it is very hard to use currency. Finland is one case. And (b) is that going to help deal with the problem at hand, as Ken and others suggest, or are you more skeptical?

JOHN WILLIAMS: If we can get rid of currency, which has a 0 percent interest rate, then basically you could lower interest rates to minus 1, 2, 3, 4, 5 percent, or whatever was appropriate, because then there wouldn't be this alternate investment with a safe, 0 percent yield. Of course, we know from the ECB, Switzerland, and Sweden that they were able to push interest rates well below zero, even with currency. So, it's not in actual fact a zero lower bound. Despite that, I think everyone understands you can't go to minus 2 or 3 or 4 percent interest rates.

So, what's happened? I've studied what's happening with currency demand in the US and the amount of currency outstanding is growing 6 or 7 percent a year. It's not going away. In the US, a lot of it is hundreds that go outside the country. But even transactional demand is still growing in the US. It would be a really big shift for the US for currency to go away.

There are other innovative ideas. Marvin Goodfriend spoke about this in Jackson Hole, and others have thought about it: Could you create a negative return on currency held at the central bank? Some economists are thinking along those lines. But I would point to some of the research that has examined the experience with negative interest rates. Here's the way I would summarize it. Clearly, negative rates affect rates in capital markets. You see the pass-through from these negative rates into commercial paper rates and bond rates, for example. On the other hand, there seem to be some negative effects, too, in terms of profitability of banks and other parts of the financial system. So, my reading right now is that the boost to the incremental economy you get from lowering interest rates declines as interest rates get below zero.

BEAT SIEGENTHALER: I work for UBS, and in the market we always love a good conspiracy theory. You told us that the price-level targeting discussion was really a long-term discussion, nothing to do with the current situation. But in the market, people would say, "Well, it is also a very convenient cover right now to accept higher inflation." So, if we go above the 2 percent target, then you could say, "Well, of course, that's because we have a symmetric target and we have undershot for so long." But where would be the limit for inflation? And could the symmetry of the target and the long undershot be a reason to accept a significantly higher inflation in the current situation or more immediate future? Thank you.

JOHN WILLIAMS: I'm going to break that into a couple of pieces. And remember what I said in the beginning, that I'm going to express my own views, and not necessarily those of other people in the Federal Reserve System.

The first, with the symmetric goal, I'm just going to do basic statistics. If you have a 2 percent goal, and you're managing that goal well, you're spending roughly half the time above, half the time below, hopefully, being in the vicinity. And I think that's how I interpret my view of where the economy is, the forecasts that we put out in March and our FOMC statements. It's about an expectation that inflation will be around 2 percent, maybe a little bit above, a little bit below, but averaging roughly around 2 percent.

I started talking about the monetary policy framework question publicly about a year ago, when this was not an active policy issue. Inflation was coming back, we were normalizing monetary policy, this is not a backdoor way to do price-level targeting. I don't think that's a good way to think about this. When you think about frameworks and strategies, you do this in terms of a commitment to a longer-term, consistent, coherent strategy and not as part of an opportunistic effort to achieve some shorter-term goal. And that's the way I think about it. You know, Fed time is not weeks or months. I'm not predicting things, but we'll discuss this over a long period of time. I expect that to happen in other countries so that, like our 2012 decision, we'll have thought it through, heard all of the different views, and then come to a decision.

Our framework today is inflation targeting. It's a framework that says we want to get inflation back to 2 percent and keep it near that.

Introduction

Charles I. Plosser

Someone made a comment in the last session regarding the goals of monetary policy. I'm going to take the liberty of asking people, if you haven't read the Federal Reserve Act recently, go back and read Section 2A on the conduct of monetary policy. It's very interesting when you actually read what it says about the goals of monetary policy. And rather than try to quote it, I'll paraphrase it as follows: it says that monetary policy should control the long-run growth of money and credit aggregates consistent with the economy's long-run potential to produce so as to promote effectively maximum employment, stable prices, and moderate long-term interest rates. Notice it talks about the instruments of policy, long-run ability of the economy to produce, and goals of monetary policy. It says almost nothing about the Phillips curve or short-term stabilization policy. Many will read more or less into this statement, but I urge you to go back and read it as you contemplate the actions and demands of monetary policy making.

Anyway, it's great to be here in the last panel of the day. It's been a long day, but it's been a fascinating day, as usual at this conference. I want to thank John and John for inviting me to come back. I was looking up at the history of these conferences and thinking, I think I've been a participant in some way or another in all but one. And so I'm going to take that as a good sign as they keep inviting me back to participate in some way. So, I'm delighted to be here.

The tradition of this last panel has always been one of having actual policy makers engage in a conversation with the audience and talk about practical policy issues. And if you think we don't have any of those to talk about, just think about the last eight hours and the issues that have been broached in this conference, everything from international coordination— although I know Raghu doesn't like to use that phrase—so we'll say from international activities, to the balance sheet, which we've just had two sessions about. John Williams gave us a very interesting and thoughtful conversation about different ways of thinking about policy regimes and strategies and how to conduct the choices that the Fed has about something other than inflation targeting—maybe we should have some different strategy? So, there've been lots of issues on the table today that really speak to challenges facing policy makers. One way I like to think of it is, some people like to say, "Well, we had this crisis, we had the Great Recession, and lo and behold, we had a recovery, the recovery's been going on for nine years now. Let's just pat ourselves on the back and talk about a job well done." But the fact of the matter is that the crisis, the unconventional monetary policy that was adopted, that we are still debating about its merits or demerits, a lot of the issues of that period are still with us. As we have discussed today, the Fed and monetary policy still face the challenges going forward of those unconventional monetary policies.

So, this is an opportunity to have real-life policy makers on a panel who are doing day-to-day decision making, to share some of their thoughts about those policies, to share some of their thoughts about current challenges that the Fed has, and also the opportunity for you in the audience to prod them with some questions and see what their reactions will be.

It's really exciting to have the final panel of the day and I'm delighted to be here, since I've sat in their seats at least two or three times over the last four or five years. I'm glad they get to answer the questions today and not me.

CHAPTER THIRTEEN

Monetary Policy and Reform in Practice

Esther L. George

Thank you for the opportunity to offer my views on monetary policy and reform in practice. I appreciate the Hoover Institution bringing together leading academics and monetary policy makers to share ideas about the practical issues facing central banks today. We have much to learn from each other.

My comments this afternoon focus on some of the practical issues I think about as I formulate my own policy views. As I do so, you'll hear me describe these issues with more questions than answers, reflecting the nature of the policy landscape today.

Before I continue, however, I want to note that these are my own views and are not necessarily representative of others in the Federal Reserve System.

TODAY'S POLICY LANDSCAPE

Nine years after the financial crisis, the Fed has, at least for the moment, achieved its objectives of maximum employment and price stability. Yet the legacy of the crisis—through the response of the Fed and fiscal authorities—has left us in a very different place than before the crisis in a number of ways. The equilibrium nominal policy rate is low by historical standards. The current target for the federal funds rate is considerably lower than the Federal Open Market Committee's (FOMC) projection of its longer-run value.

Our balance sheet is almost five times its pre-crisis size. The Fed's footprint in financial markets is considerably larger than before the crisis. The banking sector is consolidating and big banks have gotten even bigger. Federal deficits and debt are high and projected to rise to unprecedented levels.

Despite this legacy, many of the structural developments that dominate our thinking today were well under way before the onset of the financial crisis and Great Recession. An aging population, slowing productivity growth, rising globalization and declining equilibrium interest rates all predate the crisis. In this sense, things have not changed. Moreover, since the mid-1990s and through the financial crisis, Great Recession, and current expansion, core inflation—as measured by the personal consumption expenditure price index—has fluctuated in a relatively narrow range of roughly 1 percent to 2 ½ percent.

Given the structural changes that have been developing over the last several decades, it may well be that we are in a low-growth, low-interest-rate environment. Yet, from a cyclical perspective, the economy appears to be operating at or beyond full employment with inflation expected to rise over the medium term, while the FOMC's funds rate target of 1½ percent to 1¾ percent remains well below the FOMC's projection of its longer-run level of about 3 percent. The current gradual normalization of interest rates is geared toward removing accommodation at a pace that is expected to sustain the expansion without generating undesired increases in inflation, on the one hand, or creating financial instability, on the other. But there are clearly risks.

And there are still uncertainties about how the landscape will look once policy has achieved a "new normal." In particular, questions remain to be answered about the Fed's future operating framework, its strategic framework, and its role in promoting financial stability. I'll discuss each of these issues in turn.

DETERMINING A LONG-RUN
OPERATING FRAMEWORK

In 2016, the FOMC held lengthy discussions about potential long-run frameworks for monetary policy implementation. The committee discussed the merits of maintaining an abundance of reserves in the banking system versus returning to a framework of reserve scarcity. With an abundance of reserves, the Fed would rely on interest on reserves and the overnight reverse repurchase agreement (ON RRP) to maintain control over short-term market rates. With a scarcity of reserves, the open market desk at the New York Fed would control market rates through its control over the supply of reserves. The discussion ended with agreement that "decisions regarding the long-run implementation framework were not necessary at this time."[1] Since that time, however, we have begun to normalize our balance sheet with an understanding that the balance sheet will be smaller than it is today but larger than it was in 2007. As the balance sheet continues its steady decline, I would suggest that we again need to consider the appropriate long-run size of the balance sheet and our related operating framework.

While it may simply be a case of nostalgia on my part, I found our minimalist pre-crisis operating framework to have a number of features that served us well for many years. We maintained a small balance sheet with liabilities that were comprised almost entirely of currency in circulation with reserves averaging about $10 billion, compared with more than $2 trillion today. We maintained a Treasuries-only balance sheet with duration-matching Treasury issuance to maintain a neutral influence on financial markets. We had a small number of counterparties and we managed the supply

---

1. Federal Open Market Committee Minutes, November 1–2, 2016, accessed August 9, 2018, https://www.federalreserve.gov/monetarypolicy/fomcminutes20161102.htm.

of reserves to achieve the target federal funds rate. As a result, our footprint in the financial markets was relatively small.

Relative to this pre-crisis framework, the current operating framework—made necessary by a large balance sheet—has had a number of undesirable consequences, some of which were unintended. The Fed now owns significant outstanding shares of Treasuries and mortgage-backed securities (MBS) and is no longer a neutral influence on financial markets. We have a large number of counterparties, including nonbanks, made necessary by the ON RRP facility. Increases in the funds rate are achieved by raising an administered rate—the interest rate on excess reserves (IOER). Some have expressed concern that as IOER goes up, payments to banks—including to foreign banks—go up. Finally, the nature of unconventional policies has drawn both attention and criticism to the Federal Reserve's large balance sheet with consequences for central bank independence and fiscal discipline. Congress has begun to see the Federal Reserve as a source for plugging spending gaps, drawing on the Fed to fund the Consumer Financial Protection Bureau, finance highway spending, and, more recently, to contribute $2.5 billion to the federal government from its capital surplus as part of the budget deal passed in February after the brief government shutdown.

Given these developments, the current thrust of policy can become more difficult to gauge. At the same time the funds rate is being normalized, we have embarked on a program to gradually reduce the Fed's security holdings by decreasing reinvestment of principal payments. While I support this policy—with balance sheet normalization occurring largely on autopilot and in the background—it does pose challenges as we try to understand the implications for the stance of policy. Is policy tighter than we think because the balance sheet is shrinking? Or is the still-large balance sheet putting downward pressure on longer-term rates, making policy more accommodative than we think?

Whether it is desirable or even possible to return to our pre-crisis operating framework remains an open question for the FOMC. Can we return to the corridor-like framework with scarce reserves? Or will we need to retain the current floor system? If we maintain the current system, by how much can we reduce the supply of reserves? And what is the eventual role of the ON RRP facility? Can IOER guide the funds rate without reliance on the floor established by the rate on ON RRPs? Answers to these questions will be shaped by the FOMC's future discussions.

STRATEGIC FRAMEWORK

In addition to uncertainties about the longer-run operating framework, a number of strategic challenges and uncertainties pose practical issues for policy makers. With little countercyclical policy space available to respond to a future downturn, monetary policy options must contemplate how interest rate and balance sheet policies will work before, during, and after a crisis. Aggressively purchasing assets in a downturn and only gradually allowing them to roll off once the economy has fully recovered suggests the possibility of a balance sheet that grows bigger and bigger over time.

This dynamic, combined with varying degrees of uncertainty about the efficacy of asset purchases, has led to calls for a discussion about future policy strategies for the next encounter with the zero lower bound. Ideas like price-level targeting, a higher inflation objective, or nominal GDP targeting all offer worthwhile and intellectually stimulating debate. And certainly the time is right to consider the trade-offs around various strategies, but determining if these ideas might work in practice is challenging.

PROMOTING FINANCIAL STABILITY

These uncertainties make it all the more important to ensure the current economic expansion is sustained as interest rates rise and the balance sheet normalizes. We should take every measure possible to *prevent* a crisis rather than hope that we can devise a monetary policy *cure* after the fact.

As the FOMC gradually moves away from the zero lower bound, with a slowly shrinking but still-large balance sheet and growing federal debt, maintaining financial stability is paramount.

Here, I would like to make two key points:

- First, in contemplating a future bout of financial instability, we should be realistic about the robustness of macroprudential tools with a good dose of humility around the necessary finesse to deploy them in a timely fashion.
- Second, we should not waver in our aims to bolster resilience in our banking system, especially for the largest banks.[2]

There is little dispute that financial stability is a necessary condition for achieving the FOMC's employment and price stability mandates. It is recognized in the FOMC's "Statement of Longer-Run Goals and Strategies" as well as being the objective of macroprudential policies. However, there remains a tension as to the trade-off between macroeconomic goals and financial stability. The "lean or clean" debate is ongoing. Specifically, some argue that the output losses associated with using monetary policy to lean against growing financial imbalances far outweigh the possible benefits. Instead, they suggest that macroprudential policies are the appropriate response to financial instability. In my view, this approach might be more effective in theory than in practice.

---

2. The eight US global systemically important banks (GSIBs) held $11 trillion in total assets at the end of 2017, an amount equal to 57 percent of US gross domestic product.

A few years ago, I participated with some of my colleagues in a tabletop exercise designed to assess the efficacy of certain macroprudential policy tools in responding to a hypothetical financial crisis. In the exercise, we examined the use of capital-based, liquidity-based, and credit-based tools, along with stress testing and supervisory guidance, in mitigating the effects of an overheating of the financial markets. What we discovered in conducting the exercise was that the effectiveness of the tools varied because of realities like implementation lags and/or limited scope. In addition, monetary policy looked to be a relatively more attractive option than some might have expected before the exercise.[3] Obviously, this particular exercise is not conclusive in all scenarios, but rather a caution about becoming overly confident in relying on macroprudential tools to address growing financial imbalances.

In thinking about the role of financial stability in the conduct of monetary policy, I find recent research from the Bank for International Settlements (BIS) to be compelling. This research sees financial market deregulation from the 1980s and 1990s as having increased the likelihood of crises and posits a growing financial cycle in which monetary policy responds asymmetrically over time to crises, easing rates aggressively during the crisis but raising rates only gradually after the crisis has subsided. Their prescription is for policy makers to break this cycle by making policy more attentive to financial imbalances and more symmetrical in the response.[4]

We should take advantage of the current economic conditions to bolster resilience in the financial system. Instead, the United States has yet to implement a countercyclical buffer and the banking

---

3. Tobias Adrian, Patrick de Fontnouvelle, Emily Yang, and Andrei Zlate, "Macroprudential Policy: A Case Study from a Tabletop Exercise," *FRBNY Economic Policy Review* 23, no. 1 (February 2017), accessed August 9, 2018, https://www.newyorkfed.org/research/epr/2016/epr_2016-adrian-macroprudential-policy.

4. Claudio Borio, Piti Disyatat, Mikael Juselius, and Phurichai Rungcharoenkitkul, "Monetary Policy in the Grip of a Pincer Movement," BIS working paper no. 706, March 1, 2016, accessed August 9, 2018, https://www.bis.org/publ/work706.htm.

agencies contemplate steps in the direction of relaxing capital requirements. Recently issued for comment is a proposal to modify the enhanced supplementary leverage ratio on global systemically important banks (GSIBs) that would have the effect of lowering capital requirements.[5] With the US economy in a sustained expansion and at risk of growing financial imbalances, this is a time in the credit cycle when GSIBs and other banking organizations should be building capital instead of increasing leverage.

CONCLUSION

The financial crisis and Great Recession left a legacy of low interest rates, a big balance sheet, and large fiscal deficits. And a number of long-running structural trends have become prominent considerations for understanding their implications for future growth. This landscape is accompanied by an economy growing at or above trend with full employment, stable prices, and easy settings for monetary policy. Whatever the "new normal" is, monetary policy is not yet there. When times are good, as they are now, it is an opportune time to resolve some of the uncertainties around how we will implement monetary policy in the future, what strategies we will employ in response to the next downturn, and how we can best promote resilience and stability in our financial system. I hope we do so before we find ourselves cleaning up after the next crisis.

---

5. Board of Governors of the Federal Reserve System, "Rule Proposed to Tailor 'Enhanced Supplementary Leverage Ratio' Requirements," news release, April 11, 2018, accessed August 9, 2018, https://www.federalreserve.gov/newsevents/pressreleases/bcreg20180411a.htm.

CHAPTER FOURTEEN

US Economic Conditions and Monetary Policy Considerations

Robert S. Kaplan

Thank you for inviting me. Congratulations to John Cochrane and John Taylor on this conference.

One of the main reasons I came to the Fed was because I thought "normalization" of monetary policy was going to be very challenging. As difficult as the crisis was, it has been my view that normalization would be as or more challenging. I think this conference and today's debate reinforce that view. While we have talked about normalizing the federal funds rate, how we deal with the balance sheet is going to be just as important. With that background, I'm going to talk about some of the challenges I see in the US economy and then address four or five points which pertain to the key themes of this conference. I look forward to expanding on these points in the Q&A.

So, let me start with my view of the economy. While the near-term outlook for the US economy is very positive, and we're making very good progress in meeting our dual-mandate objectives of full employment and price stability, I think the medium-term picture is much more challenging. Dallas Fed economists expect US gross domestic product (GDP) growth to be strong in 2018, but we also expect growth to moderate in 2019 and by 2020. It is our forecast that GDP growth in the United States will ultimately drift down toward "potential" of somewhere between 1¾ and 2 percent by 2020.

Why do we expect this move down to potential? Why is potential growth so low? There are four key structural drivers that are critical to this analysis. While the news and the press headlines tend to be focused on the shorter-term cyclical developments and the near-term growth of the US economy, these structural drivers get far less attention. But I believe they are much more important to understanding the situation we're facing.

KEY STRUCTURAL DRIVERS

Aging Population

The first structural driver is the aging population in the United States, which translates into slowing workforce growth. We've made much of the fact that the labor force participation rate has declined from 66 percent in 2007 to approximately 62.8 percent today, and it's our view at the Dallas Fed that this participation rate will decline below 61 percent over the next ten years.[1] While we're very hopeful that discouraged workers and other workers on the sideline may come into the workforce, we don't think there's going to be a magic bullet to offset this inexorable trend of slowing workforce growth due to aging demographics. This trend has a substantial impact on GDP growth. It certainly should have profound impacts on how we think about updating our immigration policies as well as other policies which affect workforce growth. GDP growth is made up of growth in the workforce plus growth in productivity—and, based on demographics, we believe growth in the workforce is going to be sluggish.

---

1. Bureau of Labor Statistics, April 2018.

Technology-Enabled Disruption and Its Implications for Education and Skill Levels

The second structural issue relates to productivity. It is our view at the Dallas Fed that, while technological advances and increases in overall capital spending should help improve productivity in a variety of industries in the United States, we are concerned that lagging educational achievement and skill levels will mute these gains for the US workforce. In particular, we note that approximately 46 million workers in this country (age twenty-five and over) have a high school education or less.[2] In terms of the talent pipeline, we note that US students are lagging in terms of math, science, and reading skills. We rank twenty-fourth out of thirty-five OECD (Organization for Economic Cooperation and Development) countries in terms of math, science, and reading skills among fifteen-year-olds.[3]

While we're improving middle-skills training in the United States, we are not improving fast enough to keep up with the skills needs of employers. This may help explain why approximately half of all small businesses in the United States report they are unable to find enough "qualified" workers to fill open positions.[4]

While companies and industries are improving their productivity (and profitability), overall workforce productivity growth has been sluggish. It is our hypothesis at the Dallas Fed that this could be at least partially explained by lagging educational achievement and insufficient progress in ramping up skills training to meet the "skills gap" in our economy. Specifically, if you're one of those

---

2. Ibid.

3. According to the Program for International Student Assessment (2015) by the Organization for Economic Cooperation and Development (OECD), the United States ranks nineteenth in science, twentieth in reading, and thirty-first in mathematics out of thirty-five OECD countries. An average of scores across the three categories places the United States twenty-fourth.

4. National Federation of Independent Business.

46 million workers who has a high school education or less, it's likely you're seeing your job either restructured or eliminated. In a good job market, you'll likely find another job. But, unless you get retrained—easy to say, harder to do in practice—it's likely that you will go to a job where your productivity is lower. Because we measure productivity workforce-wide, it's our concern that lagging educational levels as well as lagging skill levels are not improving sufficiently to keep up with the changing workforce needs created by technology-enabled disruption. As a result of these human capital issues, I am concerned that productivity growth is going to remain sluggish.

Potentially Unsustainable Path of Government Debt to GDP

The third structural issue is the expected path of government debt to GDP. I think this path is likely to be unsustainable. US government debt held by the public is now 77 percent of GDP.[5] The present value of unfunded entitlements is now $54 trillion.[6] This high level of indebtedness will likely squeeze out the opportunity for fiscal policy in the next downturn, and it may, depending on how it's managed, create other headwinds for economic growth in the future.

Globalization

The last big structural trend is globalization. Of course, the trend toward globalization has been going on for most of our lives. We

---

5. US Department of the Treasury and Bureau of Economic Analysis as of first quarter 2018.

6. "The 2018 Annual Report of the Board of Trustees of the Federal Old-Age and Survivors Insurance and Federal Disability Insurance Trust Funds," US Social Security Administration, June 5, 2018; "The 2018 Annual Report of the Boards of Trustees of the Federal Hospital Insurance and Federal Supplementary Medical Insurance Trust Funds," Centers for Medicare and Medicaid Services, June 5, 2018.

know that financial flows and our economies are much more integrated, and global competitiveness is more important, than ever before. The issue is how we handle this trend—is it a threat, or is it an opportunity? I will put forward the view that while trade and immigration may have been threats to jobs in the United States fifteen years ago, today they are more likely to be opportunities for growth at a time when we need to grow faster in order to service government debt and entitlement obligations.

The development of integrated supply-chain and logistical arrangements with Mexico is an example of how trade may help improve US jobs and competiveness. While the North American Free Trade Agreement (NAFTA) needs to be modernized, our research at the Dallas Fed indicates that in excess of 70 percent of US imports from Mexico are "intermediate goods"—that is, part of complex logistical and supply-chain arrangements that our research shows help the United States and North America take share from Asia.[7] Our research indicates that these arrangements improve our competitiveness and add jobs in the United States which might otherwise be lost to other regions of the world.

In addition, while other countries, particularly China, are making dramatic investments (and maybe overinvestments) in improving their education, their infrastructure, and their technology, America appears to be lagging in terms of making these investments—particularly in education and infrastructure. We have to be concerned that unless policy makers make the right decisions on globalization and make key investments in improving our global capabilities, we will in fact lose global competitiveness in the United States, even though the short-term prospects for GDP growth look good.

---

7. Jesus Cañas, Aldo Heffner, and Jorge Herrera Hernández, "Intra-Industry Trade with Mexico May Aid U.S. Global Competitiveness," *Southwest Economy*, Federal Reserve Bank of Dallas, second quarter 2017, accessed August 10, 2018, www.dallasfed.org/~/media/documents/research/swe/2017/swe1702b.pdf.

IMPLICATIONS

So, these are four key forces that we closely monitor at the Dallas Fed. Of course, policy solutions to deal with many of these structural drivers are outside the control, to a great extent, of the Federal Reserve. However, how these drivers are managed is going to play a key role in how well we are able to meet our dual-mandate objectives of full employment and price stability. These forces may help explain why potential GDP growth is only 1¾ to 2 percent. These sluggish medium-term and longer-term growth expectations may help explain why the yield curve has been flattening and why the expectations for the longer-run federal funds rate by Federal Open Market Committee (FOMC) participants have declined substantially in the Fed's Summary of Economic Projections from 2012 through today. This may also help explain why forecasts for r-star are historically low.

As John Williams said at lunch today, a lower r-star means there's less room for the FOMC to deal with the next downturn or the next shock. As most of you who've heard me speak before have heard me say, I believe the Fed should be gradually removing accommodation, moving toward a neutral stance in monetary policy, and I do believe we should be gradually reducing our balance sheet. However, due to the structural drivers discussed here, I think the path of rate hikes is likely to be much flatter than we've historically been accustomed. More important for the subject of this conference, I think, in the next downturn there's likely to be less capacity for fiscal stimulus, which means that the Fed may well need more tools beyond the federal funds rate in order to address economic conditions in that scenario.

THE FED BALANCE SHEET

With that backdrop, let me just address three or four points pertaining to the Fed's balance sheet. Point number one, I was very struck by Charlie Plosser's paper on the use of the Fed balance sheet and the risks of having a large balance sheet.[8] I was particularly struck by the thought that the willingness of the Fed to use its balance sheet might be having an effect on fiscal policy, i.e., may be leading to a lack of discipline in fiscal policy. This is a jarring issue to consider, and I think it *should* be considered.

The second point I want to address relates to Peter Fisher's comments about whether we should be "presuming" that the Fed will use quantitative easing in the next downturn. My own view is that, as we've said in our policy normalization principles and plans, the Fed should be prepared to consider using a full range of tools in the next downturn, including making use of the balance sheet. This conference is raising a question about whether we should be more fully debating this thinking. I think this is a healthy debate.

I also agree with John Williams that, in addition to our normal conversations at FOMC meetings, we should be doing a periodic strategic review of our frameworks and our approaches. I think the issues debated at this conference fall into this strategic review. I think it is very healthy to debate these questions. They need to be debated, and as a member of the FOMC, I would welcome the discussion.

Lastly, I feel very strongly that the Fed needs to continue making demonstrable progress in reducing its balance sheet. I think this progress gives us operating flexibility so that, in the event of an economic shock or downturn, we at least have the option of deciding whether and how to use the balance sheet. I think the country

---

8. Charles I. Plosser, "The Risks of a Fed Balance Sheet Unconstrained by Monetary Policy," Economics Working Paper no. 17102, Hoover Institution, Stanford University, Palo Alto, CA, May 4, 2017.

is well served by the Fed having a wide range of tools beyond the federal funds rate.

I believe that, over time, it would be preferable for the Fed to have a balance sheet primarily comprised of Treasury securities. I am struck by the argument that the Fed being a large owner of mortgage-backed securities made sense during the crisis. However, it is a legitimate question as to whether, at this point, it makes sense for the Fed to have such significant influence on housing policy.

In addition, I think the balance sheet issue and the low r-star issues are related, and we would also be well served by a broad discussion of whether some type of price-level or nominal GDP targeting is appropriate. In this regard, I would particularly look forward to a discussion of nominal GDP targeting. I'm not sold yet on this approach, but I do feel strongly that a broad policy debate on these issues would be healthy and advisable. My colleague Evan Koenig of the Dallas Fed has done substantial work on the subject of nominal GDP targeting and the wisdom of making greater use of this approach in monetary policy.[9] The debate on nominal GDP targeting may affect how we think about the appropriate size of the Fed balance sheet and how we might use the balance sheet in a future downturn.

MACROPRUDENTIAL POLICY CONSIDERATIONS

Macroprudential policy is also an element of these considerations. I believe that the extraordinary policies implemented by the Fed in response to the Great Recession—various rounds of quantitative easing—were necessary because we had a severe financial crisis and we had severe financial instability. So, with that in mind, I'm

---

9. See Evan F. Koenig, "Like a Good Neighbor: Monetary Policy, Financial Stability, and the Distribution of Risk," *International Journal of Central Banking* 9, no. 2 (June 2013): 57–82. Also see Evan F. Koenig, "All in the Family: The Close Connection Between Nominal-GDP Targeting and the Taylor Rule," Staff Papers, Federal Reserve Bank of Dallas, no. 17 (March 2012).

particularly attuned to our policies in place today, to make sure we don't have this type of financial crisis in the future. In this regard, I think we've been extremely well served over the last eight or nine years by having very tough capital requirements and rigorous stress testing for large, systemically important financial institutions. As we look to find ways, which I favor, to tailor requirements for small to midsize banks, I would be very concerned if we went too far in relaxing capital standards and stress-testing approaches for large, systemically risky institutions. I think the economy has been very well served, and I think it will continue to be well served, by having very tough requirements for large financial institutions.

In addition, as we think about the next crisis and financial instability, I am very concerned about the shadow financial system. In particular, we need to be cognizant of excess debt buildup, possibly in the form of derivatives and volatility-targeting strategies and other forms of risk-parity investing. I'm concerned that visibility into these areas is poor. It's not that we don't have data—it's that derivatives are netted, and sometimes, as we learned in the first two weeks of February, it's difficult to realize how much leverage is out there until you have a stress event. The volume of short "put" positions may not look excessive until you have a stress event. What happened in early February, I would hope, is a healthy warning to us that we probably need more oversight. While the Fed does not regulate or oversee nonbank financials, I hope that we and other agencies try to gain better visibility in these areas. I'm concerned that the next crisis will likely come from embedded leverage that is not visible to us, à la credit default swaps and other put-like structures. So I hope there is stronger oversight and monitoring of the shadow financial system—e.g., the nonbank financials.

CHAPTER FIFTEEN

When the Data Aren't Enough: Facing a Challenge of Policy Implementation

Raphael Bostic

Good afternoon, everyone. It's good to be here. I want to thank the organizers for inviting me to be part of this panel with two great colleagues. This is something of a homecoming for me, as I got my PhD just across the way at Stanford's Economics Department. It's been nice to walk around campus and see so many familiar sights. But in a very obvious sense, I'm a newbie here at this conference. So I may be the one person who didn't know what I was in for when I came.

As the newest member of the Fed on this panel, I agreed to defer to my colleagues and allow them to speak before me. With my time, I thought I might first respond to what Presidents George and Kaplan said and then talk about policy from an implementation perspective.

First, I totally agree with President George's comment that we should be thinking about our strategic framework. She mentioned price-level targeting. President Kaplan mentioned nominal GDP targeting. We at the Atlanta Fed have also jumped into this conversation. We have a four-part series on our economics blog that tries to talk to the public about why we might think about changing the strategic framework. We use price-level targeting as an example. The whole point of this, I think, is that you're going to hear consistent voices from just about all of us that periodically there's value in reexamining strategy to make sure that it's delivering the goods that we hope. And this is a time that I think is particularly ripe for that.

A second thing I would say is that, to me, the two things in the regulatory environment established by the Dodd-Frank Act that are most important are the increases in required capital and the introduction of stress tests. The capital is critical, because we learned very quickly that there wasn't enough capital in the system to withstand the turmoil. The stress test is quite important because it addresses a culture of risk management that was absent at many of our institutions. Having the stress test in place is a signal that banking institutions need to be thinking about the possibility of very adverse events, in advance and continuously. My hope is that these institutions don't just use scenarios that we come up with, but rather run through a whole host of other scenarios, so they are prepared and are as resilient as they possibly can be. That philosophy is an important one and needs to prevail throughout the industry.

I want to also say that for me, the most important aspect of our ability as the Federal Reserve to conduct our policy is the preservation of independence. Anything that might risk that independence needs to be considered seriously. I talk with our folks, including Presidents George, Kaplan, and Williams, about this all the time. Further, Governor Quarles has commented about what things we can do to make sure we are not giving any perceptions that we are moving beyond our mandate or our authorities, because it is those scenarios or situations that I think pose the greatest risk to our independence. We should be having conversations on this in a serious and urgent way, because Washington, when it moves, moves fast. We need to make sure we understand the implications of every one of our actions as we take them.

And then I wanted to talk a little bit about the economy, just briefly, in the sense that President Kaplan talked about the medium term as where there's uncertainty. His projections show growth less than 2 percent. My projections for the medium term show basically the same. I'm exactly where he is, largely because of the four things he highlighted.

But I would also say that part of the issue that we face in this economy—not just in the United States, but worldwide—is that disruption is happening. I believe it's happening at an accelerated pace, and it's happening in a broader scope of industries or sectors than we have seen before. The scale of the problem, and our response to disruption, is something that has real implications for how productive the economy can be moving forward. And it's my view that we don't have the institutions in place to help facilitate a seamless and low-cost response to that disruption. In fact, we have not really talked to our workforce about what skills they're going to need to be successful in tomorrow's economy. Without that conversation, it's hard for me to imagine how we get to a higher trajectory in terms of economic performance.

And so we're focusing on this. The Atlanta Fed recently launched the Center for Workforce and Economic Opportunity to establish a forum for engaging with the many stakeholders who are critical for making progress here. We recognize that success will require participation from institutions far beyond the Federal Reserve, as we do not have tools to really affect these issues directly. But these issues do have direct implications for our mandate, and so I think that it's important we talk about them.

Let me now turn to the issue of policy implementation. I'll try to be brief. When I was working at the Department of Housing and Urban Development, it was during the housing crisis. We designed many programs that we thought were addressing very specific issues that were underlying some of the distress that was happening in the economy. To be completely honest, some of them didn't work. But in many instances, the failures had less to do with the design of the program and more to do with the implementation of the program: making sure that institutions that were charged with delivering policy actually had the capability, the capacity, the resources, and the authority to do those policies. In that crisis time, that wasn't the case for a number of programs. I came out of that experience with a new commitment to pay attention to implementation issues. I think that implementation issues are underappreciated as challenges for the execution of policy, and I think that's something that all of us would do well to think about more in terms of the integration of policy design.

In that regard, I wanted to highlight one implementation issue that hit me almost immediately once I arrived in Atlanta. And that was the question of how we should execute policy when the data aren't enough. There are two dimensions where the data might not be enough. One is that the signals the data provide can be ambiguous, and that's been happening pretty consistently the whole time I've been in my current role. This has actually been true for an extended period. How should we deal with that? A second way that data might not be enough is if the data we look at are not the data that are going to move the market tomorrow, or the next month, or the year after. With this, I think about the Great Recession and all the distress that was happening in terms of housing markets. A lot of stuff was going on there, including the extreme leverage that was being taken on by financial market players. Some of these things had not customarily been in our "box" of things to look at and study in determining what appropriate policy should look like. I'm worried about that. People tell me this, and I'm sure you've heard it too: "Regarding tomorrow's crisis, the one thing we know is it won't look like yesterday's crisis. It's going to look different."

So how do we get focused on that wide range of things? That's a question we've been thinking about at the Atlanta Fed. And I will say that for me, I got lucky, in that the Bank had already put in place a structure to make sure we get on-the-ground intelligence on a regular basis. We use this approach to inform our thinking about a host of questions we don't have answers for. Because ultimately, if the data are not enough, then we've got to find nontraditional sources of information and find ways to integrate that into our policy making.

The Atlanta Fed has something called a Regional Economic Information Network, or REIN. My district is divided into six subdistricts and we've deployed staff in each of the subdistricts and tasked them with talking to people—CEOs, leaders of community groups, and public officials. The approach is to ask questions. What are you seeing? What are the challenges you're facing? What are the opportunities you have? What things are you experiencing that you don't see in the newspaper? The goal is to gather a collection of information that allows us to get a sense of whether noteworthy or markedly different things are happening.

With these sorts of approaches, there's always a risk that what we hear is just ad hoc, that it's one person's story. How can we ensure our policy is not dependent or driven by anecdotal experiences that are really just one-offs? We try to respond to that in the context of scale. Because we have so many people out there, we can talk to dozens of leaders. And then we bring all that information back. So this last policy cycle, we talked to about one hundred leaders from across the region, across sectors in different parts of our district, to see if there are similarities that point to common themes.

I think this has been quite useful, and there are a number of benefits associated with this. First, it allows for a more organic flow of information, so that we're not predetermining what's interesting or useful, but rather are allowing our interactions to guide us. The second is it helps us to focus on what we need to know. If we hear stories that are coalescing, we can then find relevant data that can help us get a deeper insight into those spaces.

Third, I think it increases the likelihood of finding out something that's happening that hasn't yet shown up in the data. As you know, our policies don't operate instantaneously. This places a premium on timeliness. The more timely we can be in learning things, the more timely we can be in deploying our policy and have it hit in the right way.

Fourth, it guides our future strategy. Once we determine the conundrums we seek to better understand, we can send our REIN executives out armed with questions that can help us get useful answers. So, in addition to letting our contacts tell us about what they are seeing, we can guide our conversations with them to achieve a more fruitful interaction.

The last thing I would say on this is that it has changed how we approach information-gathering more broadly. My bank is now engaged with a number of partners to do surveys that can help us get insights into key questions. In fact, we're doing one about business activity with researchers here at Stanford and at the University of Chicago.

In this context, I would like to tell one story, because I think it's instructive. President Kaplan talked about how the productivity of our labor force is quite low. We see this in the data. But the thing that has always struck me is that whenever I talk to CEOs, CFOs, and other business leaders, they all tell me they're investing tremendously in technology. They're trying to increase the efficiency of their workforce and that should translate to more productivity. So, are they wrong? Are we just missing something? I don't think they're wrong. Another thing we also hear all the time from businesses is that they are spending a whole lot of money in a new area, which is cybersecurity. And the expenditures in that area have gone up tremendously. In many ways, cybersecurity is like hiring accountants or regulatory compliance officers. They are a cost that doesn't translate, necessarily, into any kind of additional output or productivity. So we're going to look into this and see if there are ways to measure, you might call it, a cyber-adjusted productivity rate for labor to see if these new line items are changing the reality of business. And maybe our current assessments of productivity in a historical context have turned into something of an apples-versus-oranges comparison. So, hope may not be lost—all lost, at least. And we may be seeing progress in this regard.

My point here is that these conversations can spark insights that lead to directions for research. I have found real value in the type of information that we get from our on-the-ground, nontraditional engagements.

A lot of the discussions we have today come down to the question of whether our models really work, particularly in today's environment. This is a really important question and is one that we wrestle with, because sometimes they don't work so well. They're not matching up as much as we'd like. And we've got to figure out what to do with that. I don't know that I have an answer for this question, but I think this is another area where you guys can help us, and I think that can be quite useful.

Let me close by noting that I've really come to appreciate the power and the value of surveys of regular people and businesses. So, as you are wrestling with your questions, talk to the folks here at Hoover. See if they might fund or support a survey to try to get some new information that allows us to get a deeper insight as to what's really happening on the ground and a better understanding of some of the pressing challenges we're facing. What I've heard consistently at this conference is that there's a lot we still don't know. I think we're going to have to use some different approaches to get information that can help us make better policy.

GENERAL DISCUSSION

PAUL TUCKER: Two things, if I may. The first is that each of you, and John at lunchtime, talked about a clear desire to review the whole monetary framework that you have here, and you mentioned price-level targeting and some of the things that Ben Bernanke has talked about. But the question I have is this: if I think about the mainstream monetary policy frameworks over the past half century, the Fed was never the innovator, and in a sense that was good for the world, because you matter so much. Is there a real-world example of price-level targeting or nominal GDP targeting that you're looking at and saying, "Yeah, that has really kind of worked in a medium-size country, and we think we can adapt that to the US"?

The second thing is that a number of you, I think all of you actually, said—and I certainly completely agree with this— something along the lines of, "It's very important that we must not go beyond the boundaries of our powers." You also said that it's vitally important to preserve a resilient financial system. And yet through the whole day, almost nothing has been said about resolution policy. And if I may say so, this is absolutely typical of the Fed, because resolution policy belongs to the FDIC, and the Fed prefers always to talk about what you, the Fed, can do. I want to suggest to you that these two things are linked. The perception, fair or unfair, that you went beyond your powers during the crisis concerns, broadly speaking, lender-of-last-resort operations. If the resolution powers that the FDIC and others have got are as workable as others and I think they can be, that would in the future relieve the pressure on you to go beyond into the unknown with your lender-of-last-resort powers. Are you prepared to talk more about resolution policy in the future and to make it work in order to help build credibility that you will stay within the proper confines of LOLR policy?

ROBERT KAPLAN: I'll take a stab at both, and I guess I'll comment on both. The point is not whether we ultimately adopt nominal GDP targeting or price-level targeting. The point for me is that there should be a strategic review at the Fed on a regular basis. There have been governance recommendations about the Fed, we've talked about the balance sheet today, we've talked about our frameworks, we've talked about our inflation targeting. All these topics should be discussed in a regular strategic review. We, of course, do talk about all these things regularly. But I come from the business world, and I think having a strategic review every X period of time is a healthy thing. I think we should take views from outside. We should look at what's been done in other countries. I don't think we should make changes unless we have conviction. The point on this for me is more about process rather than about debating the pros or cons of any one thing.

Second, on your comment—I'll speak as a businessman on this issue of resolution authority—someone again who worked in the industry. And I hate to use this analogy, but I'll use it. The analogy is: you smoke, you drink, you're way overweight, and everybody said for years, "Wow, I can't believe he or she is still upright after all this." And then you have a terrible event happen, and then all the discussion is about what happened in the emergency room after the traumatic event. In the aftermath, you suffered some serious damage. I'm much more of a fan of preventative care. Experience has seared into my head that, yes, we should develop effective resolution authority and living wills and all these other post-trauma elements. But if those approaches are central to your ultimate defense, we're going to be in a lot of trouble. I think we are much better served talking about sound monetary policy, how we use our balance sheet, and all these other issues, because by the time you actually have to use resolution authority, serious damage has already been done. So, I don't think these resolution frameworks take the place of or take any pressure off us figuring out sound economic policies, including how to manage the balance sheet and how we might use it in a crisis or in order to avoid a crisis.

ESTHER GEORGE: I'm not sure we need to change the framework. I think what we need to do is be open to many of the calls that we hear about what's wrong with the framework: that you can't hit 2 percent inflation and what do you mean by a symmetric target? As it was framed earlier, being open to thinking about that is healthy for the institution and helps make us more accountable.

On the resolution policy, I will just say I'm probably the skeptic here. We certainly have yet to prove that these resolution regimes will work in practice as well as they do in theory. It's why I tend to lean more heavily on the things we do know. We do know strong leverage ratios work. We do know strong capital and liquidity are going to be key, based on experience and the research that has been done. And I still get a very strong sense that the market believes banks are too big to fail. So, when I look at the size—this is just in the US—of an $11 trillion industry, we should keep working on resolution for sure, but I'm not sure that we're there yet.

RAPHAEL BOSTIC: Totally agree with them. I would just say that prevention is a big focus for me. I think about this from a basic health perspective. If you wait until you get to a crisis situation, the disruption, the pain, is a lot worse, and it costs a lot of money. So, if we can avoid that, I think that's in our interest. And I think we should try to make sure that when you get to the crisis, the transaction happens smoothly, and as many assets are preserved, as much value is preserved as possible. But I don't think it substitutes for making sure that we minimize the likelihood that we actually get there.

And one takeaway that I hope you have is that—you guys should know—we're pretty thoughtful. And I say this because I've gotten a sense that you guys think we're locked in on things, that there's a preordained policy that we all come to, and I have to pledge fealty to, before I get my position. And that's not the case. One of the nice things with my colleagues is that we argue all the time. We're open to discussions, and conferences like this are actually quite helpful for us in terms of getting a better sense of what things we need to think harder about or know more about, because we are in uncharted territory and the transition path is not one that people have experienced before. So it's going to require thought, and we all are open to doing that.

CHARLES PLOSSER: Thank you. I'm going to use the chair's prerogative here to intervene and at least to make a comment, because Paul's suggestion and John's comments earlier today raise the issue of choosing a strategic framework for monetary policy. I think that's fine to consider, but I think, being a veteran of this war for eight or nine years when I was at the Fed, one of the things that the Fed and we often miss in that discussion is, yes, having a strategic framework is important. But where the debate ends up occurring is often not about the goals. It usually ends up a debate about how you get there, the tactics. You have lots of debates in the FOMC about rules versus discretion, strategies to adopt, about how to achieve the best goals, and so I would urge my former colleagues and the new ones in the Fed, that if you go down this road of considering a new framework, whether it be price-level targeting, nominal GDP targeting, or other such approaches, be sure you think through the implications of that for how you will conduct monetary policy. How would you conduct monetary policy in a credible—to John's point—systematic way to achieve those goals? Because, without that discussion, this is just kind of pie in the sky, and without an articulation of how that will happen or what you have to commit to do to deliver, it is all just wishful thinking.

ROBERT KAPLAN: And if it makes you feel better, Charlie, I doubt there's anyone around the table that would disagree with what you just said. I think the people around the table aren't going to be willing to be supportive of a change in framework unless they understand all the issues you just raised.

CHARLES PLOSSER: And Raphael's point about implementation becomes critical . . .

RAPHAEL BOSTIC: No, I agree. I do want to say, though, that policy is path-dependent. And we got here through a set of circumstances that I think if it were our druthers wouldn't have happened. We wouldn't be here. So, I think it's difficult to just talk about this policy as a point in time/space, without acknowledging that we came through a whole host of challenges. A lot of the policy articulation of strategy was designed to provide certainty and some stability in a space where there wasn't very much of that. Once you become identified as having that kind of stability, it becomes very dangerous to start tinkering with that, because that could have serious adverse impacts, beyond the policy itself. Actually, I haven't heard enough about the role of uncertainty today in terms of economic performance. And I know for me, in terms of the things that I spend time on, I focus a lot on how our policies will be perceived relative to the path that has been charted. I'm not a Fed guy but I have become very aware of the Fed watchers out there. They really watch us. Like, every word, every step we take, so deviations from the path we have charted can have outsize implications for the response the market will have to our policy. And that's a component that I think we've got to make sure everyone is sensitive to. You know, people watch you very closely.

MICKEY LEVY: I'd like to ask this question in the form of a hypothetical. At some point in the future, say, early next year, inflation is 2.3 percent or thereabouts, above 2 percent. And you and the median FOMC member forecast sustained healthy real economic growth, say 2.5 percent to 2.75 percent, which is way above your estimate of potential growth. And your forecast of the unemployment rate is unchanged from the current low rate, significantly below the estimate of the natural rate of unemployment. What is your inflation forecast going to be? If it's higher, which is what the Fed's macro models would forecast, you may jar inflationary expectations. If, on the other hand, you forecast that inflation is going to go back to your 2 percent target, what are you going to do with your forecast of the appropriate path of the federal funds rate (the so-called "dots")?

ESTHER GEORGE: In your hypothetical scenario here, Mickey, as you know, there are always questions about what other factors may be at play too. The committee has not committed to a path today, and notwithstanding the dot plot and the attention it gets, I'm reminded at every meeting how we are constantly recalibrating where we sit today relative to the forecast that we've set out there. So, if what you're suggesting is, we can see that there's going to be persistence in this inflation rate, that we're growing above trend, the scenario looks like the economy is overheating, then you have to revisit what your path is, and think about whether the number of rate increases that you've thought about are going to have to be steeper. And this is always the challenge. This is a challenge that we've known since the day we did liftoff, which is: Do we wait and go slow? Will we have to go faster at some point? I think we're all mindful of that. So, I get your point, and we are where we are.

ROBERT KAPLAN: I'll say one thing. The most important thing I've learned in this job—and I used to be a leader in business, and I taught leadership for a living—if I had to give one piece of advice to a leader, on what's the most important leadership quality? You must be open to learning. Don't be rigid or predetermined, and certainly don't rigidly rely only on models or on any one approach to doing your analysis. And I think I try to bring that philosophy to the FOMC table. But I've been extremely impressed as a member of the FOMC—I've only been here two years—by the prevalence of that way of thinking. We pay attention to the results of the models, and we do all the work. But I think as important as all that is a whole series of other approaches. Raphael talked about some of them. And I think this group is open to learning. It doesn't mean we won't make mistakes, but we've got an attitude where we're humble, willing to say, "I don't know," "I've changed my mind," "We've made mistakes." And I have a lot of confidence that this group has those qualities.

MICHAEL BORDO: I just want to amplify what Paul Tucker said. I think he's right. The Fed hasn't generally been the leading innovator in central bank technology and ideas, with one key exception, and that's Paul Volcker's disinflation in 1979. But to get to my question, what will be the effects of the large and rising fiscal deficits and debt-to-GDP ratio in the US on Fed policy thinking?

ROBERT KAPLAN: I may have talked more about this subject than just about anybody else around the FOMC table. My concern is that through most of our lives, we've increased debt-to-GDP in order to stimulate GDP growth. We're getting very possibly to the stage, now, where the path of government debt, especially because if you take into account the demographic trends in the United States—the path of debt growth may well be unsustainable. We actually haven't been through a period in my life—I've been through it with companies, but I don't think we've been through it in this country—where we either have to moderate debt growth or actually deleverage. Deleveraging could likely create a headwind for economic growth. And these are considerations we have to take into account. And so, when I say things are good in the short term, I'm very mindful of the fact we've just had a very large fiscal stimulus. But the underlying drivers of economic growth have not dramatically changed. I hope they do. I hope we make investments and policy decisions to address them. But I think recent fiscal policy decisions may increase the likelihood that out-year growth is going to be sluggish or disappointing.

ESTHER GEORGE: One of the things I think about, Michael, is the experience we had in '90 and '91 and the political pressure that the Fed came under. As I look at the increasing willingness of Congress to reach in, for example, to the reserve banks for funding, obviously, it doesn't affect our ability to operate. But those optics, those practices begin to chip away at issues around independence. So, coming into a time of rising rates, when you see these debt levels, I think you have to keep that in the back of your mind—that those dynamics could come into play again.

WILLIAM NELSON: I have a question for President Kaplan, President George. So, you mentioned the leverage ratio proposal. But there was, of course, also recently the proposal to change the day-to-day capital requirements to include the stress capital buffer, which, in effect, is basically just adding the GSIB surcharges to the post-stress hurdle rates. So, there's been very much a recalibration away from a leverage ratio, risk-blind measure for the largest banks to an even more robust set of requirements for the largest banks. And simultaneously, the stress tests that are going on right now include increases in the unemployment rate and declines in house prices, commercial real estate prices, and stock prices, as well as widenings in the Triple-B spread that are greater . . . all of which was worse than what was seen in the crisis. So, I just wanted to ask, it seems to me that those changes meet the criteria you just described of applying tougher standards as things continue to improve and of maintaining very strict requirements on the largest banks—and, I think, in quite a desirable way, moving away from a binding leverage requirement. I just wanted your perspectives on those two things.

ESTHER GEORGE: First of all, your stress tests are only as good as what you're modeling, and so you're putting a great deal of faith in the calibration of your models. And I'm going to assume that those scenarios are as good as we can do, and I'm supportive of running those stress tests. But we know from our experience around risk-based capital and how we calibrate that that the leverage ratio is a stronger measure. I do not see evidence that it creates incentives for risk, particularly when you combine it with the CCAR exercise that we do. And given the experience of 2008 and '09, and my own experience going back to the eighties, that leverage ratio is not a constraint in terms of lending. In fact, you see that it becomes a source of funds. It becomes a source of strength, actually. And so, given the systemic risk posed and the amount of leverage in the banking system relative to any other corporate form, I think that ought to be our strong bias in terms of strengthening the system. I think what we've seen so far as that leverage ratio has raised is that we've become far more competitive worldwide. We have become really the strongest banking system, and I don't see any reason why we ought to deviate from that.

ROBERT KAPLAN: I wouldn't add anything to that. I think we can debate exactly how we do it, and I think those are good arguments as to the best way to do it. But I think directionally—you hear where I'm coming from, I think for the big banks—I don't think the country is being hurt at all. In fact, I think it's being helped by having tough capital requirements and stress testing. And whether it's a buffer or leverage, I'm open-minded to different ways to do this. But I think that we're well served by tough capital requirements and stress testing.

At the same time, I do think we need to be giving regulatory relief to small- and mid-size banks. I think that will help spur business growth.

ANDY FILARDO: Picking up on Mickey's question, I would like to ask about the current status of the Fed's dual mandate. A number of your FOMC colleagues have recently been talking about the issue of "overheating." A lot of people outside the United States are asking what the Fed means by this term and its implication for policy trade-offs. Is this term just a euphemism for "medium-term inflation risks"? Or does it also refer to employment, the second part of the Fed's mandate? In an environment in which the Phillips curve is sending decidedly mixed signals, one wonders whether noninflationary overheating of the labor markets would prompt the Fed to normalize at a quicker pace. Or is the pace of normalization, for all intents and purposes, largely tied to inflation behaviour?

RAPHAEL BOSTIC: For me, overheating means that economic performance, in terms of the GDP growth as well as pricing, starts to go well beyond what we think is sustainable in the short to medium term. Because if we move beyond sustainable, and this is something my colleagues and my staff have really impressed upon me, once it breaks down, it ends badly. And the Fed historically has not shown a real ability to prevent that negative momentum from leading to extra disruption. So to the extent that we can start to see some signs that the economy is getting close to an unsustainable level, and I think that unsustainability will contain both dimensions, that would be a signal for us that we then need to prevent a snapback that leads to excess disruption.

ROBERT KAPLAN: I agree with everything Raphael said. I'm very conscious of the fact that the structure of the economy has changed dramatically in the last number of years. We've always had forms of automation, but what I've seen going on—at least in my business career, and I've spent my career dealing with businesses—this is something different. I think it's probably the proliferation of cloud computing and other technologies that have challenged the pricing power of business much more than any time I've seen in my career. And the ability for businesses to be disrupted is accelerating. Artificial intelligence and other things that were unthinkable are accelerating. So, to Raphael's point, I'm mindful of the fact we could dramatically overshoot full employment. And even though in the near term we don't seem to be seeing as much inflation as we expected, I'm sensitive to the fact it may take a little longer for those pressures to build, because you've got this headwind. But that doesn't mean pressures are not building. And you've got to be aware even though the data don't show you as much inflation as you expected, that doesn't mean you're not going to see it. It just means it may take a little longer, you've got a greater lag, and you've got this structural headwind. I think the Fed has been well served by this balanced approach, where you take into account the degree of the overshoot in full employment as well as the degree of the undershoot in inflation, and you balance those two, understanding there may be more of a lag. I think there's more of a lag, and we're doing a lot of work on this, and having a conference, actually, in three weeks—which you're welcome to come to—in Dallas to talk about this: whether there isn't more of a lag because of the structural changes. And so I'm sensitive to the possibility of a structural change in the inflation process. We don't know the answer. We will in hindsight. But I'm sensitive to that.

ESTHER GEORGE: I was just going to end where you started, Charlie, and say I'm careful to think only about two variables, unemployment rate and inflation right now, when I think our mandate is broader. This idea of sustainable, productive growth in the economy is hard to define sometimes. We see the Phillips curve relationships make us raise questions. We see the unemployment rate dropping. I think there are a number of variables that have to come to play, and maybe using the word "overheating" is too ambiguous, so good of you to call it out.

About the Contributors
and Discussants

ADRIEN AUCLERT is a macroeconomist whose research focuses on inequality, consumption, monetary and fiscal policy, and international economics. His recent work explores the interactions between macroeconomics and inequality as well as the redistributive effects of monetary and fiscal policy. He received his PhD in economics from MIT in 2015 and was a postdoctoral fellow at Princeton University from 2015–16. He teaches macroeconomics and international economics at Stanford, where he is a faculty member of the Stanford Institute for Economic Policy Research (SIEPR), and is a faculty research fellow at the National Bureau of Economic Research.

RAPHAEL BOSTIC became the fifteenth president of the Federal Reserve Bank of Atlanta on June 5, 2017. Before coming to the Bank, he was a professor of public policy at the University of Southern California in Los Angeles. He brings a wealth of experience from an outstanding career in academia, government, and research. Bostic served as assistant secretary for policy development and research at the Department of Housing and Urban Development. He also spent several years as an economist at the Board of Governors. He has a passion for understanding the housing sector and how credit markets, financing, and public policy work together to help people achieve the American dream. He has published extensively in academic journals. He earned a PhD in economics from Stanford University and earned his undergraduate degree at Harvard. Since joining the Atlanta Fed as president and CEO, he has spent much of his time on public outreach, sharing his deep knowledge of business and financial conditions. He is also a voting member this year on the Federal Open Market Committee, the Fed's policy-making group.

JOHN H. COCHRANE is an economist. He is the Rose-Marie and Jack Anderson Senior Fellow of the Hoover Institution at Stanford University. His academic writing focuses on monetary economics and finance. He writes op-eds in the *Wall Street Journal* and blogs as "the Grumpy Economist." Cochrane earned a bachelor's degree in physics at MIT and earned his PhD at the University of California–Berkeley. He was a professor of economics and then of finance at the University of Chicago Economics Department and then Booth School of Business before coming to Hoover.

SEBASTIAN EDWARDS is the Henry Ford II Professor of International Economics at the University of California–Los Angeles. From 1993 to 1996, he was chief economist for Latin America at the World Bank. He has published fifteen books and more than two hundred scholarly articles. He was the codirector of the National Bureau of Economic Research's Africa Project. Edwards has been an adviser to numerous governments, financial institutions, and multinational companies. He is a frequent commentator on economic matters on CNN and other cable outlets. His op-ed pieces have been published in the *Wall Street Journal*, the *Financial Times*, the *Los Angeles Times*, *El País* (Spain), *La Vanguardia* (Spain), *Clarín* (Argentina), *El Mercurio* (Chile), and other newspapers around the world. His latest book is *American Default: The Untold Story of FDR, the Supreme Court and the Battle for Gold* (Princeton University Press, 2018). Other books include *Toxic Aid: Economic Collapse and Recovery in Tanzania* (Oxford University Press, 2014), *Left Behind: Latin America and the False Promise of Populism* (University of Chicago Press, 2011), and *Crisis and Reform in Latin America: From Despair to Hope* (Oxford University Press, 1995). He has been president of the Latin American and Caribbean Economic Association and was a member of the Scientific Advisory Council of the Kiel Institute for the World Economy in Kiel, Germany. He was also a member of former California governor Arnold Schwarzenegger's Council of Economic Advisers. In 2013, he was awarded the Carlos Díaz-Alejandro Prize in recognition of his research on Latin American economies. He was educated at the Universidad Católica de Chile. He received an MA in economics in 1978 and a PhD in economics in 1981, both from the University of Chicago.

PETER R. FISHER is senior fellow at the Center for Business, Government & Society at the Tuck School of Business at Dartmouth, where he also serves as a clinical professor. He is a director of the John F. Kennedy Library Foundation and of the Peterson Institute for International Economics. He is a member of the Advisory Committee on Systemic Resolution of the Federal Deposit Insurance Corporation and of the advisory board of the MIT Golub Center for Finance and Policy. From 2004 to 2013, Fisher worked at BlackRock, where he served in several capacities, including head of fixed income portfolio management and chairman of BlackRock Asia. From 2001 to 2003, he served as undersecretary of the US Treasury for domestic finance. From 1985 to 2001, he worked at the Federal Reserve Bank of New York, concluding his service as an executive vice president and manager of the Federal Reserve System Open Market Account. Fisher has previously served as a member of the Strategic Advisory Committee of the Agence France Trésor, as a nonexecutive director of the Financial Services Authority of the United Kingdom, and as an independent director of AIG. He received a JD degree from Harvard Law School and a BA in history from Harvard College.

ESTHER L. GEORGE is president and chief executive officer of the Federal Reserve Bank of Kansas City. She is a member of the Federal Open Market Committee, which sets US monetary policy. She has more than thirty years of experience in the Federal Reserve, with her early career primarily focused on regulatory oversight of banks and financial holding companies in seven states. She was directly involved in the banking supervision and discount window lending activities during the banking crisis of the 1980s and post-9/11. During the most recent financial crisis, she served as the acting director of the Federal Reserve Board's Division of Banking Supervision and Regulation in Washington, DC. She has served as president of the Bank since October 2011 and currently leads the Federal Reserve's efforts to modernize the US payments system. She hosts the Federal Reserve Bank of Kansas City's International Economic Policy Symposium in Jackson Hole, Wyoming. She is a native of Missouri.

GITA GOPINATH is the John Zwaanstra Professor of International Studies and of Economics at Harvard University. Her research focuses on international finance and macroeconomics. She is codirector of the International Finance and Macroeconomics program at the National Bureau of Economic Research, a visiting scholar at the Federal Reserve Bank of Boston, a member of the economic advisory panel of the Federal Reserve Bank of New York, economic adviser to the chief minister of

Kerala state in India, a coeditor at the *American Economic Review*, and coeditor of the current *Handbook of International Economics*. She was managing editor of the *Review of Economic Studies*. She also served as a member of the Eminent Persons Advisory Group on G-20 Matters for India's Ministry of Finance. In 2011, she was chosen as a Young Global Leader by the World Economic Forum. In 2014, she was named one of the top twenty-five economists under age forty-five by the IMF. Before going to Harvard, she was an assistant professor of economics at the University of Chicago's Graduate School of Business.

OLEG ITSKHOKI is professor of economics and international affairs at Princeton University. His research interests are in the fields of macroeconomics and international economics. One line of his research focuses on the effects of globalization on labor markets, in particular unemployment and income inequality. Another line of his research studies the pricing policies of firms in international transactions, in particular focusing on currency choice by importing and exporting firms and its implication for macroeconomic policies. He also explores the role of large firms in international transmission of shocks. His most recent research is centered around the issue of optimal macroeconomic policies in currency unions and optimal development and industrial policies in economies with financial frictions. He was a participant in the Review of Economic Studies tour, a Sloan Research Fellow, and a recipient of the Excellence Award in Global Economic Affairs from the Kiel Institute for the World Economy. His research was supported by a National Science Foundation grant and his work is published in the *American Economic Review, Econometrica, Quarterly Journal of Economics*, and *Review of Economic Studies*. He is a research associate at the National Bureau of Economic Research and a research affiliate at the Centre for Economic and Policy Research. He earned his BA at Moscow State University, MA at the New Economics School (Moscow), and PhD at Harvard University.

ROBERT S. KAPLAN has served as the thirteenth president and CEO of the Federal Reserve Bank of Dallas since September 8, 2015. He represents the Eleventh Federal Reserve District on the Federal Open Market Committee in the formulation of US monetary policy and oversees the 1,200 employees of the Dallas Fed. Kaplan was previously the Martin Marshall Professor of Management Practice and a senior associate dean at the Harvard Business School. Before joining Harvard in 2006, Kaplan was vice chairman of the Goldman Sachs Group, with global responsibility for the firm's Investment Banking and Investment Management divisions. Previously, he served as global co-head of the Investment Banking Division. He was also a member of the firm's Management Committee and served as cochairman of the firm's Partnership Committee and chairman of the Goldman Sachs Pine Street Leadership Program. During his twenty-three-year career at Goldman Sachs, Kaplan served in various other capacities, including head of the Corporate Finance Department, the Asia-Pacific Investment Banking, and the high-yield department in Investment Banking. He became a partner in 1990. On leaving the firm in 2006, he was given the honorary title of senior director. He serves as cochairman of Project ALS and cochairman of the Draper Richards Kaplan Foundation, a global venture philanthropy firm that invests in developing nonprofit enterprises dedicated to addressing social issues. He is also a board member of Harvard Medical School. Kaplan received a bachelor's degree in business administration from the University of Kansas and a master's degree in business administration from Harvard Business School.

MICKEY D. LEVY is the chief economist for Berenberg Capital Markets, LLC. From 1998 to 2013, he was chief economist at Bank of America Corporation. He is a long-standing member of the Shadow Open Market Committee. Levy conducts research on US and global economic and fiscal policies and the influences of policies on economic and financial market performance. He testifies frequently before the US Congress on monetary policy and banking regulation, credit conditions, and fiscal and budget policies.

LORIE K. LOGAN is a senior vice president in the Markets Group of the Federal Reserve Bank of New York where she is head of Market Operations Monitoring and Analysis (MOMA). This is the area responsible for execution of monetary policy at the direction of the FOMC, provision of fiscal agent services to the Treasury in support of debt issuance and foreign exchange operations, market analysis of financial market developments to inform the policy-making process, sponsorship of the Treasury Market Practices Group (TMPG) and the Foreign Exchange Committee (FXC), and the production of the FRBNY's reference rates, including SOFR.

She is also the deputy manager of the System Open Market Account for the FOMC. Logan joined the Bank in June 1999 as a financial analyst in the bank analysis department. In 2000, she was assigned to the Markets Group. She held successive assignments in the Treasury markets directorate, and from June 2009 to March 2012 she served as the chief of staff for the Markets Group. She has held her current position since then. She played a prominent role in the development and implementation of the Federal Reserve's crisis-related activities, including the expansion of the Federal Reserve's balance sheet, the creation of several liquidity facilities to mitigate systemic risks to the financial system, and the development of the Federal Reserve's policy normalization tools. She holds a bachelor's degree from Davidson College and a master's degree in public administration from Columbia University.

PRACHI MISHRA is deputy division chief and mission chief in the Western Hemisphere Department of the IMF. Prior to this, she was specialist adviser and head of Strategic Research Unit at the Reserve Bank of India, and Senior Economist at the Ministry of Finance, Government of India. She holds a PhD in economics from Columbia University, and a masters from the Delhi School of Economics.

WILLIAM NELSON is an executive vice president and chief economist at the Bank Policy Institute. Previously, he served as executive managing director, chief economist, and head of research for The Clearing House Association and chief economist of The Clearing House Payments Company. He contributed to and oversaw research and analysis to support the advocacy of the association on behalf of TCH's owner banks. Prior to joining The Clearing House in 2016, Nelson was a deputy director of the Division of Monetary Affairs at the Federal Reserve Board, where his responsibilities included monetary policy analysis, discount window policy analysis, and financial institution supervision. He attended Federal Open Market Committee meetings and regularly briefed the Board and FOMC. He was a member of the Large Institution Supervision Coordinating Committee (LISCC) and the steering committee for Comprehensive Liquidity Analysis and Review (CLAR). He has chaired and participated in several Bank for International Settlements (BIS) working groups on the design of liquidity regulations and most recently chaired the CGFS-Markets Committee working group on regulatory change and monetary policy. He joined the Board in 1993 as an economist in the banking section of Monetary Affairs. In 2004, he was the founding chief of the new Monetary and Financial Stability section of Monetary Affairs. In 2007 and 2008, he visited BIS in Basel, Switzerland, where his responsibilities included analyzing central banks' responses to the financial crisis and researching the use of forward guidance by central banks. He returned to the Board in the fall of 2008, where he helped design and manage several of the Federal Reserve's emergency liquidity facilities. Nelson earned a PhD, an MS, and an MA in economics from Yale University and a BA from the University of Virginia. He has published research on a wide range of topics, including monetary policy rules; monetary policy communications; and the intersection of monetary policy, lender-of-last-resort policy, financial stability, and bank supervision and regulation.

JONATHAN D. OSTRY is deputy director of the Research Department at the International Monetary Fund and a research fellow at the Center for Economic Policy Research. His recent responsibilities include leading staff teams on IMF-FSB early warning exercises on global systemic macro-financial risks; multilateral exchange rate surveillance; international financial architecture and reform of the IMF's lending toolkit; capital account management and financial globalization issues; fiscal sustainability issues; and the nexus between income inequality and economic growth. Past positions include leading the division that produces the IMF's flagship publication, the *World Economic Outlook*, and leading country teams on G-3, advanced and emerging market economies. Ostry is a member of the World Economic Forum's global agenda council on inclusive growth and its risk advisory board. He is the author of a number of books on international macro policy issues, including *Taming the Tide of Capital Flows* (MIT Press, 2017) and *Confronting Inequality* (Columbia University Press, 2018), and numerous articles in scholarly journals. His work has been widely cited in print and electronic media, including the BBC, the *Economist*, the *Financial Times,* the *Wall Street Journal,* the *New York Times*, the *Washington Post, Business Week,* and National Public Radio. His work on inequality and unsustainable growth has also been cited in remarks made by President Barack Obama. He earned his BA (with distinction) from Queen's University (Canada) at age eighteen and went on to earn a BA and MA from Oxford University (Balliol College) and graduate degrees from the London School of Economics (MSc, 1984) and the University of Chicago (PhD, 1988). He is listed in *Who's Who in Economics* (2003).

KYLE PALERMO is marketing communications manager at the Hoover Institution where he reports on conferences, publications, and other institutional activities. He is a graduate of San Jose State University, where he studied political science and economics.

MONIKA PIAZZESI is the Joan Kenney Professor of Economics at Stanford University, senior fellow at the Stanford Institute for Economic Policy Research, and professor of finance, by courtesy, at the Stanford Graduate School of Business. She is the program director of the NBER Asset Pricing Program, a fellow of the Academy of Arts and Sciences and the Econometric Society, and was a Guggenheim Fellow during 2015–2016. During the years 2006–2014, she was co-editor of the *Journal of Political Economy*. Prior to joining Stanford, she taught at the University of Chicago and UCLA. She received the Elaine Bennett Research Prize and the Bernazer Prize for Research in Macroeconomics and Finance. She holds a diploma in economics from the University of Bonn and a PhD from Stanford. Her research focuses on the interactions between financial markets and the economy. Her work has studied the impact of monetary policy on the term structure of interest rates, booms and busts in housing markets, and the risk exposures of financial institutions.

CHARLES I. PLOSSER served as president and CEO of the Federal Reserve Bank of Philadelphia from 2006 to his retirement in 2015. He has been a longtime advocate of the Federal Reserve adopting an explicit inflation target, which the Federal Open Market Committee did in January 2012. Before joining the Philadelphia Fed in 2006, Plosser served as dean from 1993 to 2003 at the University of Rochester's Simon School of Business. He is a research associate of the National Bureau of Economic Research as well as a visiting scholar at the Hoover Institution. Plosser served as coeditor of the *Journal of Monetary Economics* for two decades and cochaired the Shadow Open Market Committee with Anna Schwartz.

His research and teaching interests include monetary and fiscal policy, long-term economic growth, and banking and financial markets. Plosser earned PhD and MBA degrees from the University of Chicago.

RANDAL K. QUARLES took office as a member of the Board of Governors of the Federal Reserve System and was sworn in as vice chairman for supervision on October 13, 2017. His term as vice chairman for supervision ends on October 13, 2021. Prior to his appointment to the Board, Quarles was founder and managing director of the Cynosure Group, a Utah-based investment firm. Before founding the Cynosure Group, he was a partner at The Carlyle Group, a private equity firm based in Washington, DC. From April 2002 until November 2006, Quarles served in several positions at the Treasury Department, including undersecretary of the Treasury for domestic finance and assistant secretary of the Treasury for international affairs. He also served as policy chair of the Committee on Foreign Investment in the United States and he was the US executive director of the International Monetary Fund from August 2001 to April 2002. From January 1991 to January 1993, he served in the Treasury Department as a special assistant to the secretary of the Treasury for banking legislation and as deputy assistant secretary of the Treasury for financial institutions. Prior to, and in between, his service at the Department of the Treasury, he was a partner at Davis Polk & Wardwell, serving in the New York and London offices. He received an AB in philosophy and economics, *summa cum laude*, from Columbia in 1981 and earned a law degree from the Yale Law School in 1984.

RAGHURAM RAJAN is the Katherine Dusak Miller Distinguished Service Professor of Finance at the University of Chicago's Booth School. Prior to that, he was the twenty-third governor of the Reserve Bank of India from 2013 to 2016, as well as the vice chairman of the board of the Bank for International Settlements from 2015 to 2016. He was the chief economist and director of research at the International Monetary Fund from 2003 to 2006. Rajan's research interests are in banking, corporate finance, and economic development, especially the role finance plays in it. He coauthored *Saving Capitalism from the Capitalists* with Luigi Zingales in 2003. He then wrote *Fault Lines: How Hidden Fractures Still Threaten the World Economy*, for which he was awarded the Financial Times-Goldman Sachs prize for best business book in 2010. Rajan was the president of the American Finance Association in 2011 and is a member of the American Academy of Arts and Sciences and the Group of Thirty. In January 2003, the American Finance Association awarded him the inaugural Fischer Black Prize for the best finance researcher under the age of forty. The other awards he has received include the global Indian of the year award from NASSCOM in 2011, the Infosys prize for the Economic Sciences in 2012, the Deutsche Bank Prize for Financial Economics in 2013, and *Euromoney* magazine's Central Banker of the Year Award in 2014.

THOMAS J. SARGENT, a macroeconomist, joined New York University as the first W. R. Berkley Professor in September 2002, a joint appointment by the Economics Department at NYU's Faculty of Arts and Sciences and the Stern School of Business. He was awarded the 2011 Nobel Prize in Economics, shared with Princeton University's Christopher Sims, for his empirical research on cause and effect in the macroeconomy. Sargent was a professor of economics at the University of Minnesota from 1975 to 1987, the David Rockefeller Professor at the University of Chicago from 1992 to 1998, and the Donald Lucas Professor of Economics at Stanford University from 1998 to 2002. He has been a senior fellow at the Hoover Institution since 1987. He earned his PhD from Harvard University in 1968 and was a first lieutenant and captain in the US Army. He was a university medalist as Most Distinguished Scholar in the Class of 1964 and won the Nemmers Prize in Economics in 1997. He was elected a fellow of the National Academy of Sciences and a fellow of the American Academy of Arts and Sciences, both in 1983. He is past president of the Econometric Society, the American Economic Association, and the Society for Economic Dynamics.

MARTIN SCHNEIDER is a professor of economics at Stanford University. He is also a research associate at the National Bureau of Economic Research (NBER) and a research fellow at the Center for Economic and Policy Research (CEPR). He has published widely on topics in macroeconomics, monetary policy, and financial markets. From 2005 to 2008, he served as a senior economist at the Federal Reserve Bank of Minneapolis. He has also taught at the University of Rochester, UCLA, and New York University. He holds a PhD in economics from Stanford University and a diploma in economics from the University of Bonn.

GEORGE P. SHULTZ is the Thomas W. and Susan B. Ford Distinguished Fellow at the Hoover Institution. He served as secretary of labor in 1969–70, director of the Office of Management and Budget from 1970–1972, and secretary of the Treasury from 1972 to 1974. He was sworn in on July 16, 1982, as the sixtieth US secretary of state and served until January 20, 1989. In January 1989, he was awarded the Medal of Freedom, the nation's highest civilian honor. Shultz rejoined Stanford University in 1989 as the Jack Steele Parker Professor of International Economics at the Graduate School of Business and as a distinguished fellow at the Hoover Institution. Shultz is the chair of the Precourt Institute for Energy Advisory Council at Stanford, chair of the MIT Energy Initiative External Advisory Board, and chair of the Hoover Institution's Shultz-Stephenson Task Force on Energy Policy. He is a distinguished fellow of the American Economic Association.

JOHN B. TAYLOR is the Mary and Robert Raymond Professor of Economics at Stanford University, the George P. Shultz Senior Fellow in Economics at the Hoover Institution, and the director of Stanford's Introductory Economics Center. He served as senior economist (1976–77) and member (1989–91) on the President's Council of Economic Advisers. From 2001 to 2005, he served as undersecretary of the Treasury for international affairs. He received the Adam Smith Award from the Association of Private Enterprise Education, the Truman Medal for Economic Policy for extraordinary contribution to the formation and conduct of economic policy, the Hayek Prize for his book *First Principles*, the Bradley Prize for his economic research and policy achievements, the Adam Smith Award from the National Association for Business Economics, the Alexander Hamilton Award and the Treasury Distinguished Service Award for his policy contributions at the US Treasury, and the Medal of the Republic of Uruguay for his work in resolving the 2002 financial crisis. He currently is a member of the Eminent Persons Group on Global Financial Governance. Taylor received a BA from Princeton and a PhD in economics from Stanford.

SIR PAUL TUCKER is chair of the Systemic Risk Council and a fellow at Harvard Kennedy School. His book *Unelected Power: The Quest for Legitimacy in Central Banking and the Regulatory State* was published by Princeton University Press in spring 2018. His other activities include being a director at Swiss Re, a senior fellow at the Harvard Center for European Studies, a visiting fellow of Nuffield College Oxford, a member of the Advisory Board of the Yale Program on Financial Stability, and a governor of the Ditchley Foundation. Previously, he was deputy governor at the Bank of England, sitting on its monetary policy, financial stability, and prudential policy committees. Internationally, he was a member of the G20 Financial Stability Board, chairing its group on "too big to fail," and a director of the Bank for International Settlements, chairing its Committee on Payment and Settlement Systems.

KEVIN WARSH serves as the Shepard Family Distinguished Visiting Fellow in Economics at the Hoover Institution and as lecturer at the Stanford Graduate School of Business. He advises several private and public companies, including serving on the board of directors of United Parcel Service (UPS). Warsh is a member of the Group of Thirty (G-30) and the Panel of Economic Advisers of the Congressional Budget Office (CBO). Warsh conducts extensive research in the field of economics and finance. He issued an independent report to the Bank of England proposing reforms in the conduct of monetary policy in the United Kingdom. Parliament adopted the report's recommendations. Governor Warsh served as a member of the Board of Governors of the Federal Reserve System from 2006 until 2011. Warsh served as the Federal Reserve's representative to the Group of Twenty (G-20) and as the Board's emissary to the emerging and advanced economies in Asia. In addition, he was administrative governor, managing and overseeing the Board's operations, personnel, and financial performance. Prior to his appointment to the Board, from 2002 until 2006 Warsh served as special assistant to the president for economic policy and as executive secretary of the White House National Economic Council. Previously, Warsh was a member of the Mergers & Acquisitions department at Morgan Stanley & Co. in New York, serving as vice president and executive director. Warsh received his BA from Stanford University and JD from Harvard Law School.

JOHN C. WILLIAMS is the president and chief executive officer of the Federal Reserve Bank of New York, having served in the same capacity at the Federal Reserve Bank of San Francisco from 2011 to mid-June 2018. In this role, he serves on the Federal Open Market Committee, bringing the Fed's Twelfth District's perspective to monetary policy discussions in Washington. Williams was previously the executive vice president and director of research for the San Francisco Bank, which he joined in 2002. He began his career in 1994 as an economist at the Board of Governors of the Federal Reserve System, following the completion of his PhD in economics at Stanford University. Prior to that, he earned a master of science degree from the London School of Economics and an AB from the University of California–Berkeley. His research focuses on topics including monetary policy under uncertainty, innovation, and business cycles. Additionally, he served as senior economist at the White House Council of Economic Advisers and as a lecturer at Stanford University's Graduate School of Business.

About the Hoover Institution's Working Group on Economic Policy

The Working Group on Economic Policy brings together experts on economic and financial policy at the Hoover Institution to study key developments in the US and global economies, examine their interactions, and develop specific policy proposals.

For twenty-five years starting in the early 1980s, the US economy experienced an unprecedented economic boom. Economic expansions were stronger and longer than in the past. Recessions were shorter, shallower, and less frequent. GDP doubled and household net worth increased by 250 percent in real terms. Forty-seven million jobs were created.

This quarter-century boom strengthened as its length increased. Productivity growth surged by one full percentage point per year in the United States, creating an additional $9 trillion of goods and services that would never have existed. And the long boom went global with emerging market countries from Asia to Latin America to Africa experiencing the enormous improvements in both economic growth and economic stability.

Economic policies that place greater reliance on the principles of free markets, price stability, and flexibility have been the key to these successes. Recently, however, several powerful new economic forces have begun to change the economic landscape, and these principles are being challenged with far-reaching implications for US economic policy, both domestic and international. A financial crisis flared up in 2007 and turned into a severe panic in 2008 leading to the Great Recession. How we interpret and react to these forces—and in particular whether proven policy principles prevail going forward—will determine whether strong economic growth and stability returns and again continues to spread and improve more people's lives or whether the economy stalls and stagnates.

Our Working Group organizes seminars and conferences, prepares policy papers and other publications, and serves as a resource for policy makers and interested members of the public.

Working Group on Economic Policy—Associated Publications
Many of the writings associated with this working group will be published by the Hoover Institution Press or other publishers. Materials published to date, or in production, are listed below. Books that are part of the Working Group on Economic Policy's Resolution Project are marked with an asterisk.

Index